AI-First Healthcare
AI Applications in the Business and Clinical Management of Health

Kerrie L. Holley and Siupo Becker, M.D.

Beijing · Boston · Farnham · Sebastopol · Tokyo

AI-First Healthcare

by Kerrie L. Holley and Siupo Becker, M.D.

Published by O'Reilly Media, Inc., 1005 Gravenstein Highway North, Sebastopol, CA 95472.

O'Reilly books may be purchased for educational, business, or sales promotional use. Online editions are also available for most titles (*http://oreilly.com*). For more information, contact our corporate/institutional sales department: 800-998-9938 or *corporate@oreilly.com*.

Acquisitions Editor: Michelle Smith	**Indexer:** WordCo Indexing Services, Inc.
Development Editor: Melissa Potter	**Interior Designer:** David Futato
Production Editor: Kristen Brown	**Cover Designer:** Karen Montgomery
Copyeditor: Arthur Johnson	**Illustrator:** Kate Dullea
Proofreader: Holly Bauer Forsyth	

April 2021:   First Edition

Revision History for the First Edition
2021-04-19:   First Release

See *http://oreilly.com/catalog/errata.csp?isbn=9781492063155* for release details.

978-1-492-06315-5

[LSI]

Table of Contents

Preface. vii

Introduction. xi

1. Myths and Realities of AI. 1
    AI Origins and Definition   2
        AI and Machine Learning   4
        AI Transitions   11
        AI—A General Purpose Technology   15
    AI Healthcare Myths   17
        Myth: AI Will Cure Disease   21
        Myth: AI Will Replace Doctors   25
        Myth: AI Will Fix the "Healthcare Problem"   27
        Myth: AI Will Decrease Healthcare Costs   29
    AI Myths   33
        Myth: AI Is an Existential Threat   34
        Myth: AI Is Just Machine Learning   35
        Myth: AI Overpromises and Underdelivers   36
        Myth: True Conversational AI Already Exists   37
        Myth: AI as Overlord   38
    AI Technology Myths   39
        Myth: AI Algorithms Are Biased   40
        Myth: AI Sees, Hears, and Thinks   40
        Myth: AI Diagnoses Diseases Better Than Doctors   41
        Myth: AI Systems Learn from Data   43
        Myth: AI Is a Black Box   43
        Myth: AI Is Modeled After the Brain   45
    AI-First Healthcare   45

2. Human-Centered AI... **49**

    Toward Human-Centered AI   49

        AI Centaur Health   50

        Human-Centered AI   53

    Intersection of AI and Humans   54

        AI and Human Sociocultural Values   58

        AI Understanding Humans   61

        Humans Understanding AI   64

    Human Ethics and AI   66

        Human-Centric Approach   67

        Making Human-Centered AI Work   69

    Summary   71

3. Monitoring + AI = Rx for Personal Health.............................. **73**

    Prescription (Rx) for Personal Health   76

        Three Realms Influencing Healthcare   78

        Ambient Computing and Healthcare   81

    Continuous Monitoring Using AI   83

        Continuous Monitoring   84

        Beeps, Chimes, Dings, and Dongs   85

        Health Continuum   86

    Application of IoT and AI to Medical Care   88

        IoT and AI   88

        Health Determinants and Big Data   92

    Summary   93

4. Digital Transformation and AI.. **95**

    Digital Transformation of Healthcare   97

        Path A: Creating Digital Operations and Processes   99

        Path B: Building New Capabilities   100

        Path C: Transforming Business Processes   101

        Paths to the Digital Transformation of Healthcare   102

    Digital Healthcare   102

        AI Applied to Digital Healthcare   104

        AI, Digitization, and Big Tech   105

    Preventive and Chronic Disease Management   106

        AI and Prevention   107

        AI and Chronic Disease   108

        AI and Mental Health   110

    AI and Telemedicine   111

    Medication Management and AI   113

        Medication Adherence   114

    Digital Medication   115
    AI and Digitization Applied to Administrative Tasks   117
    Summary   119

5. An Uncomfortable Truth. **121**
    Healthcare Waste   122
        Healthcare Spend and AI   123
        Treatment Decisions and AI   126
    Administrative Costs   131
        Administrative Processes and Waste   133
        Job Security and AI   135
    Clinician Time   136
        Ambient Clinical Intelligence   137
        AI Use in Diagnostic Imaging and Analysis   137
    Summary   142

6. Emerging Applications in Healthcare Using AI. **145**
    Improving Human Health   146
        Improving Human Lives   147
    Making Technology Work for Healthcare   148
        Ambient Intelligence   148
        From a Patient's Perspective   151
        From a Doctor's Perspective   153
        From a Hospital System's Perspective   156
        From an Insurer's Perspective   160
    Emerging Applications and Services   162
        Coordination of Care Platform   163
        Disease State Management Platform   164
        Human to Machine Experience Services   165
        Customer Journey Platform   166
        Clinician Decision Support Tools   167
        Ambient Intelligence Environments   167
        Digital Twin Platform   168
        Real-Time Healthcare   169
        Internet of Behaviors   170
    Summary   171

7. AI at Scale for Healthcare Organizations. **173**
    Achieving AI at Scale   173
    Transforming Healthcare   178
        The Chasm   182
    Invisible Engines—Healthcare Platforms   183

The Road to a Healthcare Platform   186
Ecosystems   190
Application Programming Interfaces (APIs)   191
Summary   191

Index. **195**

Preface

The number of books describing artificial intelligence (AI), machine learning, deep learning, natural language processing, and the full constellation of AI technologies could fill a library. Coupled with the ever-growing list of articles, videos, and blogs, there is no lack of content. Clinicians, computer scientists, technologists, physicians, philosophers, and journalists each tackle different AI issues and challenges.

However, we couldn't find a book that discussed AI from a medical doctor and a technologist's paired perspectives. This is a book that tracks the journey of a physician and a technologist working together, discussing AI's opportunity while explaining AI for the consumption of a clinician, an IT worker, a user, an executive, or a business stakeholder. Our goal is for you to understand the possibilities for improvements in healthcare supercharged by artificial intelligence.

While discussing this vast potential, we strove to maintain the awe of AI while grounding the reader in the reality of AI today. We hope that Chapter 1 will provide you with confidence that you understand the myth versus the reality. More importantly, this first chapter seeks to familiarize you with the language of AI—what is a model, an algorithm, a neural network, and more—without your needing to brush up on linear algebra or computer science.

Chapter 2 integrates human-centered design, with providers and technologists working together to build smart systems to ensure that AI is used to do good. Chapter 3 helps the reader see how combining AI with sensing and monitoring, given the growth of intelligent objects, affords unparalleled opportunity for accelerating personalized medicine. Chapter 4 describes digital transformation and AI, and the utility of AI for digital transformation.

Several opportunities exist for using AI to reduce the amount of waste in healthcare and to reduce medical errors, as addressed in Chapter 5. Chapter 6 describes several AI solutions that, when realized, materially affect the quadruple aim of healthcare. Last, Chapter 7 provides a road map for how organizations realize AI's benefits not just for a single instance but at scale.

The state of healthcare is top of mind because it touches most aspects of our lives. The COVID-19 pandemic exposes the slow train wreck of dumb systems frustrating doctors, provider systems, and patients. There is no "silver bullet," no quick fix, no one-size-fits-all solution, but the potential to transform healthcare with AI is now possible. We hope this book provides a blueprint for organizations in their journey to leverage AI to make healthcare better for everyone.

Conventions Used in This Book

The following typographical conventions are used in this book:

Italic
> Indicates new terms, URLs, email addresses, filenames, and file extensions.

O'Reilly Online Learning

 For more than 40 years, *O'Reilly Media* has provided technology and business training, knowledge, and insight to help companies succeed.

Our unique network of experts and innovators share their knowledge and expertise through books, articles, and our online learning platform. O'Reilly's online learning platform gives you on-demand access to live training courses, in-depth learning paths, interactive coding environments, and a vast collection of text and video from O'Reilly and 200+ other publishers. For more information, visit *http://oreilly.com*.

How to Contact Us

Please address comments and questions concerning this book to the publisher:

> O'Reilly Media, Inc.
> 1005 Gravenstein Highway North
> Sebastopol, CA 95472
> 800-998-9938 (in the United States or Canada)
> 707-829-0515 (international or local)
> 707-829-0104 (fax)

We have a web page for this book, where we list errata, examples, and any additional information. You can access this page at *https://oreil.ly/ai-first-healthcare*.

Email *bookquestions@oreilly.com* to comment or ask technical questions about this book.

For news and information about our books and courses, visit *http://oreilly.com*.

Find us on Facebook: *http://facebook.com/oreilly*

Follow us on Twitter: *http://twitter.com/oreillymedia*

Watch us on YouTube: *http://www.youtube.com/oreillymedia*

Acknowledgments

Thanks to Melissa Potter, our content development editor at O'Reilly Media, whose edits, suggestions, and thoughtful comments were spot on. She kept us on track, and her patience and insights throughout the process of writing this book were invaluable. We will miss our weekly meetings with Melissa.

We are grateful to Arthur Johnson, our *AI-First Healthcare* copyeditor, who not only understood the topic and validated our research but also made the book immensely better.

Special thanks are due to those who gave their time to review our manuscript. Their thoughtful comments made a huge contribution to this book: Garry Choy, Dominik Dahlem, Thomas Davenport, Carly Eckert, Jun Li, and Bharath Ramsundar.

Kerrie Holley

Working with Siupo on this project felt like being part of a dream team; her real-life perspective on clinical practices and challenges brought the technological future to life.

Without the support of my wife, Melodie Holden Holley, who allowed me to work every weekend for a year, this book would not be possible. Her nonprofit work in women's health in developing countries enlightened me on the many issues of healthcare in underserved nations. Thank you to my kids—Kier Holley and Hugo Holley for their weekly support, Aliya Holley for her perpetual optimism, and Reece Holden for our thoughtful conversations. I hope this book provides my older son, Kier, with insights that will help him reach his goal of being a doctor. And thank you to my sister Rita Olford, whose smile brightens a room even over Zoom; my niece Theressa; and my nephews Dion, Herbert, Howard, and Marcus.

Thanks to Bethanie Collins for sharing her story.

Thanks to my colleagues, who continue to enlighten me on AI and more: Dr. Garry Choy, Dominik Dahlem, PhD, Sanjeeva Fernando, Steve Graham, Galina Grunin, Ravi Kondadadi, Dan McCreary, Mark Megerian, Dima Rekesh, PhD, Dr. Vernon Smith, and Julie Zhu.

Thank you to Fei-Fei Li, PhD and Andrew Moore, PhD, who taught me more than they know in our interactions discussing AI and healthcare.

Last, a dedication to my childhood mentor and educator, Sue Duncan, and her life's work at the Sue Duncan Children's Center in Chicago. And a dedication to my late brother and sister, Laurence and Lynette Holley, whom I miss every day.

Siupo Becker

I would like to express my deepest thanks to Kerrie Holley for asking me to partner with him on the creation of this book. You have been and continue to be a phenomenal friend and colleague.

Kudos and thanks to Melissa Potter, our content development editor, without whom this book would not have come into being. Thank you to my husband, Tom, for your support during this time, and to Florinda and Neal Deloya, who kept our entire household running so that I could focus on this work. And last but not least, thank *you*, kind reader, for your interest in the rapidly developing field of AI in healthcare. I wish you all the best.

Introduction

Across the world, healthcare systems face enormous challenges, including lack of access, cost, waste, and an aging population. Pandemics like coronavirus (COVID-19) create severe strain on healthcare systems, resulting in shortages of personal protective equipment, insufficient or inaccurate diagnostic tests, overburdened clinicians, and imperfect information sharing, to name a few important effects. More importantly, a healthcare crisis such as COVID-19 or the emergence of human immunodeficiency virus (HIV) in the 1980s highlights the stark reality of shortcomings in our health systems. We can reimagine and realize systems of care and back-office healthcare systems, as healthcare crises accentuate current problems, such as:

- Inequitable access to healthcare
- Insufficient on-demand healthcare services
- High costs and lack of price transparency
- Significant waste
- Fragmented, siloed payer and provider systems
- High business frictions and poor consumer experiences
- Record keeping frozen since the 1960s
- Slow adoption of technological advances
- Burnout of healthcare providers, with the inability of clinicians to remain educated on the newest advances in medicine based on the volume of data to be absorbed

As we focus on these problems, we should recognize they are interdependent, giving the illusion of healthcare as being complex, when in reality healthcare is delivered through complex systems. That's not to say providing excellent healthcare isn't challenging; however, we can build systems with less complexity, providing better care and making the healthcare system work for everybody. AI should be a crucial enabler of simplicity in healthcare and of building intelligent systems of care. The COVID-19 crisis shows the opportunities for applying AI, ranging from diagnostics and treatment decision support to contact tracing and the use of AI-driven tools.

We think of AI as being synonymous with machine learning, and because of that, we *don't* think about building complete AI systems accounting for processes, structures, experiences, and patterns of care delivery, which can be enabled by machine learning models, natural language processing, and more. Framing the problem this way helps us understand and set the stage for developing AI systems, not just machine learning models—for building simple, intelligent, robust systems that embody remarkable, frictionless experiences for all stakeholders in the healthcare ecosystem. That's why we wrote this book, *as a primer for employing AI in healthcare* without a narrow focus on machine learning. Each chapter moves us incrementally closer to understanding how we make AI the center of everything we do in healthcare without focusing on AI, and this is what we mean by AI-First. A lot of what we discuss is both ambitious and aspirational but also realistic.

There is no magical solution or technology such as AI that fixes healthcare, just like there isn't a single technology solving all problems in banking, retail, automotive, tech, or any other industry. Existing healthcare systems are enormously complex, and multiple attempts to revamp their structure and function have failed. Repairing complex healthcare systems may not be the answer; instead, we propose rethinking how we build production-ready tools, experiences, and intelligent systems using data that work for doctors, nurses, healthcare workers, patients, and care facilities.

Today, in one process or one tool within one specialty, AI delivers value: finding cancer, diagnosing eye diseases, identifying abnormal images, enabling early detection of the onset of Alzheimer's or depression, and more. Think about the internet and the shift to web pages, and then the shift to mobility as we moved to apps. Now, with AI, we embrace natural human interface modalities such as voice. The experience of how people interface with machines should change along with the underlying systems. By applying AI to various situations/roles within healthcare, we create a more integrated and therefore less complex system for users, whether they are consumers, providers, or payers.

There are some basic tenets to ground us:

- AI systems improve every day, and continuously.
- AI systems and tools may be the only way to accelerate the delivery of healthcare to the underserved.
- AI systems will become easier to trust as they explain themselves and as user experience increases over time.

- AI systems will endow a single doctor with the experience of millions of doctors.
- AI, like mobility, will be the way of life for children born after 2010.

Each doctor's mistakes and successes have to be learned by experience and eventually become part of the standard of care and best practices. Doctors learn from other doctors, from research studies, from drug and device companies marketing products, and from their successes and failures with their own patients. Each doctor's mistake has to be discovered and actualized—sometimes to the detriment of their patients. This type of learning reflects human nature, and clinicians are not immune to the hard-wiring of our brains and learning systems. The problem is that this anecdotal experience leads to bias and limitations on the part of the provider. In fact, some physicians may inadvertently fool themselves into thinking a diagnosis is correct, or that a treatment works even though it's contrary to evidence supported by studies or outcomes of thousands of patients, based on their own anecdotal/previous experience. Sometimes a doctor is simply unaware of studies and evidence of new treatment care pathways or better diagnostic modalities. The current medical environment demands that physicians see as high a volume of patients as possible to maximize reimbursement. That leaves doctors little time to address secondary patient care tasks, let alone remain educated on the most recent advances in medicine. But doctors today have direct access to the experiences and best practices of thousands of cohorts; they don't need to wait for best practices to be codified into standards of care. With AI, we can change this calculus even more and move at a faster scale than a single doctor or institution could on their own.

The era of a doctor touting that "in my experience, this treatment works" has passed; instead, they should be saying, "My experience plus the experiences of hundreds of thousands of patients, fellow doctors, and clinical studies give me confidence in pursuing this treatment path." But how would a doctor have at their disposal, at their fingertips, the knowledge of hundreds of thousands of clinical studies, the experiences of hundreds of thousands of patient treatment pathways, and the collective experience of thousands and thousands of doctors? This requires technology; it requires AI. As humans, clinicians are subject to cognitive and cultural biases, but we can minimize and maybe even eliminate the impacts of such biases within AI by providing a technological equalizer in the knowledge base of providers.

AI can evolve to deliver best practices, cumulative knowledge, and the experiences of hundreds of thousands of doctors to the doorstep of any doctor more swiftly than any previous technology. But for this reality to materialize, AI needs to be embedded in our entire healthcare ecosystem, becoming as ubiquitous as electricity, so that it can be used and expanded to lift the practices and skills of every medical professional. This is what we mean when we use the term *AI-First*. For AI to truly drive solutions for the most pressing problems, we have to think about how to develop holistic, intelligent systems—AI systems, not just machine learning models. We must think about the structures and processes, which include patterns of diagnostics, treatments, and care delivery, that can be enabled by machine learning, computer vision, natural language processing, ambient computing, and more.

Our AI-First journey starts with a chapter describing AI and ends with a chapter describing how to make AI a reality in healthcare at scale:

Chapter 1, Myths and Realities of AI

> To understand what AI-First means, we must first understand what AI is and what it is not. We must explore the myths and realities of AI and understand the art of what's possible. Most tales have some threads of truth, but we describe them as myths because they are either false or misleading. AI and machine learning are used synonymously and interchangeably, and this can be good and bad. Machine learning is critical to the success of building AI systems, but an AI system can be a lot more than a collection of machine learning models. Computers getting better at tasks previously done only by humans does not mean machines are getting smarter and smarter, moving toward or even beyond human intelligence. It does mean, however, that we have the tools to build intelligent systems.

Chapter 2, Human-Centered AI

> The conversation around machines surpassing human intelligence is both nuanced and more philosophical than science-based. The dark and dystopian views of AI taking over the world or replacing doctors cause us to lose sight of what we can do today. The real threat is not superintelligent machines or AI; the threat comes from dumb systems. Dumb systems often create friction, are typically designed with weak user interfaces, and frequently promote a lack of interoperability. Today, the evidence is overwhelming that superior results are obtained through thoughtful pairing of humans and machines. We can use human-centered AI to usher in a new era of healthcare in which access is improved, providing everyone the opportunity to live healthier lives.

Chapter 3, Monitoring + AI = Rx for Personal Health

> The opportunity for people to play a more significant role in their healthcare has never been greater thanks to the proliferation of personal health gadgets, intelligent medical devices, and smart wearables with sensors that monitor people's vital signs. Infuse these technologies with AI and combine them with sensory-abundant ambient spaces, and a prescription emerges for improving personal health. Invisible computing is emerging, as we now see AI in our everyday lives, such as in the Apple Watch, which allows you to look at your heartbeat to check for an irregular rhythm that may be AFib (atrial fibrillation, a risk factor for stroke). This will expand to more ordinary things, like your toothbrush taking saliva samples and alerting you to changes that might indicate you are at risk for metabolic disease or infectious disease. The arrival of smart and ambient spaces

in our homes and places of work creates a future in which noninvasive technology married with AI becomes a tool, a prescription for keeping people healthy.

Chapter 4, Digital Transformation and AI

The delivery of care should be transparent to all constituents in the healthcare ecosystem, and access to services should be coordinated with all parties in real time. Back-office systems such as claims and prior authorizations should operate like other industries, in near real time or in real time. Real-time healthcare must be the norm, not the exception, such that outcomes are immediate, and prior authorizations behave the same as credit card authorizations, operating in seconds for the vast number of transactions. Digital healthcare begins and thrives with people using invisible engines that they helped design and that undergo continuous improvement based on clinician and patient experiences. This requires digital platforms, the kind we see with companies born in the internet and cloud eras. Adoption of AI and accompanying technologies can make this a reality. Digitization requires understanding and adopting AI, not just machine learning models.

Chapter 5, An Uncomfortable Truth

An uncomfortable truth must be addressed in today's healthcare: the enormous amount of waste. Suboptimal consumer outcomes from clinician visits should and can be improved with AI. Evolving to a human/machine-based healthcare system in which agency is solely in the hands of people, not "Dr. Algorithm" or "AI Doctor," will dramatically improve patient outcomes. AI and technology must be ever present, though invisible, to reduce errors and waste. There is evidence of the value AI brings in reducing waste in healthcare; today, AI is used largely to detect fraud but can also be applied to identify and reduce waste in other aspects of healthcare. This chapter examines how leveraging AI can facilitate the solutions that improve efficiency and reduce waste.

Chapter 6, Emerging Applications in Healthcare Using AI

Applications for healthcare sit in the front office and are often visible to consumers or patients; they live in our pockets via smart mobile devices, we wear them, and they live in the back offices of payers, insurers, and healthcare service providers. AI is upending all of these application types, and new application types are emerging, some of them situational applications with short lives. All of these application types must be embraced with an eye toward making healthcare operate in real time, enabling points of care to start with the patient when necessary, and enabling healthcare to be ubiquitous and on-demand. This chapter explores these new and emerging application types.

Chapter 7, AI at Scale for Healthcare Organizations

Making the promises of AI come alive will quickly become an order of magnitude more complicated than our shift to mobility was, for a number of reasons. The process will start, just as it did with mobility, with our recognizing that we must embrace a new modality and a new type of application. Every organization's journey will be different, and this chapter provides a prescriptive approach to getting started, whether the organization is big or massive.

Summary

The adoption and value of AI implementations are shaped less by the intrinsic attributes of AI technologies and more by the economics of investing in innovations that make healthcare better. It's not so much about what AI can do for you or me but about the specific benefits or transformations to be achieved through investment in AI. AI-First is not about the investment in AI but more about why this general-purpose technology, AI, should be seen as a horizontal enabling layer for the business of healthcare. AI integration into healthcare is harder than it looks, especially when we seek to reconfigure care systems, rather than just augmenting existing systems and making predictions with machine learning models.

This is a time to reimagine how we do healthcare, and to begin a transformation of the healthcare system, with AI at its core.

CHAPTER 1

Myths and Realities of AI

Pamela McCorduck, in her book *Machines Who Think* (W. H. Freeman), describes AI as an "audacious effort to duplicate in an artifact" what all of us see as our most defining attribute: human intelligence. Her 1979 book provides a fascinating glimpse into early thinking about AI—not using theorems or science, but instead describing how people came to imagine its possibilities. With something so magical and awe-inspiring as AI, it's not hard to imagine the surrounding hyperbole. This chapter hopes to maintain the awe but ground it in reality.

Stuart Russell, a computer scientist and one of the most important AI thinkers of the 21st century, discusses the past, present, and future of AI in his book *Human Compatible* (Viking). Russell writes that AI is rapidly becoming a pervasive aspect of today and will be the dominant technology of the future. Perhaps in no industry but healthcare is this so true, and we hope to address the implications of that in this book.

For most people, the term *artificial intelligence* evokes a number of attributed properties and capabilities—some real, many futuristic, and others imagined. AI does have several superpowers, but it is not a "silver bullet" that will solve skyrocketing healthcare costs and the growing burden of illness. That said, thoughtful AI use in healthcare creates an enormous opportunity to help people live healthier lives and, in doing so, control some healthcare costs and drive better outcomes. This chapter describes healthcare and technology myths surrounding AI as a prelude to discussing how AI-enhanced apps, systems, processes, and platforms provide enormous advantages in quality, speed, effectiveness, cost, and capacity, allowing clinicians to focus on people and their healthcare.

A lot of the hype accompanying AI stems from machine learning models' performance compared to that of people, often clinicians. Papers and algorithms abound describing machine learning models outperforming humans in various tasks ranging from image and voice recognition to language processing and predictions. This raises the question of whether machine learning (ML) diagnosticians will become the norm. However, the performance of these models in clinical practice often differs from their performance in the lab; machine learning models built on training and test data sometimes fail to achieve the same success in areas such as object detection (e.g., identifying a tumor) or disease prediction. Real-world data is different—that is, the training data does not match the real-world data—and this causes a data shift. For example, something as simple as variation in skin types could cause a model trained in the lab to lose accuracy in a clinical setting. ML diagnosticians may be our future, but additional innovation must occur for algorithm diagnosticians to become a reality.

The hyperbole and myths that have emerged around AI blur the art of what's possible with AI. Before discussing those myths, let's understand what we mean by AI. Descriptions of AI are abundant, but the utility of AI will be more important than a definition. Much of this book will explore the service of AI. We provide clarity in helping with understanding the context and meaning of the term *AI*. A brief look at its origin provides a useful framework for understanding how AI is understood and used today.

AI Origins and Definition

Humans imagining the art of what's possible with artificial life and machines has been centuries in the making. In her 2018 book *Gods and Robots* (Princeton University Press), Adrienne Mayor, a research scholar, paints a picture of humans envisioning artificial life in the early years of recorded history. She writes about ancient dreams and myths of technology enhancing humans. A few thousand years later, in 1943, two Chicago-area researchers introduced the notion of neural networks in a paper describing a mathematical model. The two researchers—a neuroscientist, Warren S. McCulloch, and a logician, Walter Pitts—attempted to explain how the complex decision processes of the human brain work using math. This was the birth of neural networks, and the dawn of artificial intelligence as we now know it.

Decades later, in a small town along the Connecticut River in New Hampshire, a plaque hangs in Dartmouth Hall, commemorating a 1956 summer research project, a brainstorming session conducted by mathematicians and scientists. The names of the founding fathers of AI are engraved on the plaque, recognizing them for their contributions during that summer session, which was the first time that the words "artificial intelligence" were used; John McCarthy, widely known as the father of AI, gets credit for coining the term.

The attendees at the Dartmouth summer session imagined artificial intelligence as computers doing things that we perceive as displays of human intelligence. They discussed ideas ranging from computers that understand human speech to machines that operate like the human brain, using neurons. What better display of intelligence than devices that are able to speak and understand human language, now known as natural language processing? During this summer session, AI founders drew inspiration from how the human brain works as it relays information between input receptors, neurons, and deep brain matter. Consequently, thinking emerged on using artificial neurons as a technique for mimicking the human brain.

Enthusiasm and promises for the transformation of healthcare abound, but this goal remains elusive. In the 1960s, the AI community introduced expert systems, which attempt to transfer expertise from an expert (e.g., a doctor) to computers using rules and then to apply them to a knowledge base to deduce new information, an inference. In the 1970s, rules-based systems like MYCIN, an AI system engineered to treat blood infections, held much promise. MYCIN attempted to diagnose patients using their symptoms and clinical test results. Although its results were better than or comparable to those of specialists in blood infections, its use in clinical practice did not materialize. Another medical expert system, CADUCEUS, tried to improve on MYCIN. MYCIN, CADUCEUS, and other expert systems (such as INTERNIST-I) illustrate the efforts of the AI community to create clinical diagnostic tools, but none of these systems found its way into clinical practice.

This situation persists today; AI in healthcare is not readily found at the clinical bedside. Several research papers demonstrate that AI performs better than humans at tasks such as diagnosing disease. For example, deep learning algorithms outperform radiologists at spotting malignant tumors. Yet these "superior" disease-detecting algorithms largely remain in the labs. Will these machine learning diagnostic tools meet the same fate as the expert systems of the 20th century? Will it be many years before AI substantially augments humans in clinical settings?

This is not the 1970s; AI now permeates healthcare in a variety of ways—in production, for example. Artificial intelligence helps researchers in drug creation for various diseases, such as cancer. Beth Israel Deaconess Medical Center, a teaching hospital of Harvard Medical School, uses AI to diagnose possible terminal blood diseases. It uses AI-enhanced microscopes to scan for injurious bacteria like *E. coli* in blood samples, working at a faster rate than manual scanning. Natural language processing is widely used for automating the extraction and encoding of clinical data from physician notes. Multiple tools at work in production settings today use natural language processing for clinical coding. Machine learning helps with steering patients to the optimal providers. For decades, machine learning has been used to identify fraud and reduce waste. The widespread adoption of AI in specific use cases in healthcare companies, coupled with recent innovations in AI, holds tremendous promise for expanding the use of AI in clinical settings.

This book on AI-First healthcare hopes to show a different future for the widespread adoption of AI in healthcare, including in clinical settings and in people's homes. There continues to be an active conversation among clinicians and technologists about implementing AI in healthcare. A 2019 symposium attended by clinicians, policy makers, healthcare professionals, and computer scientists profiled real-world examples of AI moving from the lab to the clinic.[1] The symposium highlighted three themes for success: life cycle planning, stakeholder involvement, and contextualizing AI products and tools in existing workflows.

A lot has changed in the years since the conception of neural networks in 1943. AI continues to evolve every decade, explaining why consensus on an AI definition remains elusive. Since we are not all operating with the same definition, there is a lot of confusion around what AI is and what it is not. How artificial intelligence is defined can depend on who provides the explanation, the context, and the reason for offering a definition. *AI is a broad term representing our intent to build humanlike intelligent entities for selected tasks. The goal is to use fields of science, mathematics, and technology to mimic or replicate human intelligence with machines, and we call this "AI."* In this book, we will explore several intelligent entities, such as augmented doctors, prediction machines, virtual care spaces, and more, that improve healthcare outcomes, patient care, experiences, and cost.

We continue to build and exhibit systems, machines, and computers that can do what we previously had understood only humans could do: win at checkers, beat a reigning world chess master, best the winningest *Jeopardy!* contestants. Famously, the computer program AlphaGo has defeated world champions in the 4,000-year-old abstract strategy game Go and excels in emulating (and surpassing) human performance of this game. Articles abound on machine learning models in labs outperforming doctors on selected tasks, such as identification of possible cancerous tumors in imaging studies; this suggests that AI may eventually replace some physician specialties, such as radiologist.

AI and Machine Learning

A tenet of this book's central message is that *artificial intelligence comprises more than machine learning.* If we think of AI solely in the context of ML, it's doubtful that we ever build intelligent systems that mirror human intelligence in the performance of clinical or healthcare activities, or that we create AI that materially enhances patient experiences, reduces costs, and improves the health of people and the quality of life for healthcare workers.

---

1 Erik Drysdale at al., "Implementing AI in Healthcare" (*https://oreil.ly/AzfGq*) (whitepaper, Vector-SickKids Health AI Deployment Symposium, Toronto, ON, October 30, 2019).

Most publicized implementations of AI showcase ML model successes, which explains why many see an equivalence between machine learning and AI. Furthermore, the most common AI applications utilizing deep learning, computer vision, or natural language processing all employ machine learning.

The supposition that machine learning is the same as AI ignores or dismisses those aspects of a software stack used to build intelligent systems that are not machine learning. Or worse, our imagination or knowledge of what's possible with AI is limited to only those functions implementable by machine learning.

AI comprises many of the components of the AI Stack in Figure 1-1, which illustrates the many capabilities of AI beyond machine learning.

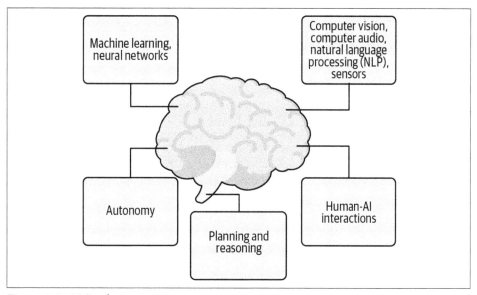

Figure 1-1. AI Stack

AI's aspiration to create machines exhibiting humanlike intelligence requires more than a learning capability. We expect and need the many AI capabilities for engineering healthcare solutions illustrated in Figure 1-1. Transforming healthcare with AI involves computer vision, language, audio, reasoning, and planning functions. For some problems, we may choose to give AI autonomy; in our discussion on ethics later in the book, we address the implications and risks of doing so.

The AI features in an implementation will vary based on the problem at hand. For example, in an ICU, we may want AI to have audio capability to enable question-and-answer capability between AI and clinicians. A clinician in conversation with AI requires language skills in AI. AI must be able to understand the natural language of people—that is, it must have natural language processing (NLP). Speech to text and text to address must be a capability of AI to enable a rich conversation. We need sensors to detect movement, such as a patient falling out of bed, with AI triggering alerts. At the heart of enabling this intelligent space in the ICU, we need continuous learning. All of these features require machine learning. Thinking of AI as a single thing or a single machine would be incorrect. For example, in the ICU, AI would be part of the environment. Embedding AI in voice speakers, sensors, and other smart things working together provides humanlike intelligence augmenting clinicians. We know that patients recall less than 50% of their physician communications during the patient-doctor interaction.[2] Therein lies one of many opportunities to use AI to improve patient-doctor interactions.

The AI Stack may comprise both a hardware and a software stack, a set of underlying components needed to create a complete solution. Using the AI Stack in Figure 1-1 as a guide, the next sections provide a brief primer on AI capabilities, starting with machine learning and neural networks.

Machine learning and neural networks

There are different types or subcategories of machine learning, such as supervised learning, unsupervised learning, and deep learning.

In supervised learning, we train the computer using data that is labeled. If we want an ML model to detect a child's mother, we provide a large number of pictures of the mother, labeling each photo as "the mother." Or if we want an ML model to detect pneumonia in an X-ray, we take many X-rays of pneumonia and label each as such. In essence, we tag the data with the correct answer. It's like having a supervisor who gives you all the right solutions for your test. A supervised machine learning algorithm learns from labeled training data. In effect, we supervise the training of the algorithm. With supervised machine learning, we effectively use a computer to identify, sort, and categorize things. If we need to pore through thousands of X-rays to identify pneumonia, we will likely perform this task more quickly with a computer using machine learning than with a doctor. However, just because the computer outperforms the doctor on this task doesn't mean the computer can do better than a doctor in clinical care.

Much of the learning we do as humans is unsupervised, without the benefit of a teacher. We don't give the answers to unsupervised learning models, and they don't use labeled data. Instead, we ask the algorithm, the model, to discover the answer. Applying this to the example of the child's mother, we provide the face recognition algorithm with features, like skin tone, eye color, facial shape, dimples, hair color, or distance between the eyes. Unsupervised machine learning recognizes the unique

---

2 Sara Heath, "Patient Recall Suffers as Patients Remember Half of Health Info" (*https://oreil.ly/bNBtT*), Patient-EngagementHIT, March 26, 2018.

features of the child's mother; learning from the data, it identifies "the mother" in images with high accuracy.

Deep learning uses a series of algorithms to derive answers. Data feeds one side, the input layer, and moves through the hidden layer(s), pulling specific information that feeds the output layer, producing an insight. We describe these layers, or series of algorithms, as a neural network. Figure 1-2 illustrates a neural network with three layers. Each layer's output is the next layer's input. The depth of the neural network reflects the number of layers traversed in order to reach the output layer. When a neural network comprises more than three layers or more than one hidden layer, it is considered deep, and we refer to this machine learning technique as deep learning. It's often said that the neural network mimics the way the human brain operates, but the reality is that the neural network is an attempt to simulate the network of neurons that make up a human brain so that machines will be able to learn like humans.

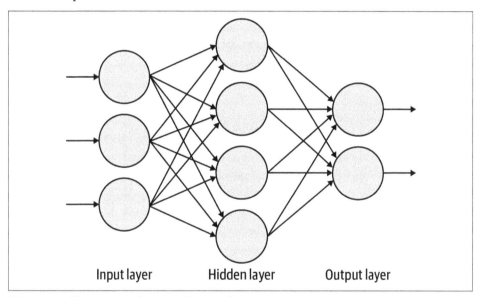

Figure 1-2. Illustration of a neural network

The neural network allows the tweaking of parameters until the model provides the desired output. Since the output can be tuned to our liking, it's a challenge to "show our work," resulting in the "black box" categorization. We're less concerned about how the model got the result and are instead focused on consistently getting the same result. The more data advances through the neural network, the less likely it is that we can pinpoint exactly why the model works, and we focus on the model accuracy.

People and machines learn differently. We teach machines to identify certain images as a tumor with predefined algorithms using labeled data (e.g., tumor or non-tumor). A child can recognize their mother with minimal training and without lots of pictures of their mother and of people who are not their mother. But a machine needs enough data (e.g., tumor/non-tumor) to build the "skill" to learn if an image is "the mother."

A machine learning model, often synonymously but inaccurately described as an algorithm, learns from data. These algorithms are implemented in code. Algorithms are just the "rules," like an algebraic expression, but a model is a solution. Machine learning algorithms are designed mechanisms that run the engineered featured inputs through the algorithms to get the probability of the targets. The option selections and hyperparameter tuning increase the model's outcome accuracy and control modeling errors. Data is split into training and test data, using training data to build a model and test data to validate the model. Cross-function validation is necessary before the model's deployment into production, to make sure the new data would get a similar outcome. Figure 1-3 illustrates a simple regression model. This figure shows a linear relationship to the target Y variable from x1, x2, ... features used in the model. An early step is to define the target to predict, find the data source to perform the feature engineering, which identifies the related variables, and test the different algorithms to best fit the data and the target. A scoring mechanism called the F1 score is used to validate the model performance.

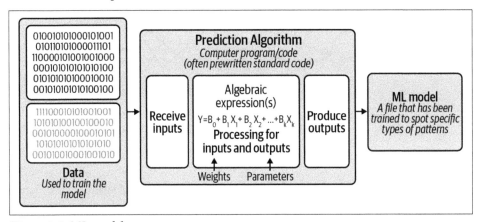

Figure 1-3. ML model

An easy example to understand is when our email is sorted into categories like "spam" and "inbox." We could write a computer program with If/Then/Else statements to perform the sorting, but this handcrafted approach would take time; it would also be fragile, because what constitutes spam changes constantly, so we would have to continuously update the computer program with more If/Then/Else computer statements as we learned more about new spam emails. Machine learning algorithms can learn how to classify email messages as spam or inbox by training on large datasets that have spam.

Once we are satisfied that the model works with different data, we incorporate the model or file and plug it into a workflow or product like email or a disease prediction tool. The model can handle new data without any hand coding, and the model gets used by different users using the email product. In this email example, we labeled data, which is supervised learning.

Computer vision and natural language processing (NLP)

Computer vision (CV), a subfield of AI, seeks to help computers understand the visual world. The visual world in healthcare encompasses many things; a short (and incomplete) list includes:

- Still images, such as X-ray images for detecting pneumonia
- Photographs showing skin lesions
- Sensors that detect movements such as falling or activities within a home
- Faxes of handwritten clinician notes
- Videos showing potential health issues

Computer vision enables machines to see and understand these visual items and then react. Often machine learning facilitates the identification and classification of objects.

Natural language processing, or NLP, provides machines with the ability to read and understand human languages. Understanding and generating speech (i.e., writing and speaking) is essential for human intelligence. NLP allows computers to read clinical notes, analyze keywords and phrases, and extract meaning from them so that people can create and use actionable insights. NLP can be useful in extracting vital elements from patient-physician interactions and automating content population in electronic medical records.

Planning and reasoning

Humans plan as a natural part of their lives. Solving many healthcare problems requires AI to realize a planning component. Planning and machine learning operate complementarily to solve challenging problems. When Google created the computer program AlphaGo to beat one of the world's best strategy players in the board game Go, the program used planning and learning. The game involved AlphaGo using a simulation model, Monte Carlo, and deep learning to predict the probability of specific outcomes. In this example, the computer must act autonomously and flexibly to construct a sequence of actions to reach a goal. It uses machine learning and techniques such as computational algorithms, aka Monte Carlo, to determine its next move. Planning may take the form of If/Then/Else logic or algorithms—whatever it takes to engineer an intelligent system necessary to solve a challenge.

Another aspect of planning addresses the black-box challenge of deep learning. The fact that we cannot explain how a model consistently gets to, say, 95% accuracy doesn't translate to not being able to explain AI outcomes. Model performance may not achieve clinical adoption, but model transparency gets us closer to that end goal, and this is part of AI planning. Like all fields of AI, interpretable AI is an area of research in which start-ups and researchers work to take the guesswork out of AI.

In addition to planning, many AI solutions must have a reasoning element. Machines make inferences using data, which is a form of reasoning. Early researchers in the field of AI developed algorithms and used If/Then/Else rules to emulate the simple step-by-step reasoning people use to solve problems and make logical inferences. The early inference engines and decision support systems in the 1960s used these kinds of techniques.

Machine learning performs many human tasks better than humans, but not reasoning. Figure 1-4 shows an image of two cylinders of different sizes and a box. Any five-year-old could answer the non-relational and relational questions shown in the image. But a computer using deep learning would not be able to understand implicit relationships between different things, something humans do quite well.

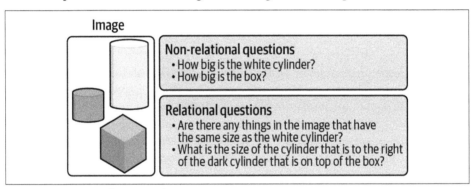

Figure 1-4. Image of various objects

In June 2017, DeepMind published a paper showing a new technique, relation networks, that can reason about relations among objects.[3] DeepMind reasoning used a variety of AI techniques in combination to get answers to relational questions. Developing reasoning in AI continues to be an evolving field of research. Healthcare solutions that need reasoning will consider both old and new AI techniques as well as emerging research.

---

3 Adam Santoro et al., "A Simple Neural Network Module for Relational Reasoning" (*https://oreil.ly/GSlLa*), DeepMind, June 2017.

Autonomy

There are instances in which we want AI to operate on its own, to make decisions and take action. An obvious example is when AI in an autonomous vehicle can save the life of a pedestrian. In healthcare, people filing claims would like instantaneous affirmative responses. Autonomous AI systems accomplish tasks like approving claims or authoring readmissions, and AI accomplishes these goals without interacting with humans. Autonomous systems may operate in an augmented fashion, answering clinicians' questions or guiding a clinician on a task. Levels of autonomy in healthcare will vary, taking cues from levels of autonomy defined for vehicles.[4] Autonomy in AI is not an all-or-nothing proposition. AI in healthcare must do no harm and in many cases should be held to a higher standard of care than AI in vehicles. Engineering autonomy in healthcare solutions must be a human-centered process. Engineers should not conflate automation, where AI can consistently repeat a task, with AI having autonomy. Humans must remain in the loop.

Human-AI interactions

Another key tenet of an AI-First approach is to make sure humans are always in the loop. AI cannot operate in a vacuum; people are needed to curate and provide data, check for biases in data, maintain machine learning models, and manage the overall efficacy of AI systems in healthcare. AI won't always be right—things can even go terribly wrong—and humans' experience and ability to react will be critical to evolving AI systems and their effectiveness in clinical settings and in healthcare at large.

It's amazing to think that AI and ML are a natural part of our lexicon and are ubiquitous terms around the world. Clearly there has been a resurgence of AI, and it's still spreading. The next section explores the diffusion of AI.

AI Transitions

Innovations in AI allow it to make giant leaps forward, toward the goal of mimicking human intelligence. Figure 1-5 highlights key innovations that became transitions for powering new AI applications and solutions in healthcare and other industries.

---

4 US Department of Transportation, NHTSA, "Automated Vehicles for Safety" (*https://oreil.ly/vp03H*), n.d.

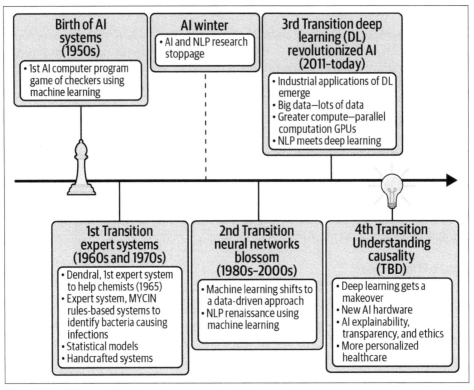

Figure 1-5. AI transitions

Arthur Samuel, a pioneer in AI, developed a checkers-playing computer program in 1952, and it is widely recognized to be the first computer program to learn on its own—the very first machine learning program. Later years saw the emergence of expert systems and decision-support systems such as MYCIN, CADUCEUS, and INTERNIST-I, which we discussed previously.

Many of the early 20th-century activities in AI used procedural programming logic as the primary programming technique and heavy lifting to provide the supporting infrastructure. The iconic display of this wave may have been when IBM's Deep Blue computer beat one of humanity's great intellectual champions in chess, Gary Kasparov. At the time, we thought this was a sign of artificial intelligence catching up to human intelligence. IBM's Deep Blue required a lot of heavy lifting; it was a specialized, purpose-built computer that many described as a brute force in both the hardware and the software. It's worth mentioning that one of Deep Blue's programmers, when asked how much effort was devoted to AI, responded "no effort." He described Deep Blue not as an AI project but as a project that played chess through the brute force of computers to do fast calculations and shift through possibilities.

AI Winter is a metaphorical description of the period of AI research and development that experienced a substantially reduced level of interest and funding. The hype and exaggeration of AI in the early 20th century backfired, as the technology at hand failed to meet expectations. Algorithmic AI did not transcend humans. The AI depicted in sci-fi movies was not real.

In 1966, government funding of research on NLP was halted, as machine translations were more expensive than using people. Governments canceled AI research, and AI researchers found it hard to find work. This was a dark period for AI, a winter. The delivery failures, runaway projects, and sunken costs of governments and industry led to the first AI Winter. AI was a dream, and it became an accepted premise that AI doesn't work. This thinking continued until analytics became the moniker. Machine learning techniques and predictive analytics were born, and the second AI transition was underway.

In 2011, IBM again made an iconic display of AI, when the IBM Watson computer system competed on *Jeopardy!* against legendary champions Brad Rutter (*https://oreil.ly/CK80K*) and Ken Jennings (*https://oreil.ly/WMWRT*) and won! This 2011 IBM Watson system took several years to build, and again brute force was used in the hardware implementation, while a lot of math, machine learning, and NLP were used on the engineering side. Neither graphical processor units (GPUs) nor deep learning characteristics of 21st-century AI found any traction. To the casual viewer, it may have seemed that IBM Watson on *Jeopardy!* was doing conversational AI, but that was not the case, as IBM Watson was not listening and processing audio. Rather, ASCII files were transmitted.

In fairness to IBM Watson and its *Jeopardy!*-winning system, its innovative work on natural language understanding advanced the field.

What we can do with AI today is of course different from what we could do in the 1950s, 1960s, 1970s, 1980s, 1990s, and early 2000s. Although we are using many of the same algorithms and much of the same computer science, a great deal of innovation has occurred in AI. Deep learning, new algorithms, GPUs, and massive amounts of data are key differences. There has been an explosion of new thinking in industry and academia, and there is a renaissance going on today, largely because of deep learning.

The demonstration of neural nets, deep learning algorithms, and the reaching of human perception in sight, sound, and language understanding set in motion a tsunami of AI research and development in academia and technology companies. The internet provided the mother lode of data, and GPUs the compute power for computation, and thus the third AI transition arrived.

In October 2015, the original AlphaGo became the first computer system to beat a human professional Go player without a handicap. In 2017, a successor, AlphaGo

Master, beat the world's top-ranked player in a three-game match. AlphaGo uses deep learning and is another iconic display of AI. In 2017, DeepMind introduced Alpha-Zero, an AI system that taught itself from scratch how to play and master the games of chess and Go and subsequently beat world champions. What's remarkable is that the system was built without providing it domain knowledge—only the rules of the game. It's also fascinating to see a computer game with its own unique, dynamic, and creative style of play.[5] AlphaZero shows the power of AI.

It's quite possible (and even likely) that many companies will see failures with their AI plans and implementations. The limitations of deep learning and AI are well known to researchers, bloggers, and a number of experts.[6] For example, deep learning cannot itself explain how it derived its answers. Deep learning does not have causality and, unlike humans, doesn't enable human reasoning, or what many describe as common sense. Deep learning needs thousands of images to learn and identify specific objects, like determining a type of cat or identifying your mother from a photo. Humans need only a handful of examples and can do it in seconds. Humans know that an image of a face in which the nose is below the mouth is not correct. Anything that approximates human reasoning is currently not viable for AI; that will be the fourth transition.

Amazing progress has been made in AI, but we have a ways to go before it achieves human-level intelligence. Research continues to advance AI. AI is aspirational, endeavoring to move as far to the right on the Artificial Intelligence Continuum as possible, and as quickly as possible, as illustrated in Figure 1-6.

In contrast to movies like *Ex Machina* or *2001: A Space Odyssey*, where AI surpasses human intelligence (reflecting strong AI), we are not yet there—we have weak AI today, or what some describe as narrow AI. It's narrow because, for example, we train machine learning models to detect pneumonia, but the same model cannot detect tumorous cancers in an X-ray. That is, a system trained to do one thing will quickly break on a related but slightly different task. Today, when we largely target well-defined problems for AI, people are needed to ensure that AI is correct. Humans must train the AI models and manage the life cycle of AI development from cradle to grave.

---

5 Matthew Sadler and Natasha Regan, *Game Changer: AlphaZero's Groundbreaking Chess Strategies and the Promise of AI* (Alkamaar, Netherlands: New in Chess, 2019).

6 Bahman Zohuri and Masoud Moghaddam, "Deep Learning Limitations and Flaws" (*https://oreil.ly/QlAAm*), *Modern Approaches on Material Science* 2, no. 3 (2020): 241–250.

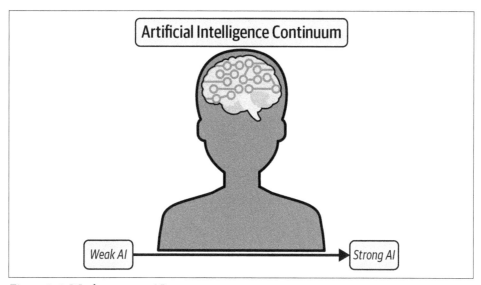

Figure 1-6. Weak to strong AI

New innovations in AI will move us further to the right along the continuum, where perhaps causality will be within our sight. We will begin to understand, for example, whether an aspirin taken before a long flight actually does operate as a blood thinner, reducing the subject's risk of blood clots related to immobility during travel. This is contrasted with the current practice of recommending that airline passengers take an aspirin as a precautionary measure.

Deep learning most likely will get a makeover with new research and innovations. Hardware will improve. There will be another AI transition like those depicted in Figure 1-5, and it will accelerate the movement of AI further to the right along the continuum depicted in Figure 1-6. Today AI and humans must work hand in hand to solve problems. AI can go wrong, and we need clinicians with intuition and experience doing healthcare augmented with AI.

AI—A General Purpose Technology

In addition to AI being a field of study in computer science, it is also proving to be a *general purpose technology* (GPT).[7] GPTs are described as engines of growth—they fuel technological progress and economic growth. That is, a handful of technologies have a dramatic effect on industries over extended periods of time. GPTs, like as the

---

7 Timothy F. Bresnahan and Manuel Trajtenberg, "General Purpose Technologies 'Engines of Growth'?" (*https://oreil.ly/olPCw*), National Bureau of Economic Research (NBER), August 1992.

steam engine, the electric motor, semiconductors, computers, and now AI, have the following characteristics:

- They are ubiquitous—the technology is pervasive, sometimes invisible, and can be used in a large number of industries and complimentary innovations.
- They spawn innovation—as a GPT improves and becomes more ubiquitous, spreading throughout the economy, more productivity gains are realized.
- They are disruptive—they can change how work is done by most if not all industries.
- They have general purposefulness—they perform generic functions, allowing their usage in a variety of products and services.

The difficulty in arriving at a single definition of artificial intelligence lies in our same disagreements about what constitutes human intelligence. The development of computer systems able to perform activities that normally require human intelligence is also a good definition of AI, but this is a very low bar, as for centuries machines have been doing tasks associated with human intelligence. Computers today can do tasks that PhDs cannot and at the same time cannot do tasks that one-year-old humans can do.

Contrary to the oft-seen nefarious machines or robots in movies like *Blade Runner, The Terminator,* and *I, Robot,* seemingly sentient, highly intelligent computers don't exist today. That would be strong and general AI. The computers seeking technological singularity (where AI surpasses human intelligence) in dystopian movies like *The Matrix* and *Transcendence* do not exist.

World-renowned scientists and "AI experts" often unanimously agree in public forums that it is possible for machines to develop superintelligence. However, the question being asked is whether it's *theoretically* possible. The trajectory of AI suggests the possibility exists. But this leads us to Moravec's paradox, which is an observation made by AI researchers that it's easy to get computers to exhibit advanced intelligence in playing chess or passing intelligence tests, yet it is difficult for machines to show the skills of a small child when it comes to perception and mobility. Intelligence and learning are complicated. Although we like to put things in buckets, such as "stupid" or "intelligent," AI is moving along a continuum, as illustrated in Figure 1-6; but AI today is not "superintelligent," nor does anyone have a time line that helps us understand when the day of superintelligent computers will arrive—it could be in five years or in a hundred years. The amount of computational resources needed to demonstrate the low-level skills humans possess is enormously reflective of the challenges ahead in creating superintelligent machines.

AI is used as shorthand for describing a varied set of concepts, architectures, technologies, and aspirations, but there is no single AI technology. AI is not a system or product that is embedded or used by such. We use the term *AI* loosely, as no computer or machine or AI with humanlike goals and intent has been developed. Nor do we know how to build such a computer or machine, as this again would be strong or general AI. When we talk about human intelligence, superintelligence, or sentience in machines, it is a future state being discussed. There is no miraculous AI fix; we cannot wave a magic AI wand that will fix healthcare or make people healthier.

Andrej Karpathy, a computer science researcher and the current director of AI at Tesla, makes a powerful case that AI changes how we build software, how we engineer applications. He argues that the way we build software/writing instructions that tell the computer what to do is slow and prone to errors. We spend a lot of time debugging—and worse, the code gets more brittle over time as more people maintain the code, often resulting in a big spaghetti of code that's difficult to change. The application locks the business into a way of doing work.

Healthcare is riddled with legacy software and/or complex applications that are so big that they themselves become impediments to innovation. Using machine learning, we can program by example—that is, we can collect many examples of what we want the application or software to do or not do, label them, and train a model to effectively learn to automate application or software development itself. Although tools to automate aspects of software engineering are starting to appear, more innovation and more tools are needed. Karpathy describes this vision as Software 2.0 (*https://oreil.ly/ 4XnWH*). In addition, few if any companies have the talent or tools to implement this vision. But we can still use machine learning rather than handcrafting for many of today's problems, allowing us to future-proof systems using machine learning as they learn with new data and to avoid programmers writing more code.

Understanding and exploring AI healthcare and technology myths illuminates our understanding and definition of AI. This will be key to understanding concepts presented in later chapters. Next, we'll turn our attention to discussing some key myths in AI healthcare.

AI Healthcare Myths

There is so much excitement involving AI in healthcare, but what exactly is AI in healthcare supposed to fix? People look to AI to predict future disease, prevent disease, enhance disease treatment, overcome obstacles to healthcare access, solve the burden of overworked and burnt-out clinicians, and improve the health of people overall while decreasing the cost of healthcare. While some of this is achievable, AI is not a miracle panacea for all health and healthcare-related problems. If AI is not applied judiciously, with human oversight and vision, then mistakes or incorrect recommendations based on faulty or inadequate data inputs and assumptions can kill the trust that AI uses in healthcare are designed to achieve. AI in healthcare must be applied for the right purpose, with review of potential risks in the forefront of developers' minds.

Roy Amara, a previous head of the Institute for the Future, coined Amara's Law, which states: "We tend to overestimate the effect of a technology in the short run and underestimate the effect in the long run." One of the major myths regarding AI is that AI will replace physicians and other healthcare providers. AI relies on the knowledge base provided by trained and experienced clinicians. AI cannot replace the "care" aspect of human interaction and its documented therapeutic effect. AI does not have the capability to determine the best solution when a holistic review of a patient would recommend an approach that relies on human creativity, judgment, and insight. For example, consider an otherwise healthy 90-year-old patient who develops an eminently treatable cancer. Logic and current medicine would support aggressive treatment to destroy the cancer. The human aspect comes into play when this same patient lets their clinician know that they are widowed and alone, and although they are not depressed, they feel they have lived a full life and thus decline treatment. AI and most physicians would argue for treatment. Holistic review of the patient's wishes and their autonomy in their healthcare decisions take priority here and would have been missed by an autonomous AI agency operating without human oversight. As this patient would be choosing a course of action that involves inaction, and the characteristics of what is included in the patient's determination of a full life are not brought into existing models, it is unlikely that AI would be able to predict this unusual but valid patient decision.

AI can apply counterintuitive strategies to health management, but the steps from raw data to decision are complex and need human perceptions and insights. The process is a progression, starting with clinical data obtained from innumerable sources that is built and developed to become relevant information, which is then used and applied to populations and/or individuals. The transformation from raw data to insights to intelligence is a process that is guided by clinicians working with data scientists using AI. The clinical interpretation of data is dependent on humans and their understanding of disease processes and its effect on the timeline of progression of disease that molds this early knowledge. Algorithms for disease management, identification of risk factors predicting the probability of development of disease—these are based on human understanding and interpretation of the disease process and the human state. The use of AI and clinicians' activities are intertwined, and together their potential for improving health is remarkable. Because there are so many potential uses for AI in healthcare, we can break them down into some of the numerous gaps identified earlier:

Inequitable access to healthcare

AI can be used to assess for social determinants of health that can predict which populations are either "at risk" or identified for underutilization of care, and tactical plans can then be developed to best address these gaps in medical usage.

Insufficient on-demand healthcare services

AI is already addressing some of these needs with applications like Lark Health, which manages using smart devices and AI with deep machine learning to manage well, at-risk, and stable chronic disease patients outside of the healthcare system.

High costs and lack of price transparency

AI can be used to predict which patients or populations are at risk of becoming "high cost," and further analysis within these populations can identify factors that can be intervened upon to prevent this outcome.

Significant waste

AI incorporation into healthcare payer systems is prevalent today. Administrative tasks and unnecessary paperwork are being removed from the patient and the provider, making their user experience that much better.

Fragmented, siloed payer and provider systems

AI has potential use here, such as in the automatic coding of office visits and the ability to automatically deduct the cost of tests/exams/visits from one's health savings account.

High business frictions and poor consumer experiences

AI uses already include the facilitation of claims payments in a timely manner and the communication of health benefits for an individual, with fewer errors and decreased processing time as compared with human-resource-dominant systems.

Record keeping frozen since the 1960s

Electronic health records and the amount of patient data available to AI applications, which can process this data and draw insights from population analysis, continue to grow and develop constantly.

Slow adoption of technological advances

AI cannot help us here. Again, the judicious application of AI to healthcare gaps is needed. AI use in healthcare should be to extend provider capabilities, ease patient access to and use of healthcare, and so on. What AI cannot answer is how we humans will accept AI-enabled solutions. AI is used in an inconspicuous manner in healthcare for the most part, due to patient and provider skepticism and resistance to change. As time progresses, and with national and international emergencies such as the COVID-19 pandemic, people are being forced to accept and even embrace technological enhancement of healthcare. To continue this trend, we need to build on success and user satisfaction with the product and process.

Burnout of healthcare providers, with an inability of clinicians to remain educated on
the newest advances in medicine based on the volume of data to be absorbed

AI can process the hundreds of new journal articles on scientific and pharmaceutical advancements that are released daily. It can also compile relevant findings on various subjects as requested by the providers so that patients can receive
the most advanced medical treatments and diagnostics relevant to their condition. AI can be used in real time to determine whether a prior authorization for a
test/procedure or medication can be given to a patient. All of these advances lead
to users' increased satisfaction with their healthcare experience, decreases in
delays in care, the removal of time and resource waste, improvement in patient
health outcomes, and increased time for doctors to be with their patients and not
on their tablets.

These are just a handful of examples of AI use in healthcare today.

Further capabilities with ongoing development and future use cases, as well as additional applications of AI to help remedy the above healthcare problems from different
angles, will be addressed throughout this book.

Now, let's take a hard example. The healthcare industry seeks to address high-cost
healthcare situations that impact patients' health. An example is maternal and fetal
mortality and morbidity and the associated astronomical costs. An initial step is to
gather as much data as possible for machine learning to occur. Training data would
need to be labeled, models developed, the models tested for accuracy, and data scored
where the outcome is unknown to identify which mothers and babies in a population
pool would be at risk for development of complications during or after pregnancy
and would be at risk for a neonatal intensive care unit (NICU) stay. This involves AI
analysis of all the patient variables to isolate the target population. It's also important
to understand whether other conditions are at play, including gestational hypertension (and perhaps its more severe manifestations), which is highly prevalent and
associated with NICU infants and complications from pregnancies.

The routine monitoring of at-risk moms from an early stage allows clinicians to
intervene with early diagnosis and management of gestational hypertension and its
manifestations to prevent maternal and fetal complications and death, with their
associated maternal and NICU costs. AI can be utilized to identify the highest-risk
moms with the greatest potential impacts from intervention. AI can assist clinicians
with identification of gestational hypertension and can then be used in disease management, with goal therapies identified by human providers and used to educate AI
tools and products. We can use AI for the analysis of these moms and infants to
determine if there is a better way to identify, diagnose, and manage this specific population. AI has inherent benefits and broad applications, but it is AI's collaboration
with the human interface that allows AI tools to be so impactful. AI will not replace
healthcare providers, but it is a powerful tool for augmenting physicians' work in

identifying and managing disease. Let's explore some of the ways that AI and health-care providers have been able to work together, while also dispelling the myth that AI can do it all on its own.

Myth: AI Will Cure Disease

AI is not a replacement for a medicinal cure that may one day end diseases (e.g., coronary artery disease and cancer); however, advances in AI, the massive accumulation of data (i.e., big data), and data sharing in healthcare could lead to what *does* end diseases. Some people believe that if AI can be used to predict who is at risk for a particular disease, then we can intervene and change behaviors or start treatment that would circumvent the disease from ever becoming present. Of course, helping people avoid getting a disease is not the same as curing the disease. Defining what we mean by a cure can be confusing, and this is never more evident than with diseases such as human immunodeficiency virus (HIV). Magic Johnson, the NBA Hall of Famer, proclaimed he was cured of HIV because doctors were unable to detect the virus in his body after ongoing treatment for HIV. Without the antiretroviral medications, HIV would have increased in number and would once again have been found in Johnson's body. Was he ever truly cured? For certain diseases, a prospective cure is not well defined. However, preventing a disease for an individual is better than trying to cure that disease.

The norm today is that we work to prevent disease, often with the use of machine learning. Routinely, healthcare companies take in data from electronic health records (EHRs), healthcare claims, prescriptions, biometrics, and numerous other data sources to create models for the identification of "at-risk" patients. For prevention to be effective, healthcare constituents need to use artificial intelligence to support decisions and make recommendations based on the assessment and findings of clinicians providing healthcare to all patients.

The healthcare ecosystem comprises consumers in need of healthcare services; clinicians and providers who deliver healthcare services; the government, which regulates healthcare; insurance companies and other payers that pay for services; and the various agencies that administer and coordinate services. In the ideal state, these ecosystem constituents are in sync, optimizing patient care. A simple example is medical coding, where the medical jargon does not always sync with the coding terminology, resulting in gaps in care in identifying the true disease process of an individual patient. The current system is heavily dependent on coding of diagnoses by hospitals, providers, medical coders, and billing agents. This medical coding process has improved as we see greater AI adoption, increasing the opportunity to prevent diseases.

AI can provide clinicians with more and better tools, augmenting a clinician's diagnostic capabilities by analyzing a holistic picture of the individual patient with broader data streams and technological understanding of the disease process and of who is at risk and will be most impacted. AI has become a more accurate tool for identifying disease in images, and with the rise of intelligent spaces (e.g., hospitals, homes, clinicians' work spaces), AI triggers a more viable source of diagnostic information. We will examine this in greater detail in Chapter 3, in which the world of intelligent machines and ambient computing and its impact on healthcare is discussed. The volume of data streams makes this unmanageable for a human but highly possible for intelligent machines supported by AI. By identifying and stratifying individuals most at risk, AI can alert physicians and healthcare companies to intervene and address modifiable risk factors to prevent disease.

AI algorithms, personalized medicine, and predictive patient outcomes can be used to study different diseases and identify the best practice treatments and outcomes, leading to an increased likelihood of curing a specific disease. AI can further analyze whether and why a specific population may not respond to certain treatments versus another treatment. In 2014, Hawaii's attorney general sued the makers of a drug called Plavix[8] (used to thin the blood to prevent stroke and heart attack). The suit alleged that Plavix did not work for a large proportion of Pacific Islanders due to a metabolic deficiency in that population and that the makers of the medication were aware of this anomaly. Although the drug maker would not have known of this genetic difference originally, as it did not include Pacific Islanders in its initial clinical trials, it was aware of the anomaly in efficacy later on, during widespread patient use. AI algorithms were not used to identify the increase in poor outcomes related to Plavix's use as a preventive medication within this population. But AI's application to such a use case—that is, following a population after a medication's release to look for aberrancy points in data and then drawing conclusions from these findings—is a perfect use of AI, which would have led to alternative therapy recommendations for blood thinners to prevent cardiovascular complications and recurrence of disease in a much more timely manner. The alternative was a drawn-out process occurring over several years in which a finding was noted by clinicians and then reported, and eventually the finding was made regarding the lack of efficacy of Plavix among Pacific Islanders.

The application of AI to cancer is garnering a huge amount of interest, prompting thinking that we may be able to substantially reduce annual deaths from cancer. A large proportion of our world population develops cancer—in 2018 alone, about 10 million people died of cancer worldwide (*https://oreil.ly/JeN64*). The data from these individuals prior to their development of disease, after diagnosis, and during treatment, along with the use of AI, has the potential to improve oncologic care and effect more cures from treatment. Embedding AI technology in cancer treatment acceler-

---

8 "State Sues Maker of Plavix for Misleading Marketing in Hawaii" (*https://oreil.ly/skpnk*), *Hawaii News Now*, March 19, 2014.

ates the speed of diagnostics, leading to improved clinical decision making, which in turn improves cancer patient outcomes. AI can also be useful in managing advanced stages of cancer, through the ability to predict end-of-life care needs to facilitate a patient's quality of life.

One area in which AI has the potential for significant impact is the identification of cancer in radiologic studies. The University of Southern California's Keck School of Medicine published a study in 2019 showing improved cancer detection using AI.[9] Specifically, "a blinded retrospective study was performed with a panel of seven radiologists using a cancer-enriched dataset from 122 patients that included 90 false-negative mammograms." Findings showed that all radiologists experienced a significant improvement in their cancer detection rate. The mean rate of cancer detection by radiologists increased from 51% to 62% with the use of AI, while false positives (a determination of cancer when cancer is not actually present) remained essentially the same.

Early detection of disease states has an enormous positive impact on treatment and cure in cancer outcomes not just with radiologists but also with dermatologists. Computer scientists at Stanford created an AI skin cancer detection algorithm using deep learning for detection of malignant melanoma (a form of skin cancer) and found that AI identified cancers as accurately as dermatologists. China has used AI in the analysis of brain tumors. Previously, neurosurgeons performed tumor segmentation (used in diagnosis of brain cancer) manually. With AI, the results were accurate and reliable and created greater efficiency. Wherever early and accurate detection can lead to a cure, AI has a proven place in the diagnosis of cancers.

AI continues to evolve in its use and role in cancer detection. Currently, genetic mutations are determined through DNA analysis. AI is widely used in companies like Foundation Medicine (Roche) and Tempus to recommend treatments for particular tumor genomes. Also, AI has been used in radiogenomics, where radiographic image analysis is used to predict underlying genetic traits. That is, AI has been used to analyze and interpret magnetic resonance imaging (MRI) to determine whether a mutation representing cancer is present. In one Chinese study, AI analysis of MRIs predicted the presence of low-grade glioma (brain tumor) in patients with 83–95% accuracy. In the past decade, AI has been applied to cancer treatment drug development, with one study showing AI ability to predict the likelihood of failure in a clinical trial testing more than 200 sample drugs. Another study applied AI to the prediction of cancer cell response to treatment.

---

9 Alyssa T. Watanabe et al., "Improved Cancer Detection Using Artificial Intelligence: A Retrospective Evaluation of Missed Cancers on Mammography" (*https://oreil.ly/r1ISv*), *Journal of Digital Imaging* 32, no. 4 (August 2019): 625–637.

Identifying and diagnosing cancer in its early stages, coupled with proper care treatment, increases the opportunity to cure patients of cancer. AI can significantly contribute to the diagnosis of patients based on signals or symptoms missed by human detection. Gathering data from large population pools allows an understanding and awareness of the most effective plans for treatment. This leads to better treatment for individual patients based on what have been proven to be the most effective treatment plans for other patients who have had similar types of cancers. This is where AI—specifically, deep learning algorithms using large datasets containing the data of millions of patients diagnosed with cancer all over the world—could play a major role. Unfortunately, access to and accumulation of such massive datasets does not yet exist. Nations would have to agree to share data, while within countries patients would have to grant general access to their private data; technological systems to aggregate all this disparate data with different measures and norms would have to be built. All of which leads to worldwide health data aggregates being a thing of the future. The technological ability is there, but the ethicality of such datasets and their use may prohibit their creation. That said, if given large enough data sources for analysis, AI can provide clinicians with evidence-based recommendations for the treatment plans with the greatest opportunity for positive outcomes.

Human error that results in a delay in diagnosis, or a misdiagnosis, can be a matter of life or death for cancer patients; detecting cancer early makes all the difference. AI helps with early detection and diagnosis by augmenting current diagnostic tools for clinicians. An important part of detecting lung cancer is finding if there are small lesions on the lungs through computed tomography (CT) scans. There is some chance for human error, and this is where artificial intelligence plays a role. Clinicians using AI could potentially increase the likelihood of early detection and diagnosis. With the data available in relation to cancer and its treatment, AI has the potential to assist in creating structure out of these databases and pulling relevant information to guide patient decision making and treatment in the near future.

Giving patients tools that help them also helps their doctors; we will discuss this in more detail in Chapter 3. Tools that rapidly analyze large amounts of patient data to provide signals that may otherwise go undetected should increasingly play a role in healthcare, as should machine learning algorithms that can learn about a patient continuously. In Chapter 3 we explore the synergy between increasingly instrumented patients, doctors, and clinical care. The shift from largely using computers to using devices that patients wear for early detection of disease states is well underway. Despite the plethora of seemingly almost daily news stories about new machine learning algorithms or new devices or AI products improving healthcare, AI alone will not fix the healthcare problems confronting societies. There are many challenges that need to be solved to make our healthcare system work better, and AI will help, but let's dispel the next myth about AI alone fixing the problems facing healthcare.

Myth: AI Will Replace Doctors

AI will not replace doctors, either now or in the near future, despite much discussion suggesting that it will happen. In 2012, entrepreneur and Sun Microsystems co-founder Vinod Khosla wrote an article with the provocative title, "Do We Need Doctors or Algorithms?" (*https://oreil.ly/vnsQJ*), in which he asserts that computers will replace 80% of what doctors do. Vinod saw a healthcare future driven by entrepreneurs, not by medical professionals.

We can look at AI as a doctor replacement *or* as a doctor enhancement. AI can perform a double check and see patterns among millions of patients that one doctor cannot possibly see. A single doctor would not be able to see a million patients across their lifetime, but AI can. The diagnostic work done by a doctor arguably focuses heavily on pattern recognition. So augmenting diagnoses with AI makes sense.

Key arguments for AI replacing doctors include the following:

- AI can get more accurate every day, every year, every decade, at a rate and scale not possible for human doctors.
- AI will be able to explain possibilities and results with confidence scores.
- AI can improve the knowledge set, raising the insight of a doctor (who is perhaps not trained in a specific specialty).
- AI may be the only way to provide access to best-in-class healthcare to millions of people who don't have access to healthcare services or can't afford healthcare services.

Arguments *against* AI replacing doctors include the following:

- Human doctors are better at making decisions in collaboration with other humans.
- Doctors have empathy, which is critical to clinical care.
- Doctors can make a human connection, which may directly influence how a patient feels and can facilitate a patient adhering to a treatment plan.
- The *AMA Journal of Ethics* states that "patients' desire for emotional connection, reassurance, and a healing touch from their caregivers is well documented."[10]
- Doctors may observe or detect critical signals because of their human senses.
- AI cannot yet converse with patients in the manner that a human doctor can.

---

10 James E. Bailey, "Does Health Information Technology Dehumanize Health Care?" (*https://oreil.ly/akbGm*), *Virtual Mentor* 13, no. 3 (2011): 181–185.

- Subconscious factors that may influence a doctor's ability to treat, if not explicitly identified for AI, will be missed.

The role of radiologist has come under a lot of scrutiny as one that AI could potentially replace. It's worth looking at some tasks that a radiologist performs and recognizing that AI won't be able to take over these tasks, although it might augment the radiologist in performing some of them:

- Supervising residents and medical students
- Participating in research projects
- Performing treatment
- Helping with quality improvements
- Administering substances to render internal structures visible in imaging studies
- Developing or monitoring procedures for quality
- Coordinating radiological services with other medical activities
- Providing counseling to radiologic patients for things such as risky or alternative treatments
- Conversing with referring doctors on examination results or diagnostic information
- Performing interventional procedures

All this said, radiologists are the group most likely to be considered "replaceable" by AI, as they have zero to minimal direct patient contact, and not all of them perform all of the tasks listed here. There are many tasks that AI can do better than a doctor, but rarely if ever will AI replace entire business processes or operations or an entire occupation or profession. The most likely scenario is that doctors in the foreseeable future will transition to wielding AI with an understanding of how to use AI tools to deliver more efficient and better clinical care. AI today provides a lot of point solutions, and its opportunity to improve diagnostics is significant. Treatment pathways and even many diagnostics today require decision making, something AI is not good at.

AI and physicians can work together as a team because the stakes are high. AI can facilitate active learning (as a mentor to the clinician) by paying attention to aspects that are highly uncertain and can potentially contribute to a positive or negative outcome. The AI can receive feedback and insights (as a mentee of the clinician) to improve in particular ways.

A practical problem exists in that AI must live in our current brownfield world, where several barriers to AI replacing doctors must be overcome. Today we have a proliferation of systems that do not integrate well with each other. For example, a patient who is cared for at a hospital, an urgent care center, or a provider office may have their data spread across several different systems with varying degrees of integration. A doctor's ability to navigate the healthcare system and pull together this disparate data is critical to patient care.

The reality is that there is not going to be a computer, a machine, or an AI that solves healthcare, just like there isn't one solution to all banking, retail, or manufacturing problems. The path to digitization differs based on clinical specialty and most likely will occur one process at a time within each domain or specialty. AI systems are here and on the horizon for assessing mental health, diagnosing disease states, identifying abnormalities, and more.

Myth: AI Will Fix the "Healthcare Problem"

Most assuredly, AI fixing the myriad of healthcare problems is a myth. In the United States, the current healthcare system has a large ecosystem of providers, insurer systems, payers, and government agencies who must play well together to increase access to healthcare, reduce costs, reduce waste, and improve care. Generally, when governments discuss the "healthcare problem," they are referring mainly to our nation's exponentially increasing expenditures on healthcare. Most nations continue to address an aging population that is consuming more resources on an ever-growing basis. The ability of AI to overcome obstacles to healthcare access, solve the burden of overworked and burnt-out clinicians, and improve the health of people while decreasing the cost of healthcare is possible but exaggerated.

The Committee for a Responsible Federal Budget reports (*https://oreil.ly/sPFmk*) that the US spent more than $3 trillion on healthcare expenditures in 2017, equating to approximately $9,500 per person. The Deloitte consulting firm states that America spends more per capita on healthcare than any other country in the world, while also holding the unpleasant distinction of ranking near the bottom in objective measures, such as access, efficiency, and efficacy. Administrative costs are adding additional burden to the healthcare system, along with the rise in healthcare costs as medical advances lead to prolonged longevity and the associated costs of an aging population.

Neither technology nor AI can fix all of these problems, so realistically, the question is: how can AI help address some of the healthcare issues? First is the issue of access, as access to healthcare is composed of three parts:

- Gaining entry into the care system (usually through insurers)
- Having access to a location where healthcare is provided (i.e., geographic availability)
- Having access to a healthcare provider (limited number of providers)

The Patient Protection and Affordable Care Act (ACA) of 2010 led to an additional 20 million adults gaining health insurance coverage. However, the US population still has millions of uncovered people. This gap is so relevant as a major healthcare problem because the evidence shows that people without insurance are sicker and die younger, burdening the healthcare system and contributing to higher government costs. The American Medical Association (AMA) has endorsed the ACA and is committed to expanding healthcare coverage and the protection of people from potential insurance industry abuse, which increases access to healthcare and thus increases the likelihood of people living healthier lives, thereby reducing the costs of healthcare.

Although AI alone cannot fix all healthcare problems, it can play an enormous role in helping to fix some issues in healthcare, a major one being access to healthcare services. While governments work on addressing insurance coverage reform, AI is gaining a foothold in increasing healthcare accessibility. Apps such as Lark now use AI and chatbots, along with personal data from patients and smart devices, to provide health recommendations for preventive care, reduction of healthcare risks (such as obesity), and management of stable chronic medical conditions, such as diabetes, without direct clinician interaction. Thus AI is being used to identify at-risk patients, prevent disease, and focus on best practices for current disease conditions while addressing provider access issues. AI has been shown to be more effective than providers in certain areas, such as disease identification (as we saw earlier regarding cancer identification). As AI is applied to more functions associated with nurses, doctors, and hospitals, it will relieve some of the burden on healthcare access, freeing providers to perform more directly patient-related activities.

China provides an illuminating case study for how AI can help to reform healthcare access. China is facing arguably the largest healthcare challenges in the world. With a population of 1.4 billion, China is having enormous difficulty addressing the needs of its population with limited resources. A Chinese doctor will frequently see more than 50 patients daily in an outpatient setting.[11] The general practitioner is in high demand in China, and there is a shortage of qualified general practitioners. Poor working conditions, threats of violence, low salaries, and low social status are challenges contributing to the shortage, and they are compounded by patient concerns about the quality of care provided by general practitioners. Patients recognize differences in the academic and professional qualities of specialists versus those of general practitioners. This is where new technologies like AI can create breakthroughs by augmenting general practitioners with better diagnostic tools and clinical care treatment guidance. So China has relied heavily on AI to address its healthcare issues. From medical speech recognition and documentation to diagnostic identification and best practice

---

11 Xiangyi Kong et al., "Artificial intelligence: a key to relieve China's insufficient and unequally-distributed medical resources" (*https://oreil.ly/XrPSA*), *American Journal of Translational Research* 11, no. 5 (2019): 2632–2640.

treatment algorithms, China is utilizing AI to decrease the work burden for its providers. The further integration of these technologies into the healthcare system opens up accessibility to providers in both direct and remote care, thus providing a potential solution to the issue of resource limitation in both quantity and location. The advantages of AI in China's system as opposed to that of the US are certainly linked to the fact that China's system is government-run; with a centralized, controlled healthcare system in which all data is accessible by a single entity, utilization of AI is more impactful.

However, even with our disparate systems in the US, direct and remote access to clinicians will be improved as AI is further adopted and integrated into our healthcare system. There are several prime applications for AI, including clinical decision support, patient monitoring and guidance (remote or direct patient management), surgical assistance with automated devices, and healthcare systems management. Each of these and more will be discussed in later chapters.

Myth: AI Will Decrease Healthcare Costs

US health expenditure projections for 2018–2027 from the Centers for Medicare & Medicaid Services (*https://www.cms.gov*) show that the projected average growth rate on healthcare spend is 5.5%, with expectations of meeting $6 trillion in spend by 2027. Looking at these numbers, it's clear that healthcare spending will outstrip economic growth. All components of healthcare are projected to increase at exceedingly high annual rates over the next decade. For example, inpatient hospital care, which is the largest component of national health expenditures, is expected to grow at an annual average rate of 5.6%, which is above its recent five-year average growth rate of 5%. AI alone won't fix these problems, but it can help with cost containment and cost reduction.

The myth regarding AI and healthcare costs is the thinking that AI will completely reinvent or overturn the existing healthcare or medical models in practice today, or that AI use alone will be able to contain healthcare costs. AI is not a magic wand, but it can make a big difference by streamlining inefficiencies, finding some innovative ways to look at data and member health, and providing new use cases to impact patient health and cause improvement in overall health, which may well cause a decline in medical spend (though that will be offset by the cost of the technology and its supporting infrastructure). Tremendous evidence abounds that the big technology companies and start-ups will transform how healthcare is done. AI will be the tool of trade that makes many of these transformations possible. You might see this as splitting hairs, but the point is that the problems facing healthcare have lain in resistance to change, historical inefficiencies and inertia, lack of cooperation for the greater good by companies designed to compete with each other, and the lack of a game-changing technology. Now we have the game-changing technology: AI.

Given this background, how and where will AI have an impact? One major area of spend is management of chronic disease. When people with a chronic condition are not adherent to treatment plans, then complications related to the underlying disease occur, which can result in expensive hospitalizations and/or the need to institute high-cost specialty pharmacy therapies. For example, diabetic retinopathy (or DR), an eye disease of diabetes, is responsible for 24,000 Americans going blind annually, as reported by the Centers for Disease Control and Prevention (*https://oreil.ly/ccB5V*) (CDC). This is a preventable problem; routine exams with early diagnosis and treatment can prevent blindness in up to 95% of diabetics. And yet more than 50% of diabetics don't get their eyes examined, or they do so too late to receive effective treatment. The cost of treating diabetes-related disease and blindness is estimated to total more than $500 million per year.

AI can address cost spending in chronic disease by increasing efficacy and ease of obtaining eye exams in diabetics. AI using machine learning and deep learning has been adopted by various groups to develop automated DR-detection algorithms, some of which are commercially available. Although binocular slit-lamp ophthalmoscopy remains the standard against which other DR-screening approaches are compared, AI applications with fundus photography are more cost effective and do not require an ophthalmologist consultation. Fundus photography involves photographing the rear of the eye (fundus) using specialized flash cameras with microscopic detail. The scarcity of ophthalmologists who can perform this exam necessitates the use of nonphysicians who can carry out the DR screening using AI algorithms (deep learning) embedded in various tools, such as a mobile device. Such solutions are already used in developing nations with a shortage of ophthalmologists, demonstrating that a highly trained doctor is not required for disease detection when AI can be trained to do the same.

Cost savings from using AI and fundus photography have been reported at 16–17% (due to fewer unnecessary referrals). A cost effectiveness study from China (*https://oreil.ly/Tj19e*) showed that though the screening cost per patient increased by 35%, the cost per quality-adjusted life year was reduced by 45%. Taking this a step further, to help diabetics with existing eye-related disease, AT&T partnered with Aira in a research study combining smart glasses with AI algorithms to improve patients' quality of life, which resulted in increased medication adherence through medication recognition technology. The technologies for medication adherence are varied, such as tracking when patients open their pill bottle using sensors in the bottle cap or sensors in the bottle that show weight decline. Mobile apps or smart speakers that alert patients to take their medications can also be armed with machine learning to teach the patients habits, and instead of sending repeated and annoying alerts they learn the optimal time of day to send a reminder to the patient.

All of these strategies using AI in chronic condition management lead to a waterfall of positive health effects and cost savings. In this case, the diabetic is now screened for diabetic eye-related disease through the ease and efficacy of AI; if they are found to have significant disease, then the AT&T/Aira "pill bottle reader project" can facilitate medication adherence, and issues such as falls related to poor vision, fractures or other musculoskeletal trauma, hospital admissions for poor blood sugar control, infections related to poor blood sugar control, and so on, can all be avoided, with significant cost savings as well as quality-of-life improvement for patients.

AI can assist in the standardization and identification of best practice management of chronic disease. It has always been known in the medical community that there is a wide variation in practices, and economists have pointed out that treatment variability results in wasteful healthcare spending. As an example of how treatment management can impact healthcare spend, let's examine low back pain. More than 80% of Americans experience low back pain at some point in their lives. Of those people with low back pain, 1.2% account for about 30% of expenditures. When treatment guidelines were adhered to, costs were less. The pattern for increasing costs to both the overall healthcare system and patients is reflected in Figure 1-7, illustrating the impact on costs when consumers (that is, patients) fail to adhere to treatment guidelines.[12]

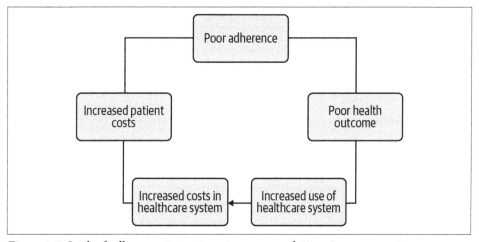

Figure 1-7. Lack of adherence to treatment recommendations increases costs

---

12 Lily H. Kim et al., "Expenditures and Health Care Utilization Among Adults with Newly Diagnosed Low Back and Lower Extremity Pain" (https://oreil.ly/nRW06), JAMA Network Open 2, no. 5 (2019); James D. Owens et al., "Impacts of Adherence to Evidence-Based Medicine Guidelines for the Management of Acute Low Back Pain on Costs of Worker's Compensation Claims" (https://oreil.ly/ztgvJ), Journal of Occupational and Environmental Medicine 61, no. 6 (2019): 445–452.

AI can reduce treatment variability by applying itself to the myriad of siloed data sources to identify optimal care pathways, leading to the updating of current guidelines and improvements in cost expenditure. As a caveat, health savings are associated with the application of evidence-based medicine treatment guidelines; the issue is that they are not strictly adhered to in medical practice. AI would facilitate application of treatment guidelines by helping to facilitate doctor decisions on plan of care. (This will be explored further in Chapter 4.) Some have asked: what if AI makes the wrong recommendation? As AI would be augmenting and facilitating the physician's decision, the ultimate treatment decision and responsibility for verifying AI recommendations would likely lie with the provider.

Hospitalization and administrative costs are also a major driver for US healthcare. "More than $1 trillion is wasted each year on costly administration and avoidable hospital readmissions," according to Orion Health CEO Ian McCrae.[13] Orion Health used AI to predict patient costs and readmission risks, while analyzing clinical and financial outliers to improve the treatment and practice management at the point of care. AI is being applied to the large data pools coming in through numerous inputs, including socioeconomic data, behavioral data, biometric data, demographics, geographic location, and so on, all in an effort to more accurately predict who would benefit from more aggressive treatment management, with the goal of avoiding hospitalizations.

Another area of high healthcare spend is medication research and discovery. Historically, the development of new medications and vaccines has taken a long time, and demonstrating safety and efficacy is a tedious and time-consuming process. Now AI could facilitate this process by expediting the analysis and research components. This will be discussed further in Chapter 5.

Accenture performed a study in 2017 that showed a potential savings of $150 billion in annual healthcare cost savings by 2026 through the application of AI to healthcare in the areas of robot-assisted surgery ($40B), virtual nursing assistants ($20B), administrative workflow assistance ($18B), fraud detection ($17B), dosage error reduction ($16B), connected machines ($14B), clinical trial participant identifier ($13B), preliminary diagnosis ($5B), automated image diagnosis ($3B), and cybersecurity ($2B).[14] These statistics show the potential value and transformative effect in adopting AI to reduce costs. But this is potential future costs reduction; the real rub lies in translating these costs to reduced patient costs.

---

13 "Orion Health Unveils New Predictive Intelligence Using Machine Learning to Help Save Billions in Healthcare Costs" (*https://oreil.ly/GkURv*), *The Journal of Precision Medicine*, March 7, 2018.

14 "Future AI Opportunities for Improving Care Delivery, Cost, and Efficacy" (*https://oreil.ly/pm1V2*), *HealthITAnalytics*, July 29, 2019.

Translational challenges continue to exist and include issues such as costs of implementing this technology and cultural acceptance of AI in healthcare. All of these continue to act as barriers to AI use in helping to control healthcare spend. Investments in AI can take away from short-term financial goals. Legacy systems usually exist as silos, and the time and expense of creating interoperability can be prohibitive. Providers themselves may be unaware of the benefits of AI and its applications to their practices in improving the lives of their patients. Safely and respectfully controlling the confidentiality of patient information through these systems and the use of AI is another potential barrier. That said, the future of AI in assisting in the control of healthcare costs and improving the health of our population is clear. AI has opened a world of potential opportunities for working with clinicians and healthcare systems to better the lives and health of our population. The future is full of potential for AI use in healthcare, but it is not limitless.

A surge in new healthcare products powered by AI technologies is on the horizon. AI is causing a paradigm shift in healthcare, and there is significant value in the application of AI to a host of challenges. So far we have provided a brief history of AI, offered a definition of AI, and dispelled some overarching expectations, i.e., AI healthcare myths. Next, we will explore some AI myths and AI technology myths, which will further enhance your understanding of the art of the possible when applying artificial intelligence.

AI Myths

Who can deny that sci-fi movies influence and shape how we think about AI? Movies provide aspirational views of AI, as well as at times depicting a dystopian future in which AI surpasses human intelligence and becomes our overlord. We also have interviews and quotes from notable scientists, inventors, and entrepreneurs suggesting that a sentient AI—a superintelligent AI that will create its own rules—is coming, and that an AI apocalypse is possible as AI becomes more advanced. All of this raises questions about what AI is now and what it will be in the near and distant future. Can AI reason?[15] Will AI become sentient and make decisions? Should we be concerned about the arrival of an AI overlord? The following sections answer these questions and more, dispelling several myths about AI.

---

15 Gary Marcus and Ernest Davis, "GPT-3, Bloviator: OpenAI's Language Generator Has No Idea What It's Talking About" (*https://oreil.ly/by9Xn*), *MIT Technology Review*, August 22, 2020.

Myth: AI Is an Existential Threat

The existential threat narrative reinforces a sense that it's too late to do anything. While fears of superintelligence are overblown, the rapid advancement of general purpose reasoning technology and AI poses an existential risk worth assessing and monitoring. The use of AI for positive or nefarious purposes remains a choice for people, as with any technology or tool. There is nothing in AI today that possesses and acts with motivations, goals, intent, or a sense of purpose. Strong AI would need to be a reality for this to be true. It is strong AI or general AI that some have used as the basis for the speculative, dystopian AI future. However, it's possible and maybe even likely that humans will weaponize AI or negligently apply AI, resulting in an existential threat—if not to humanity, then to selected groups such as minorities.

A machine that can understand or learn any task that a human can is strong AI. Some describe this as passing the Turing test, developed by Alan Turing in 1950 and based on a computer's ability to exhibit intelligence indistinguishable from that of a human being. Perhaps we should use another test demonstrating strong AI—maybe a Hassabis test, after Demis Hassabis, who, in a 2019 podcast, suggested that when an AI system wins a Nobel Prize for scientific discovery, then we will know that general intelligence has arrived for AI. To date no computer or machine has passed the Turing test or the Hassabis test.

Strong AI is a future state, a world in which computers or machines, like humans, can do the following:

- Move from one knowledge domain to another
- Converse in natural language, with all of its nuances and context
- Self-learn without human intervention
- Ideate and possess their own ideas and goals
- Manipulate the physical world to engineer and create new things

These are just a few characteristics of human intelligence, and AI systems that can do any of these things don't exist. Presently we don't know how to build such systems. Google's AlphaGo can play the game of Go but can't play poker or chess. Each AI system is purpose-built, often described as narrow AI, or weak AI; this is the current state of the art. Most likely, we need more innovations, more inventions in algorithms, science, and hardware, to achieve strong AI.

In 2014 the professor and physicist Stephen Hawking told the BBC, "The development of full artificial intelligence could spell the end of the human race." Maybe that would be true if we knew how to build full artificial intelligence—an AI that has intentions and goals and operates with autonomy, and that has the means to manipulate the physical world. Hawking did not define comprehensive artificial intelligence, but we can presume he meant strong AI.

The speculations, misleading statements, and criticism around AI and its potential future prompted AI researchers and academia to respond to this growing set of AI warnings by providing an objective and fact-based discussion. A 2016 *MIT Technology Review* headline (*https://oreil.ly/iXXvz*) states that "the experts don't think super-intelligent AI is a threat to humanity." It's difficult to predict the future, and there are prominent AI researchers who correctly assert that general AI poses an existential risk. However, is that risk in 5 years or in 50 years? The mere fact that it is a risk means we must take that risk seriously while allowing innovation to continue.

The notion of humans being replaced or surpassed by machines is based on a variety of suspicious assumptions, several of which Tony Prescott identifies in a paper titled "The AI Singularity and Runaway Human Intelligence." He asserts that instead of comparing AI to a single average human, we should look at the collective and ever-advancing intelligence of the human species. We will create technologies that complement human's natural intelligence—i.e., AI—as we have done with computers, the internet, and the cloud, and before that with papyrus, the electric motor, the abacus, the telephone, and so on. AI complements clinicians and the healthcare system.

Myth: AI Is Just Machine Learning

There is significant work underway by academia and industry under the moniker of AI. Of course, it "begs the question" to argue that AI is not a big fat lie (*https://oreil.ly/nVgcc*) because researchers or academia describe their work as AI. Today, arguably, artificial intelligence cannot flourish without machine learning, while machine learning lives without AI, and therein lies the rub. Like AI, ML is a field of study using algorithms and statistical models to perform tasks relying on patterns and inference. ML is more concrete because we can identify specific algorithms as ML.

When computers first came on the scene, we built systems to do human tasks that we associate with human intelligence and that previously could not be done by machines, like playing checkers or backgammon. We didn't use machine learning but described this as an intelligent system, or AI. AI is not defined by the use of ML, although today we might debate whether systems not using ML are intelligent or AI.

We've described the achievements of computers doing tasks that previously were the exclusive domain of human intelligence, like a computer winning *Jeopardy!*, as AI. The IBM Watson achievement was not possible solely using machine learning; it required a custom-built computing infrastructure. It required NLP techniques, a custom-built framework, architecture for processing text, massive parallel processing, and more. The 2011 IBM Watson is an example of AI, a concrete example that uses more than machine learning to achieve its end.

AI is real; it's not snake oil, vaporware, a hoax, or a big fat lie. AI is a lot more than machine learning. More importantly, AI is about building systems that do tasks previously requiring human intelligence. Arguably, equating AI to ML is cognitive bias, the overreliance on a familiar tool. As Abraham Maslow said in 1966, "I suppose it is tempting, if the only tool you have is a hammer, to treat everything as if it were a nail." In later chapters, we will see more concrete examples of future AI systems that apply more than ML for intelligence in performing tasks previously done only by humans.

AI simulates human intelligence by way of heuristics (i.e., machine learning) and by way of analysis. Reaching general purpose AI solutions requires the full stack, which is more than machine learning; this is much like a human needing sensors (modes of data collection), nerves, arteries, heart, kidneys, lungs, and so on, to function. AI, like the human body, is a lot more than meets the eye, because systems need to be in place to bring it to life, to mimic human intelligence.

Myth: AI Overpromises and Underdelivers

Stakeholders betting on AI to deliver results will be disappointed. Stakeholders using AI to deliver results will be delighted. Machine learning is AI's most influential technology, and its potential for immediate and powerful results is impressive, especially in healthcare.[16] Machine learning applications are increasing and becoming ubiquitous. The techniques and architectures for building ML applications are much different than those for building apps or web-based applications. ML applications must be concerned with data, the ML model, and supporting code. ML applications require different testing approaches, keeping bias out of data, ensuring explainability, and implementing continuous improvement. Building ML applications requires a different kind of talent in the business, AI product managers, and in technology, AI engineers.

AI engineering differs from procedural traditional software in multiple ways. Developing ML models is often more a testing exercise, trial and error, than a development life cycle. In terms of QA/testing, it's a departure from traditional testing in that deployed ML models must be defended with tests that don't test functionality but do test for bias, data shift, efficacy, and more. The model in production sets a benchmark that should not deteriorate when models are retrained in production. Every model should improve upon the previous one.

Many businesses will seek to buy versus build, and these stakeholders are the most vulnerable to purchasing AI products that apply techniques of the 1960s through the

---

16 See Sam Daley's article, "32 Examples of AI in Healthcare That Will Make You Feel Better About the Future" (*https://oreil.ly/r8Zaz*), Built In, July 4, 2019.

1990s, versus post-2012 techniques in which deep learning and NLP go hand in hand or deep learning is the preferred technique. Business stakeholders must understand the differences and employ AI technology sniffers to detect false claims and help select the right fit. Failure to adequately do this may result in disappointment in AI for the business.

Myth: True Conversational AI Already Exists

The promise of conversational AI to augment and enable physician care at the right time and the right place is enormous. True conversational AI is aspirational; we don't have the technology to fully get there right now. AI technologies are rapidly moving us toward a world in which AI can use natural language to engage with patients in a normal human conversation, but that is not the reality today. So conversational AI today is on the weak end of the continuum of weak to strong AI but is moving toward strong AI, where a natural conversation between machine and human can occur. Today we often experience a search or Q&A-type dialog with "things," as opposed to a natural language conversation.

Star Trek popularized the idea of conversational AI, with its Voice-First computer. Google would later name its first voice technology Majel in honor of Majel Barrett, the human voice behind *Star Trek*'s computer voice. Today we romanticize this capability as it is beginning to take shape, as evidenced by voice speakers like Alexa, Google Assistant, and Siri. However, today's AI does not deliver the same level of human voice interactions, the human-to-machine conversational capability seen in the various *Star Trek* voice computers. Everyone using the voice speaker technology of today knows that the conversation in no way compares to a human-to-human interaction or communication. The general notion of AI talking like a human, or conversational AI, is not a well-defined problem. Today, computers and AI can only solve problems that are well defined. How we speak as humans is nuanced and complex and often based on context, background knowledge about the topic, domain assumptions, or even the timing of when the content is expressed. *Star Trek* is our future—true conversational AI, where the machine understands the nuance of language and engages in a conversation.

IBM Watson's *Jeopardy!* win was an iconic display of AI, enabling the world to see the potential of AI. Ken Jennings, one of the human contestants, said after the show that he "welcomes the new computer overlords." IBM's director of research, John E. Kelley III, described IBM Watson as a "question and answering Machine," a computer akin to the one on *Star Trek* that can understand questions posed in natural language and answer them.[17] IBM Watson used a custom-built massive parallel computing system

---

17 Cameron Martin, "'Jeopardy!' Man vs. Machine: Who (or What) Should You Root For?" (*https://oreil.ly/cdJ7c*), *The Atlantic*, February 14, 2011.

(no graphical processing units, as there was no deep learning) to convert every *Jeopardy!* question into a yes/no prediction. The difficulty was to do it with speed, trying out thousands of options and then answering the question with high confidence before a competing contestant answered; this required a different approach to NLP than what had previously been done by AI engineers.

During the *Jeopardy!* episode, Watson was not listening to Alex Trebek or the contestants; this was evident when human contestant Ken Jennings gave a wrong answer, and Watson repeated it. The *Jeopardy!* producers and IBM agreed to a set of rules that excluded audiovisual questions that would require contestants to listen to audio or watch an image or a video to determine a correct answer, because Watson couldn't handle these input types. Watson did not have audio capability to process sounds as input; it could not hear the spoken questions but rather was fed each item as typed text at the same speed. Other contestants were hearing or reading the clue. IBM Watson's appearance on *Jeopardy!* was a fantastic performance in 2011, but it was not equal to the Voice-First computer on *Star Trek* back in the 1960s, and we still don't have that technology today. Watson largely represents where we were in 2011.

However, with the advances in language models that represent text in a form understandable by machines, we are seeing rapid improvement toward reaching a *Star Trek*–like future. OpenAI, a nonprofit AI research and development organization, is building better language models. Google built a language model with a Sesame Street character's name, BERT. Applying BERT in the clinical domain (clinical BERT) helps AI understand the language of healthcare. This in turn enables many use cases in telemedicine, patient-physician conversations, helping patients recall doctor interactions, clinical coding, and more. Conversational AI technologies exist today and this technology continues to mature, suggesting that conversational AI in healthcare is on the horizon. Virtual assistants like Google Home, Apple's Siri, and Amazon Alexa are examples of conversational AI technologies.

We can use AI with voice speakers, mobile phones, and other devices to do fantastic healthcare: sending reminders on medications, helping patients find providers, answering healthcare questions, providing basic education on medical conditions, addressing healthcare benefit concerns, or replacing the often frustrating use of virtual assistants that ask you to push buttons or simply don't recognize your intonation with voice. Chapter 4 on digitization will explore the modality of voice for healthcare in more detail.

Myth: AI as Overlord

We use AI to describe various applications and products exhibiting attributes of human intelligence, but there is no AI overlord. AI technologies are embedded in products we use, but always with human intention and decision making. We can build products that tell us whom to give or deny credit to. We can use AI to prioritize patient care. We can build a self-driving car that navigates through city streets it hasn't seen before. In each example, a person, a *human*, decided to take action, not the algorithm. Of course, this doesn't stop people (the government, the media, or the entity using the algorithm) from abdicating responsibility and blaming AI.

Businesses and people decide to give up their agency to AI products, allowing the outputs of AI products to become decisions. AI doesn't make decisions; it only becomes the scapegoat for biases and the unintended consequences of the choices people make. Reasoning and decision making are essential attributes required for doctors, and there is no AI overlord with those capabilities. We don't presently have machines that we can sit down with and have a conversation or debate a potential decision; we need humans.

AI has no current capability to be a runaway, self-learning, self-improving technology with decision making. Today we can construct systems, apps, and tools that exhibit attributes of human intelligence. We must care for and feed them to ensure they operate successfully for the well-defined and intended problem space. We don't know how to build systems that can work independently and continuously learn without human intervention or switch between domains (e.g., from oncology to chess).

However, let's say that AI is developed and deployed to recommend certain actions to a healthcare stakeholder. The stakeholder begins to trust the recommendations and reinforces the underlying mechanism to distill the corresponding insight. This feedback loop goes from first-generation AI that learned from human data collection to second- and later-generation AI that learned from the same AI. While it is not an AI with the intention to do harm, it can potentially do harm as a consequence of prescribed learning over time.

Some business leaders think of AI as an automation opportunity. But automation needs checks and balances to ensure it evolves in a safe fashion. AI needs checks and balances. This has to be a design decision; it is important to acknowledge the human factors at play, such as a stakeholder becoming lazy and yielding their agency to the AI because they have a perception that AI is good enough or perhaps even better than themselves. Cathy O'Neil covers this scenario in her book *Weapons of Math Destruction* (*https://weaponsofmathdestructionbook.com*) (Crown).

AI Technology Myths

Numerous myths surround AI as it becomes more pervasive in our lives, work, and play. This next section addresses some of the big ones, such as the reality of anthropomorphism often assigned to AI, the notion of AI as a black box, and more.

Myth: AI Algorithms Are Biased

AI algorithms are not biased; people and data are biased. People select the data to train AI algorithms. People construct, annotate, create, and determine the datasets used for training AI algorithms. Human decision making without algorithms is often biased. If AI were a thing, if it could voice an opinion, it might tell humans that the data it's being fed doesn't include enough women or people of color to produce accurate, unbiased results. AI algorithms don't think for themselves; they are simply a mirror, reflecting the data people provide. Bias in algorithms comes from data, and the data comes from people; therefore, the bias in algorithms also comes from people. Cassie Kozyrkov (*https://hackernoon.com/@kozyrkov*), Chief Decision Intelligence Engineer at Google and a prolific blogger, says it beautifully: "All technology is an echo of the wishes of whoever built it," and "Bias doesn't come from AI algorithms, it comes from people" (*http://bit.ly/quaesita_biasdef*).

Myth: AI Sees, Hears, and Thinks

Using anthropomorphism in terminology to describe AI can be a hurdle to truly understanding AI solution capabilities or understanding what a current AI system is doing. Assigning blame and credit to AI systems (*https://oreil.ly/8fgiF*) can hinder our ability to understand AI's capabilities and arguably hinders our ability to define how AI should be used in healthcare. AI is not actively sensing like humans; hence AI does not see, hear, or think like humans. The day after the three-day contest between IBM Watson and *Jeopardy*'s top human contestants, Brad Rutter and Ken Jennings, Ted.com hosted a live webstream. Stephen Baker, author of *Final Jeopardy: Man vs. Machine and the Quest to Know Everything* (Houghton Mifflin Harcourt), hosted a panel of IBMers, Dr. David Ferrucci, and IBM Fellow Kerrie Holley. A question was asked of the IBM team: "Do computers think?" Watson's principal investigator, David Ferrucci, responded, "Do submarines swim?" Submarines *don't* swim. And computers don't think, they don't see, and they don't hear.

Computers do computation—it's a function they do very well. Today, computers and AI can do things better than humans as long as those things are well defined, and issues arise when this is not the case. At almost any task in which computation matters, machines outperform humans.

Assigning anthropomorphic characteristics such as sight, hearing, or thought to AI is misleading. Doing so deprives us of fully understanding both the potential and the current limitations of AI. Computer vision uses deep learning (DL) to increase its accuracy. Still, ultimately the DL model predicts accuracy on whether an image or object consisting of pixels—constituted as 1s and 0s—is actually "Kerrie Holley" or "Siupo Becker." Machines don't experience sight the same way as humans. It's common to see someone write of an AI that thinks and learns, and it's often unclear if that person is speaking literally or metaphorically.

Facial recognition's nearly human-level performance can be misleading and false, depending on the context. With some images, computer vision is better than humans at detecting. Of course, a deep learning model can run through many more pictures than a single doctor, so in some examples, computer vision outperforms humans. Deep learning makes computer vision work well—and in some cases, even better than the human eye—but there are challenges that we cannot address with computer vision.

For example, at a single glance, a person can estimate another person's size, age, or gender; AI, computer vision, does not do so well at that. People can quickly determine whether something is edible, while computer vision is not as accurate. If we show AI an image of your spouse with their lips moved between their eyes and nose, AI may not detect the anomaly, but your child would say, "Yeah, that looks like you, but it's not you, your mouth is not in the right place." If we combine the human eye with computer vision, we can do something special in healthcare.

The challenge in clinical care lies not only in detecting a tumor but also in making a judgment about it. In healthcare, doctors must find things that they were not looking for—anomalies. Finding disease states and defects that an AI model is not trained for is challenging. Finding what one isn't looking for is very hard for doctors and even more difficult for an AI model, as it will only observe and detect what a trained model teaches it to do.

Myth: AI Diagnoses Diseases Better Than Doctors

AI does not diagnose disease conditions better than doctors because the diagnostic process is a complex, collaborative activity that involves clinical reasoning. It would be more accurate to say that AI makes the diagnosis better than doctors in discrete situations in which AI is asked only a specific question.

A doctor approaches a patient's diagnostic question by first obtaining a history of the patient's symptoms and then examining the patient to find physical signs of disease; then the doctor must scan their personal knowledge base and augment it with diagnostic guidelines once potential differential diagnoses (i.e., potential disease states) are identified. The process is then to perform laboratory and imaging studies, as well as refer to specialists in specific areas to further delineate the exact condition. Sometimes this process is simple. Some symptoms are pathognomonic (i.e., true harbinger symptoms for certain conditions), and thus the diagnosis is clear. For example, when a patient complains of a stiff neck and fever, and Kernig's and Brudzinski's signs (physical exam tests) further support, the diagnosis of meningitis is almost always certain. The problem is when the symptoms and signs are specific but not sensitive; not all patients have the same symptoms or exhibit the clear physical signs on exam.

So even relatively simple diagnoses can become complex, as more tests and further evaluation must be performed to get to the underlying diagnosis. This stepwise process of taking a world of data and funneling it down and then choosing diagnostic tools that will further help require judgment and an overall knowledge of how patient internal organs and systems are interrelated and are not compartmentalized. AI can take one area under question and perform a deeper analysis and provide helpful knowledge, but it cannot take over the ability to holistically process a system as complex as a human.

That said, in discrete tasks, studies abound that demonstrate AI models outperforming radiologists, cardiologists, or other clinicians. Stanford researchers published a study in which they describe a model they developed that "can diagnose irregular heart rhythms, also known as arrhythmias, from single-lead ECG signals better than a cardiologist." Other studies by Stanford University researchers created an algorithm, CheXNeXt, that "reads" X-rays for 14 distinct pathologies in seconds. We should jump for joy, because this is the power of AI in healthcare screening; detecting 14 different pathologies or arrhythmias in seconds with AI is nothing short of amazing.

However, we should also understand that the algorithm(s) performed a screening. The algorithm did not provide clinical care or determine care treatment. An algorithm doesn't have a concept of who a patient is. It doesn't have an idea of what it means to be human beyond a collection of lines and shapes, ones and zeros—so what are we next asking the algorithm to do? AI won't think to ask the patient if this disease or condition may be related to a growth on their neck, such as dry skin due to an underactive thyroid. Does the algorithm know the patient has the wrong balance of electrolytes (such as sodium or potassium)? Does it see that the patient is healing after heart surgery? There are so many questions that a clinician must ask and know beyond the algorithm. It's great that in the seconds it takes you to read this sentence, CheXNeXt can detect 14 pathologies just as well as a radiologist can, but that makes it a great tool to augment clinical care, not a replacement for doctors.

AI has an infinite information horizon. There are several touch points where AI can remove friction in the system and personalize the healthcare experience. Consider, for example, the use of AI for triage in emergency rooms. AI-assisted ER could help to reduce wait times dramatically for patients where the AI has identified with high probability a disease status that requires attention. The aim should be less focused on using AI to replace doctors and instead on helping doctors spend more time on providing care than on administrative tasks or intensive evaluation scenarios. AI is here to help.

There is often a man-versus-machine argument with AI, and this is very constructive, but there are many use cases and studies where AI is truly shape shifting. The clinical program that the van der Schaar Lab at the University of Cambridge brought forward with AutoPrognosis and Clairvoyance illustrates the art of what's possible. There are other impediments, as clinicians are not educated alongside AI, and healthcare information systems are often archaic. This is not a shortcoming of AI, though.

Transforming healthcare with AI will not be about providing patient care, and that is the myth regarding AI performing healthcare. Or to put this in concrete terms: AI cannot stop a patient from bleeding; we need clinicians. There is no doubt that AI can do some things better than doctors as long as those things are well defined, clearly explainable, and reproducible. Issues arise when any of these requirements fail.

AI's transformative ability will mean better tools for clinicians and better tools for consumers, enabling more vital healthcare services to the underserved. Innovators will use AI to disrupt incumbent business models and make the healthcare system work better while providing better tools for providers.

We can cherry-pick tasks that computers and AI do faster or better, but the reality is that in the present day, computers and AI have done little to help a clinician make better judgments, and that's where AI needs to go. The idea that AI simplifies doctors' lives by doing tasks in less time is often too simplistic. AI needs to be invisible and yet available at the time of care—not just scribing, but being an actual assistant to the doctor, resulting in better care for the patient.

Myth: AI Systems Learn from Data

Production AI systems learn from humans, not data. Machine learning models learn from data. Humans gather more data when a model does not know or provide the right answer or adequately respond to specific conditions or inputs. Human annotators are often engaged. Humans retrain the model to increase its knowledge base and increase the confidence of the model. Humans must annotate, label, and regularly scrub data. Humans must be in the loop for AI models to work correctly in production. This is especially true in healthcare, where humans must make sure that bias is removed from data and that the right features are highlighted and given the proper weights in neural networks. Without human oversight, models may drift as real-world data changes over time. Predictive modeling learns from historical data and uses the model to make predictions on new data where the answer is not known. In healthcare, often only clinicians know that changes in data must be accommodated, and the model retrained.

Myth: AI Is a Black Box

There is a myth describing AI as a black box. Black boxes are viewed as unfavorable because the implication is that we don't know how they work. How can we expect the medical field and clinicians to use things they don't fully understand? This might be overstated, but clinicians use several medical devices (stethoscopes and sphygmomanometers, for example) and don't know how they work, i.e., they're black boxes. But doctors do know how to use those medical devices, and most importantly, they trust their use of the devices. So it's not a black-box issue—it's an issue of explaining how software or AI comes to its conclusions, predictions, or outputs and whether clinicians can trust those outcomes.

Another part of the myth is that machine learning deep neural networks are opaque, offering few clues about how they arrive at their conclusions. This notion that AI technology is indescribable even by the most talented AI engineers is false. There are plenty of methods that allow the interpretability of ML results. Algorithms or neural networks are largely deterministic; they are subject to the laws of nature and thus are describable and repeatable. The black-box problem is that some AI solutions are not described, not that they cannot be described. However, we don't wish to discount the fact that understanding deep neural networks remains difficult. With that said, randomness can be inserted in machine learning models.

Stochastic in machine learning algorithms refers to the behavior and performance of such models where some randomness and uncertainty is involved in the outcomes—stochastic being a synonym for probabilistic and random. A machine learning model is stochastic, for example, if it is making decisions based on random-number generators to shuffle data. So algorithms are deterministic if they do not include any stochastic components. This discussion of AI as a black box is nuanced, because AI can be a black box, but in many cases we can open up the black box.

Explainable AI and black-box AI are two different concepts, and we have an explainable AI challenge. That is, clinicians and healthcare providers need explainable and comprehensible AI. Explainable AI allows the users of AI to understand both the algorithm and the inputs (or parameters) used. The targeted audience, users, should understand the outputs and the why of AI systems. Clinicians must trust the AI tools and systems they employ. Because we have an explainable AI challenge doesn't mean AI is a black box; it means we must make AI systems explainable and understandable to their targeted users and consumers.

The black-box myth is discussed often, but we see little if any conversation about the non-AI black boxes abundant in the healthcare world, such as claim-processing systems. How many users of claim-processing systems know how they work? We know the expected inputs and outputs, but we also know those with AI systems. We know with existing claims systems that there is minimal explainability. If there was explainability, why are providers and others always on the phone with insurance call centers asking the most simple question, such as, Why was my claim denied? Why can the agent not consistently and rapidly answer the question about the denial? Why do claim systems not clearly explain why a claim that passes through such a system is denied? One reason is that engineers often build systems without explainable solutions, both in AI and in non-AI programs. In previous computing eras, and today with usability and user-centered design, explainability is usually not a significant factor in building computer systems. Still, it needs to be, and all the more so with AI systems. It's natural to expect diagnosis- and treatment-oriented models to have greater explainability than administrative ones such as claim processing.

Myth: AI Is Modeled After the Brain

It's a myth that AI is loosely modeled after the human brain. AI is inspired by what the human brain can do but is not loosely modeled after the brain—it couldn't be, because we know so little about how the brain operates. Dr. Thomas Insel, the former director of the National Institute of Mental Health, gave a talk on how much we know about the human brain. He explained it this way: "In the 1970s, we had a pretty good understanding of how the kidney serves as a filter, how the heart serves as a pump, what lungs do...; but today, in 2015, I can't tell you—nor can anyone else—how the brain functions as an information processing organ." The American neuroscientist Sebastian Seung, in his book *Connectome: How the Brain's Wiring Makes Us Who We Are* (Mariner Books), writes eloquently about how vastly unknown the human brain is. He describes the brain as a forest growing from 100 billion seeds that no road can penetrate. As an organ, Seung writes, the brain remains an enigma.

Keep in mind that neural networks—unlike the human brain—must be "trained" on vast amounts of data. The algorithm or neural network produces an output, a decision or prediction, related to whatever question the model was built to ask. *Who in this population might get diabetes in the next 24 months? Is this tumor cancerous?* Often this process is described as an anthropomorphic characteristic: machine learning or AI "learned." This is not how people learn—we don't need massive amounts of labeled data to discern a cat from a muffin. We are not like a neural network using mathematically based algorithms, picking out and recognizing patterns and ultimately making a prediction. You can hack a neural network, modifying the facial image by moving the nose under the mouth, as in our previous example, and AI may not notice, but people will see it 100% of the time.

But perhaps this conversation should have begun by asking the question, what *isn't* AI?

AI-First Healthcare

Industry and companies have huge expectations for AI based on what we know now and what we anticipate for future innovations. For many organizations, these expectations won't be reached, because key stakeholders who control the purse strings will underestimate the disruptive nature of AI, as did other leaders before who underestimated the impact of the internet. Except this time is different, as AI will disrupt far more than the internet did, and maybe more than any computer technology we have ever witnessed.

However, the vision that companies and industry have for AI cannot be reached by one algorithm or one machine learning model at a time; reaching it requires a whole new orientation to thinking about what AI is and is not. There should be no doubt that the future lies in AI-First thinking for organizations seeking to build great experiences and great products. AI-First thinking reflects what Google's CEO, Sundar Pichai, said at the 2017 Google I/O developer conference: "Computing is evolving again...shift[ing] computing from a mobile-first to an AI-first approach.... In an AI-first world, we are rethinking all our products and applying machine learning and AI to solve user problems."

AI-First for healthcare means adopting direction and strategy for AI that goes beyond just machine learning. A common industry definition of AI may not exist, nor will it be a necessity for advancing an AI-First agenda for healthcare. Companies without an AI strategy operate like a machine coasting downhill, with no direction, no goals, no plans for how to use AI to make their business work better, create awesome experiences, make digitization work, or make their products better.

Now that we are grounded in what AI is and what it is not, we will explore what AI-First healthcare means to clinicians, patients, providers, and healthcare companies. The next chapters will explore AI-First healthcare by describing how AI usage makes a difference. We'll explore several topics, including the following:

- Understanding human-centered AI—what it is and how to make it a reality
- Using AI technologies to build superior products and better patient and clinician experiences
- Delivering better patient care at home, on the go, and at provider locations, made possible with AI-First healthcare thinking
- Reducing waste in the healthcare system, which requires that we rethink how we do healthcare
- Building an AI-First approach and strategy, whether you're a small or a large organization, which is key to making AI-First healthcare a reality

AI-First healthcare does not equate to an AI-First company. AI-First is not a technology statement. It does not equate to healthcare incumbents competing with technology companies. It means thinking about whether applying AI in any of its facets would make a difference in the patient journey, in the patient experience, in patient care. Or we can reimagine healthcare in the ICU, the home, or elsewhere, with AI infused into environments or intelligent objects. AI-First means bringing about a change in thinking and culture such that we consistently build smart systems and products in healthcare. Healthcare companies should create the same awesome experiences of consumer-based companies. Many if not all of consumer-based companies, including Netflix, Amazon, and Uber, use AI to understand their consumers and create memorable moments and experiences—healthcare companies should have the same vision. AI-First is, if anything, a call to action.

AI-First for healthcare companies means fostering an interdisciplinary team across all levels (executive leaders, program managers, engineers, healthcare experts) and fostering an AI mindset to solve important healthcare issues. It requires a business area and the organization at large to have an AI strategy defining what AI means to them and how they will leverage it. The AI strategy may live as part of a larger strategy of the business area.

Importantly, to understand how to transform healthcare, we need to ask what recent trends and innovations in AI we should explore and leverage. Where does healthcare need to evolve, and where can we reimagine it? From a software engineering perspective, AI introduces a significant shift. Fostering an AI mindset changes for the better how we think about products and software engineering. In our next chapter, we begin this journey with a focus on human-centered AI.

CHAPTER 2

Human-Centered AI

We often measure the success of AI by comparing it to human performance on similar tasks. AI model creators use human accuracy as a benchmark against which model performance is measured. The public at large often expects AI to be perfect, or at minimum always accurate, although we don't expect this of people. Human-centered AI focuses on pairing humans and AI where neither competes with the other; rather, they amplify and complement each other, enabling or creating optimal results. In this chapter, we define the principles of human-centered AI and explain why it's essential for building excellent AI healthcare tools and systems of care. This chapter will help with understanding the importance of human-centered AI and how to accomplish it.

Toward Human-Centered AI

A great place to start when thinking about human-centered AI is the world of gaming. AI can be great at playing games like checkers, chess, *Jeopardy!*, or the ancient strategy game Go. Healthcare is an entirely different domain because of the potential consequences, and because of the absence of a simple set of rules that govern how patients and diseases should behave and how care should be administered. The goal of human-centered AI is not to compete with humans but to enhance human performance and improve collaborations among caregivers. But we have learned that even in competition, such as in games between a computer and the world's best chess player, machines and people do better when they work together, utilizing the best talents of both. Centaur chess was born from this concept, and so is the concept of AI centaur health, which is at the heart of human-centered AI: AI and clinicians collaborating.

AI Centaur Health

Most people know the story of the Russian chess grandmaster Garry Kasparov, former world chess champion, playing a machine in chess. Although Garry would win the first six-game match in 1996, he lost the rematch with IBM's Deep Blue a year later. The symbolic significance was enormous. It signaled to many that machines/computers/AI were catching up to humans. After all, Garry had previously asserted that he would never lose to a computer. The story of Deep Blue and Kasparov tells us a lot about machines and intelligence, and about how artificial intelligence might manifest in healthcare and why it must be human centered.

Out of Kasparov's defeat, he developed a new kind of chess tournament, and a new type of chess player, illustrating reciprocity between man and computer: centaur chess. Kasparov set out to demonstrate that if you combine human and computer, you achieve better results than either can alone. Teaming machines and humans in chess creates a better chess player than either a human or a computer alone.[1] Centaur chess is all about augmenting and improving human performance. That is, you increase the level of performance and reduce the number of errors, thereby improving the quality. AlphaZero seemingly negates centaur chess, as it can teach itself chess and could most likely beat the world's best chess player, Magnus Carlsen. It's unclear who would win if we were to pair Magnus Carlsen with a computer against Alpha-Zero. But the point of centaur chess is to augment human performance with machines. This story illuminates the complementary role of man and machine, and at the same time, as we fast-forward, it demonstrates the increasing power of AI. However, what doctors do in healthcare is a lot more complex than chess or other games, and pairing doctors and AI gives us the best of both worlds.

In a like manner, AI combined with clinicians will amplify the skills and capabilities of human doctors, other clinicians (such as physician assistants and nurse practitioners), and other providers of healthcare services. In his 2013 book, *Smarter Than You Think* (Penguin Press), Clive Thompson describes a new style of intelligence where we can augment human minds in innovative ways. Today is the Age of Centaurs for healthcare. Intelligent systems and AI systems of care can transform healthcare.

IBM Deep Blue exhibited AI[2] because it beat a grandmaster at chess, something previously only other humans could do. IBM Watson, using machine learning and natural language processing, demonstrated intelligence because it bested the most successful *Jeopardy!* players in a trivia game, also something we thought could be done only with human knowledge. AlphaGo, developed by Google, showed intelligence as an AI

---

1 See Mike Cassidy, "Centaur Chess Shows Power of Teaming Human and Machine" (*https://oreil.ly/k9xqN*), *HuffPost*, updated December 6, 2017.

2 See Richard E. Korf's "Does Deep Blue Use AI?" (*https://oreil.ly/mO2KY*) for the rationale for describing Deep Blue as AI, in contrast to a programmer of Deep Blue saying otherwise (*https://oreil.ly/fIyje*).

system that beat 18-time world champion Lee Sedol in the 4,000-year-old strategy game Go.

In each win by AI over humans, we can identify common AI characteristics, which, by the way, also describe the limits of AI today and thus are the keys to implementing human-centered AI. Let's compare AI characteristics in games and healthcare, as doing so will help us understand the symbiotic relationship between humans and AI, the basis of human-centered AI healthcare—see Table 2-1.

Table 2-1. AI characteristics in games versus AI characteristics in healthcare

AI characteristics: Examples in games (e.g., *Jeopardy!*)	AI characteristics: Examples in healthcare
AI was tasked with a single goal (e.g., to win the *Jeopardy!* match, or to best Kasparov at chess), AND it was a goal previously achieved only by other humans, AND we view achieving the goal as exhibiting human intelligence.	AI is tasked with a single goal: making a diagnosis based on a medical image. The goal might be to detect a specific disease, or to detect cancer. In many cases, AI outperforms humans (*https://oreil.ly/VB1eT*). Often, unique AI entities are necessary for each goal; the AI detecting cancer is different from the AI detecting diabetes.
AI performed a specific, well-defined task, a single job, and that job was not to show human cognitive capabilities but simply to win the game at hand.	An AI diagnostic tool does a single task, detecting a specific disease state using a medical image or other factors in an algorithm. Although AI can make treatment recommendations and have confidence, AI doesn't show human cognitive capabilities such as making definitive treatment decisions based on diagnosis. That is, AI hasn't been given the role of autonomous agent making decisions on behalf of the clinician.
If humans don't think about it, AI can't do it; that is, each intelligent entity, AI, was purpose-built to show human "intelligence" for a very specific task. Using the IBM Watson purpose-built for *Jeopardy!* to play any other game would result in an obvious failure.	The AI diagnostic tool was purpose-built to detect disease states, but it was not designed to make treatment or care pathway recommendations. It has no such capability. That is, humans must tell AI what it has to do. The engineering of AI systems and models requires human intent and design. Problems arise when we don't recognize the duality of technology, as technology has an intended use, and there are unintended consequences when the technology is used for something it was not designed to do. Since AI designers don't know how people will use the technology, we must be aware of the duality.
AI has enough evidence or data about a subject to know it has a high probability of being correct, but it does not have enough knowledge/data to know if it is wrong.	The AI diagnostic tool cannot deal with missing data, and it may be unable to accommodate conflicts in clinical data from a doctor-patient interaction. So, for example, the AI tool doesn't know it doesn't have enough COVID-19 pneumonia images to distinguish bacterial pneumonia from COVID-19–associated pneumonia.
Humans were required to make the AI system work and perform its single task.	Developers, along with clinician subject matter experts working alongside the developers, must provide input to ensure the AI tool is as unbiased as possible and that the datasets used by the deep learning model represent current standards of care. Subject matter experts must make sure that a medical image dataset used to train a machine learning model has the proper number of medical images accommodating both the obvious and the not-so-obvious.

The Age of Centaurs, and of centaur healthcare, keeps humans in charge of decision making; agency is always with the doctor, and now AI augments the physician's capabilities. An example of the centaur healthcare concept is the true story of a patient we will describe as Patient K. Patient K visited his primary care physician (PCP) because of a lump growing on the left side of his neck. Upon examination, his PCP concluded it was a lipoma (fatty tissue) and harmless. A few days later, Patient K was in the presence of a doctor trained in internal medicine who saw the lump and expressed concern. Patient K and his wife said, "Oh, it's nothing. Our other doctor felt it and concluded it is harmless fatty tissue." The internist asked Patient K if he would mind if she touched the lump on his neck, and he obliged. To her, it felt hard, like a tumor, and not rubbery and mobile like a benign fat mass. She suggested Patient K get a CAT scan, but he and his wife were not in favor; after all, their PCP had assured them the lump was harmless. After much prodding by the internist, they reluctantly decided to get the CAT scan, which found that the lump was likely a cancerous tumor. Early detection meant that this cancer was able to be resected/removed while it was still localized, and Patient K did not require more systemic therapies, such as chemotherapy. To this day, the couple are grateful to the internist for her insistence on getting the CAT scan. The story informs us that we need to raise the capabilities of all physicians so that they, too, see what a specialist sees. Doctors have a common saying: "If you don't think about it, you can't find it." The story tells a tale of why augmentation of doctors with AI plays a role. The marriage of a PCP with AI tools, i.e., centaur healthcare, can make a huge difference.

Centaur healthcare is essential, as in some countries, such as the US, the confidence patients have in their caregiver may not always be warranted. In China, just the opposite mindset occurs: the population at large recognizes the difference between their general practitioners and specialists, as the differences in professional training between the two are vast. China is looking to use AI to correct these imbalances of training.[3] China has a shortage of general practitioners and knows it must improve their effectiveness without requiring all general practitioners to undergo another three or four years of training. The Ping An Good Doctor platform, which has almost 300 million registered users, provides AI-assisted diagnosis systems and illustrates a production system in which AI is a primary care physician's assistant.

The same challenge is real in the US, although it is not widely known among the general population. In the US, a PCP generally completes medical school and a three-year residency. A general practitioner (GP) completes one year of residency after medical school, and that's it. A specialist such as an endocrinologist completes the same education, including residency, plus an additional three to four years of

---

3 Xiangyi Kong et al., "Artificial intelligence: a key to relieve China's insufficient and unequally-distributed medical resources" (*https://oreil.ly/bN7mX*), *American Journal of Translational Research* 11, no. 5 (2019): 2632–2640.

training. As a result, the knowledge base difference between a GP, a PCP, and a specialist can be huge. A GP's or PCP's knowledge is often broad and shallow, while a specialist's is narrow and deep. Patients like Patient K think their training is the same. Common ailments are typical, but specialists see rare things more often than a PCP. For them, unusual things are ordinary. Because specialists tend to have more training, they "think about it," so they can "find it." Unintended consequences might be more unnecessary testing and waste in healthcare spend. We need AI to raise the capabilities of doctors by facilitating their knowledge base. In this example, AI could augment differential diagnosis and then could assist the provider in determining best diagnostic approaches while limiting unnecessary testing. Centaur health is a concept and approach facilitating human-centered AI, or humans and machines working in concert to amplify each other's strengths. The next section defines more clearly human-centered AI.

Human-Centered AI

J. C. R., or "Lick," is not a well-known figure in the world of AI. However, he has been called computing's Johnny Appleseed for planting the seeds for computing in the 1950s and 1960s. Lick, whose full name was Joseph Carl Robnett Licklider, published a paper in 1960, "Man-Computer Symbiosis" (*https://oreil.ly/EuooQ*), in which he discusses the symbiotic relationship between man and machines, writing that "men will set the goals, formulate the hypothesis, determine the criteria, and perform the evaluations. Computing machines will do the routinizable work." Lick envisioned a world in the 1960s in which humans and machines were not competing against each other (playing chess or Go, for example) but were instead working together to amplify each other's strengths, i.e., intelligence amplification (IA). We would most likely think differently about artificial intelligence today if IA was the moniker of choice rather than AI. Lick saw a cooperative interaction between humans and machines, the basic premise of human-centered AI.

Fei-Fei Li, a computer scientist and professor and the co-director of Stanford's Human-Centered AI Institute, makes the point that AI is very task focused but lacks both contextual awareness and the flexible learning seen with humans. In a 2017 *MIT Technology Review* article (*https://oreil.ly/sTfag*), Fei-Fei quotes a phrase from the 1970s: "The definition of today's AI is a machine that can make a perfect chess move while the room is on fire." She goes on to say that if we want to make AI more helpful, we must bring back contextual understanding, and this is especially true in healthcare.

The quote from the 1970s stresses the importance of AI integration and adoption in healthcare being human-centered. What does human-centered AI mean? As we integrate and connect with AI on a more routine basis, human-centered AI focuses on creating AI systems for human consumption. AI must focus on the impact such technology will have on humans. From this perspective, Mark O. Riedl, in his article

"Human-Centered Artificial Intelligence and Machine Learning" (*https://oreil.ly/HRZd1*), breaks down human-centered AI into two components:

- AI systems that take into account the human sociocultural perspective
- AI systems that facilitate human understanding of these systems, i.e., explainable AI

There is growing awareness that advances in AI alone are insufficient when building applications designed to augment human tasks. For example, suppose we develop an AI system of care to work with elderly patients, and the AI engineering team comprises a brilliant team of engineers and scientists who are all in or around their mid-thirties. The team's educational background, work experience, and body of work are impressive. However, they're still lacking a key ingredient for developing a human-centered AI system of care for seniors: not a single team member has ever walked in the shoes of an older adult. Their ability to design a user interface adapted for elder use is limited. Human-centered AI finds a way to ensure that we build systems that account for sociocultural perspectives such as age, ethnic background, socioeconomic status, and more. The young engineers may get the AI right but may miss on creating a user interface that will enable the elderly to actually use the system.

Our energies and our design of AI systems should start with the intersection of people and machines. Understanding the symbiotic relationship between AI and humans helps us build better AI applications.

Intersection of AI and Humans

One of the issues that human-centered AI must deal with is a lack of human understanding of how AI answers problems. In our social world, humans have a good understanding of context. Humans would react to the room on fire while playing a game of chess and have grown up learning how to respond to problems through human interaction. Although there are those with a computer science background or interest who understand the AI process entirely, the majority of people working with AI do not. While humans can understand the motivations and intentions of other humans in problem solving, how intelligent systems address problems is different from us and may be a "black box."

Trust of technology is critical to embracing AI in clinical applications. We deal with black boxes throughout our lives. Most doctors probably don't know how a stethoscope works; it's a black box to them. But doctors trust and use stethoscopes with confidence because they believe in the technology. In building AI tools and systems of care, we must spend time describing how machine learning models work or how AI systems of care work. In some cases, this requires that we build interpretable interfaces that clinicians can use to see whether they would have made the same determination as the AI system. *Black-box AI* refers to situations in which humans may not understand the algorithms used by AI or the complex systems created by AI to address specific issues. Explainable AI helps make this understandable for humans, which we touched on briefly in Chapter 1. Explainable AI also gives users an indication of what the model took into account about the individual or the situation and what was deemed important in order to fine-tune the machine learning model. Explainable AI is about transparency related to data provenance, feature engineering, and more.

This black-box issue is a concern, as it gives credibility to the myth that because humans do not understand the processes of AI, AI has the potential to take control over humans. We debunked this myth in Chapter 1. Grounded in reality are the questions that human-centered AI must address, such as: If AI systems are not immediately understandable to humans, then how do we close this gap? How do we ensure that trust in the AI solution is not compromised? If humans cannot intuitively understand AI, then there is natural skepticism about the AI solution. The goal of human-centered AI is to bridge this gap. Caution must be top of mind when deploying AI systems that are not well understood by the users, such as doctors or healthcare systems.

For instance, Stanford University, UC Berkeley, and MIT have established human-centered AI (HAI) research institutes in part to address the issue of making AI more understandable to humans. A focus on explainable AI will ensure people's trust in AI. A principle of human-centered AI research is that AI should enhance human lives and thoughts, not replace them.

Human-centered AI recognizes the richness and vastness of human intelligence and does not conflate human intelligence with machine intelligence. It knows that comparing AI to collective human knowledge is a false comparison. Just like Lick in the 1960s (*https://oreil.ly/OyFsQ*), human-centered AI sees the value in augmenting and amplifying a healthcare worker's cognitive abilities—improving a doctor's capabilities, not replacing them—and in recognizing that we must understand how an AI solution impacts all stakeholders affected by its implementation—patients, clinicians, and others. We have been down this road before; in fact, the field of business process reengineering and design thinking informs us about human-centered AI. Figure 2-1 describes a simple framework addressing four main components.

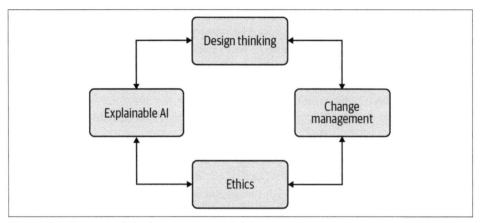

Figure 2-1. Framework for human-centered AI

Design thinking is used by countless entities to imagine products that delight. Apple is known for creating products like the iPhone that revolutionized mobile computing and our experiences. Apple has embraced design thinking for decades (*https://oreil.ly/ sT5Pw*). What if we designed AI tools and AI systems of care the same way Apple designed the iPhone, iTunes, or the MacBook? There is a plethora of literature on design thinking. It's about thinking differently about a process, the environment, and the conditions in which the product must thrive. It's about understanding how a doctor or nurse interacts with the product in context, which might be a doctor's office, an urgent care center, a home, or a patient on the go. Building and engineering with AI requires organizations to embrace design thinking. Design thinking for AI must ensure that AI solutions do not replace human decision making.

Change management was prevalent during the 1980s when business process redesign was rampant. Today we seem to have lost sight of the fact that getting people to do things differently requires us to manage the change. Change management addresses the transition of people, processes, and technology from the current to the future state. There is an old adage—"Change occurs one death at a time"—that was adapted from something that the German physicist Max Planck wrote in his *Scientific Autobiography*: "A new scientific truth does not triumph by convincing its opponents and making them see the light, but rather because its opponents eventually die, and a new generation grows up that is familiar with it." Interestingly, a 2019 study (*https:// oreil.ly/OnPZN*) supports what Planck wrote in 1950.

We don't need people to die for change management to work, but often we do need old thinking or settled ways of doing things to die for change to occur. The same is true with design thinking. AI requires both design thinking and change management when we decide to transform a way of doing business, whether that means establishing centaur healthcare, making healthcare real-time, or even undertaking a less ambitious project like making an AI that accurately diagnoses and recommends evidence-based medicine treatment plans. Adopting systems of care requires AI transformation work. We must reimagine how technology and clinicians interact.

Inserting machine learning models into workflows or using ML for diagnostic tools will require change management and design thinking. Madeleine Clare Elish and Elizabeth Anne Watkins, in a groundbreaking study on integrating AI in clinical care, writes:

> If the introductions of new technologies like AI are beneficial because they are disruptive in the sense of creating new pathways to achieve a goal, this disruption is also a kind of breakage that must be *repaired* in order for the intervention to work effectively in a particular context.[4]

Their study, *Repairing Innovation: A Study of Integrating AI in Clinical Care*, identifies the notion of "repair work" to enable effective innovation of AI in clinical care. Repair work may entail emotional support, experts providing justification, or more. This repair work often remains invisible, like the change agents in business process reengineering. For AI innovation success, the study asserts, we need fewer studies proposing how AI could be used and more on how AI technologies could be integrated into as-is business, social, and process states of current organizations.

Explainable AI focuses on ensuring that all stakeholders who must use AI directly or indirectly understand how the AI works. We wouldn't want to be in a self-driving car as the driver without understanding the role of AI versus that of the driver. That is, does the human driver or AI own the agency for decision making in collision avoidance? Does that change if a death is highly probable? As a user of AI, we need to understand who has agency, humans or AI. In healthcare, physicians won't know what datasets are used to train the model, how complete or diverse the datasets are, what assumptions were made, or the priority of goals decided on in building the model. If AI is making decisions, what's the impact of a decision being wrong? Can I, as a physician, override the decision? Can I verify the decision? The transparency or explainability of the black box must be provided to clinicians for them to be willing to adapt this technology. Without understanding any of the parameters that go into the AI solution, doctors will be hesitant to adopt this technology to augment their practice. With a clear understanding and explanation of the AI inputs, just as with a stethoscope, physicians will be more open to AI solutions and their use in healthcare. In many cases, explainability should be a requirement for AI solutions. The ability to explain may be necessary to warrant trust.

---

4 Madeleine Clare Elish and Elizabeth Anne Watkins, *Repairing Innovation: A Study of Integrating AI into Clinical Care* (*https://oreil.ly/tkHyJ*) (New York: Data & Society Research Institute, 2020).

Ethical considerations addressing model fairness, transparency, and bias must be identified. A 2019 *Nature Medicine* article provides a road map for deploying responsible machine learning solutions in healthcare.[5] The first step in the authors' road map is picking the right problem, which includes identifying and collaborating with the necessary stakeholders: knowledge experts, decision makers, and users. Understanding that models developed during product development will most likely operate differently when faced with real-world data means that finding the appropriate data is imperative, and thus data governance becomes paramount.

Data is not pixie dust; we cannot learn everything we want from any one dataset. Data is created for a purpose and carries the patterns of that purpose, both good and bad. The more information that we collect about people, the more vulnerable those people become to discrimination and intrusion into their privacy. So we must be good stewards of data. Evidence of efficacy and transparency becomes essential to building trust with patients and consumers and establishing accountability with stakeholders in the organizations creating the AI solutions. Recognizing that ethical problems may arise at any point in building and deploying AI healthcare solutions helps address ethical issues.

This framework or some derivative should be part of any human-centered AI. We must design and build with empathy and understanding; design thinking helps with this. For many systems, we must accommodate the need for the workforce to operate differently; this is where change management plays a role. It often requires extensive training and continuous learning to make the AI system better. Transparency is an essential component of human-centered AI; we must make sure healthcare providers understand how the AI works, including building the AI to work with humans, and factoring in human and sociocultural values. Physicians, nurses, care managers, and others know how electricity works, how computers work—they may not know the intricacies, but they understand the basic principles and functions of these general purpose technologies; this same basic literacy must be provided for AI.

AI and Human Sociocultural Values

Humans can be equally confusing to intelligent systems. Natural language processing (NLP) and speech processing using automatic speech recognition (ASR) systems show understanding of the English language. However, ASR may not understand all English language speakers equally well. Stanford Engineering researchers have shown that the AI embedded into many ASR systems makes twice as many errors in interpreting the words spoken by African Americans as when interpreting words

---

5 Jenna Wiens et al., "Do no harm: a roadmap for responsible machine learning for health care" (*https://oreil.ly/ 5JUA8*), *Nature Medicine* 25 (2019): 1337–1340.

spoken by whites.[6] This is an example of sociocultural values not being accommodated by AI.

The repercussions for people when companies use ASR technology can be devastating. The impact of this disparity in recognizing white and nonwhite speakers may have significant negative consequences for people's job prospects and lives. Does the company know the ASR is not reliable? Does it know its error rates depend on socioeconomic variables such as class and race? Disabled citizens accessing healthcare services through voice suddenly may not have access to working healthcare services. A likely remedy is to add a lot more voice data to train the speech recognition systems with dialects from a diverse set of English speakers.

AI also needs to understand human motivation or behaviors underlying humans' actions, i.e., the sociocultural perspective of humans. Our rearing, generation, and geography impact our social practices and decisions. Human-centered artificial intelligence means building AI applications and corresponding algorithms with the understanding that AI is part of something bigger. If the ASRs employed human-centered AI thinking and practices, the technology would have been trained and tested using voice data from a broad spectrum of people, ensuring it worked, or else a warning label would be placed on it: "Works only for native-English-speaking people with no accents." Of course, the latter would be absurd, but it points out that we must build AI systems with a broader and more precise understanding of their usage.

Human-centered artificial intelligence in healthcare requires us to design and build AI tools and applications with the awareness of the impact on stakeholders who come in contact with the AI. In healthcare, that connection could be direct (the doctor using an AI diagnostic tool), or indirect (a patient receiving a diagnostic result without knowing it was the output of AI rather than an actual doctor who examined a test or procedure result). AI design must accommodate an awareness that the AI is part of a more extensive system consisting of human stakeholders: nurses, patients, clinicians, operators, clients, and other people. Some AI researchers and practitioners use the term *human-centered AI t*o refer to intelligent systems designed with social responsibility in mind. They are addressing issues of fairness, accountability, interpretability, and transparency. Ensuring patients are treated as equitably as possible in their healthcare and not allowing racial or gender bias to influence a diagnosis make issues of fairness and accountability top of mind in applying AI for healthcare.

Solutions incorporating AI that accounts for sociocultural realities may be more understandable to humans. When we ignore these sociocultural beliefs, AI misses the mark, or mistakes occur. For example, when we leverage AI to detect people with high potential for chronic disease, we must understand the AI goal. Is the purpose of

---

6 Edmund L. Andrews, "Stanford researchers find that automated speech recognition is more likely to misinterpret black speakers" (*https://oreil.ly/sXp1C*), *Stanford News*, March 23, 2020.

the AI to make people with that disease process healthier, or is it to reduce costs? In the former case, the AI would prioritize the highest-risk patients to receive healthcare that would intervene in or even prevent development of the disease. In the latter case, the AI would appear discriminatory if it prioritized on the low end those who were at highest risk for poor outcomes, with the result that they received the least amount of healthcare.

Consider the elderly patient with the newly diagnosed cancer that we introduced in Chapter 1 as an example of where AI fails. In that example, we had an otherwise healthy elderly patient with a new diagnosis of easily treatable cancer. AI without knowledge of human values would not take into account that human autonomy in decision making would take priority over the logical decision to treat the disease. That is, AI cannot recognize that the patient's age or quality of life may make them not want to consider treatment options. The scenario is not technically a miss on AI's part. Decision and logic would argue for treatment, but a gap appeared, because AI did not take into consideration the very human concept of autonomy in a specific patient's choice. Human-centered AI would factor in sociocultural values, such as patient autonomy, in the creation of an intelligent structure addressing patient decision support. Human-centered AI ethics would argue that AI cannot and *must* not dictate the course of treatment. At best, the AI can inform treatment decisions rather than advise. The ultimate decision is with the patient, based on advice from their healthcare team, which is augmented with information generated by AI.

In this patient example, clinical knowledge of cancer treatment and factoring in known prognoses and treatment strategies encompass the explicit understanding of AI. What was missing was the implicit recognition of the importance humans give a patient's right to decide on treatment. This right is paramount and independent of AI. Human-centered AI works to bring that tacit knowledge into the creation of our intelligent structures. Currently, AI is capable of tasks associated with explicit and implied human knowledge. Explicit instruction is generally accepted wisdom and could be considered "book learning." Implicit knowledge often derives from intuition. Intuition relies on experience acquired over time and of varying factors that lead humans to have an instinctive understanding of a situation or problem. Explicit learning informs the physician that the patient warrants clinical treatment. Sociocultural values and implicit learning lead to withholding treatment. Although not in practice today, AI is at the earliest stages of obtaining a tacit understanding of humans.

The growth of affective computing is a complementary field to AI. It's the study of systems and devices that can recognize and interpret human experiences of feelings, emotions, or moods. The growth of affective computing combined with AI facial recognition, or biometric monitors, may in some cases substitute for markers of human emotion the ability to interpret facial gestures or expressions without the spoken word.

The current capabilities and aspirations of AI make it tempting to state that AI has an understanding of humans. But this would not be accurate. AI demonstrates human-like implicit knowledge, but AI must be constructed and trained using data that encodes this implicit knowledge—that is, data based on human interactions and experiences. While big data and AI algorithms, using deep and machine learning, enable the creation of AI processes simulating humanlike understanding, this is different from AI originating human meaning. That is, AI does not have an inherent knowledge of humans. Humans create the expertise and constructs for AI to understand, which is why we must recognize that AI has to understand people.

AI Understanding Humans

Several AI-associated failures are attributable, at least in part, to a lack of human-centric design. One study estimated that 60% of "big data" projects fail to be operationalized (*https://oreil.ly/BUi1s*), meaning they were never put into production for clinicians or others to experience and use. For example, in 2013, there was great excitement as the University of Texas MD Anderson Cancer Center partnered with Watson for Oncology (IBM) in using Watson's cognitive computing to help eradicate cancer by identifying the best treatment options. Watson used patient and research databases to recommend cancer treatments. What happened? The joint venture between MD Anderson and IBM did not meet expectations, and the reasons differ based on perspectives. This collaboration may well be a case study in why human-centered AI is required up front in enabling AI systems to delight users and meet stated goals. Because human-centered AI requires design thinking and getting all stakeholders working together toward a common goal, failure or success is a team effort. Human-centered AI requires a partnership among all involved parties. Human-centered AI design is not a silver bullet, and there are many reasons that AI systems fail to meet expectations; a big one is that models or the AI fail to perform as well in a production-live environment as they do in a lab. But this is a chicken and egg situation: if there was a partnership between the intended users and engineers, i.e., human-centered AI, would we see a different outcome?

Physicians look at individual patients initially through the lens of the immediate underlying disease process but then expand this to a holistic analysis, as all parts of an individual can be involved in and impact disease management. Holistic patient analysis examines, among other things, medical factors, medications, safety, social stability, and support. Physicians consider behavioral health factors, baseline health before disease onset, socioeconomic background, and values. The patient's relationship with/ trust in their physician partner, access to treatment facilities and location, and numerous other variables are also included in the physician's holistic analysis. These factors will have varying significance and weight in the treatment decision based on the physician's explicit and implicit understanding of the patient and the disease process. When so many variables are not taken into account by AI, how could humans have imagined a functional system? Constructing an AI that accounts for all these variables requires cooperation and a meeting of the minds between engineers and stakeholders. The sheer number of distinct stakeholders in healthcare heightens the need to focus on change management and human-centered design. Stakeholders must consider the user's limitations in understanding AI and ensure that AI has the constructs relevant to a humanlike decision.

Machine learning models, like any technology, possess a duality issue, wherein a model built for one purpose may later be used for another purpose. For example, let's say that an original model design is focused on employer-funded populations with the goal of predicting diabetes for proactive prevention. Later, another business unit adopts the model for a Medicare or Medicaid population with the goal of disease management and care. However, the model has not been evolved to address a new goal.

So the same machine learning model is used for two different goals: (1) to assist diabetes management among a self-funded population, where the employer assumes all healthcare costs for the members; and (2) to assist diabetes management for Medicaid or Medicare, where the government pays for a majority of each member's healthcare. The characteristics of the underlying population types vary significantly between these two goals, impacting their management and how the model gets used.

A self-funded population (i.e., employer funded) is employment aged, generally younger, and assumed to be healthier. In contrast, a Medicare population will be older, retired, and more likely to have chronic medical conditions. So an AI model goal for one community would potentially be inappropriate for the other population. As an example, AI models detecting and recommending treatment plans will be different for the two populations. Nurses might need to be more proactive and plan in-home patient visits for the more senior population. Dealing with comorbidities, aging at home, or even the primary modality of engagement might vary.

The medical community knows that average laboratory values, or test results, are not based on typical findings for the national population. Instead, an average laboratory value range reflects the average values for a middle-aged Caucasian male, as this was determined to be the norm during the initial laboratory standard setting. As an example, the average white blood cell (WBC) count for a Caucasian male ranges from 4,500 to 11,000 WBCs per microliter. The average WBC for Blacks is as much as 50% lower.[7] If attention were not paid to this bias in the underlying data ranges for "normal" when applied to specific populations with AI, then the bias would be propagated. We might see unnecessary medical testing to evaluate so-called abnormal values.

---

7 See Dawn Hershman et al., "Ethnic Neutropenia and Treatment Delay in African American Women Undergoing Chemotherapy for Early-Stage Breast Cancer" (*https://oreil.ly/WGJ6H*), *Journal of the National Cancer Institute* 95, no. 20 (2003): 1545–1548.

AI use of the "normal" lab values in any construct, even in a human-centric construct, would be limited by this inherent bias in the underlying data. That is, ethnic differences are often not reflected in the widely adopted average laboratory ranges, which could potentially result in lower-quality healthcare. AI, together with big data, could be used to personalize the "normal" ranges of lab values for each individual or population by analyzing population-wide lab values and correlating those values with outcomes across an entire population.

Compared to large-population-generated reference ranges, individual baselines or ethnic-specific laboratory ranges may improve the diagnosis of disease states, resulting in improved monitoring of patients' health, better clinical decision making, and improved healthcare in general. Why is it so crucial that AI tries to work beyond these biases and apply sociocultural human relevance? One main reason is goal relevance. AI applications are most valuable when they are relevant to human end users.

The relevance of the result is essential. A Black male could be subjected to expensive and potentially injurious further testing, including possible bone marrow biopsy (the invasive sampling of bone marrow). To further complicate matters, the context of the lab result matters as well. Whereas a low WBC could lead to further testing in a Black male, in the case of infection or even cancer, an elevated WBC for that same patient could appear to be within normal range, and thus testing to evaluate for infection or other causes would not be pursued. In the one case, unnecessary testing; in the other, necessary testing not pursued. Given that specific context is needed to interpret laboratory findings in the preceding examples, humans are an important component of both AI design and interpretation. AI cannot provide relevant solutions without human regard.

Another example of how AI's understanding of human context is essential is when human handoff must occur. However, when human-centric AI is applied, AI is aware of its limitations. We design AI to trigger handoff to humans for further contextual analysis. That is an application of implicit knowledge to obtain an adequate solution for the patient. Consider the WBC example that was just discussed. In the example, the intelligent lab system is given the additional information that normal WBC ranges may differ by ethnicity and gender. Handoff to a clinician for further review would show that the patient's WBC is ordinary, and the patient would not undergo unnecessary testing. Human-centric AI can help to determine, based on the human context, where handoffs for human intervention should occur and when. Journey maps are visual handoffs that illustrate how a clinician, a patient, or any stakeholder goes through the process of achieving the desired goal with the introduction of the new technology.

As another example of where AI can go wrong without the inclusion of human norms, in 2016 Microsoft made headlines when it announced its new chatbot, Tay. Tay utilized teenage voice and jargon and could automatically reply to people and engage in casual "fun" conversation on Twitter. In less than 24 hours, internet trolls corrupted Tay's personality by flooding it with racist, misogynistic, and anti-Semitic tweets. Chatbot Tay went from altruistic human-loving chatbot to full-on racist based on learnings from trolls, and so Tay was deactivated. Tay, through automated algorithmic decisions, reflected and amplified undesirable responses or patterns based on conversations with its users. If Tay's design had addressed the inclusion of societal norms (rules of human society), then Tay might have been highly successful. Human-centric AI could address these types of issues by creating feedback loops to inform the intelligent system of potential underlying behavior and societal bias encoded in the responses.

Humans Understanding AI

Humans understanding AI is critical to AI success and adoption in transforming healthcare, and we describe this under the umbrella of explainable AI. When a plane goes down unexplainably, the Federal Aviation Administration will look at the "black box" data to help determine where a process or system went wrong. Likewise, in our automated intelligent systems, when a breakdown occurs, we as humans want to know why. Often AI neural networks show up as uninterpretable, just as in a black aviation box, but there are strategies for addressing interpretability. It may take a tremendous amount of time and energy to understand an autonomous AI decision-making process, or why a specific outcome came about. It is usually the AI experts who perform this type of analysis, and their goal is generally to debug or improve a particular AI system. The work of making AI understandable to nonexpert humans is called explainable AI.

As in other AI applications, the issue of transparency is a human problem, and a technical one. From a healthcare perspective, the goal of explainable AI is to provide enough education about these intelligent systems for others to understand how they work and how they were made. This understanding, as described previously, must be shared by all stakeholders affected by or using the AI. In practice, providing an understanding of the underlying hypothesis, assumptions, goals, datasets, and scope of the model helps with model usage. There is natural skepticism toward acceptance of any system that is not understandable to the human end user. In healthcare this issue is accentuated because of the sensitive and personal nature of our health.

There are various options for helping humans understand intelligent systems. All focus to some extent on the amount of information that must be shared to create understanding and therefore acceptance. One option in helping to explain AI is to develop descriptions of how the algorithm processes input. Describing the goals of the model, its intended use cases, helps explain the model. Another option is to develop rationales for why decisions come about. We produce rationales through experiences collected from explanations to intelligent systems of humans performing similar tasks. Intelligent systems can then take these human-explained examples and translate them into automated reasoning that is similar to social rationales, including culturally specific idioms. However, some intelligent systems defy a natural explanation. In a sense, this is not unlike human processing. Doctors' clinical decisions may be transparent at times and may almost seem automated as they follow clinical practice guidelines for a specific disease condition, such as hypertension. Once complexity is added to a patient's story, then our human thinking may not be so transparent or "explainable."

Consider this AI system example, where AI is used in determining the site of discharge from a hospital setting—that is, a home, nursing home, or rehabilitation facility. Phil, a 65-year-old patient with known hypertension, was hospitalized due to a stroke. If AI were applied, information would suggest that as long as the patient was still neurologically impaired to a significant extent, he should remain hospitalized for his safety. However, Phil left the hospital against medical advice. While at home, Phil called to be admitted for further care at a rehabilitation facility. The standard process is to move from acute inpatient hospitalization straight to a rehabilitation facility with no intermittent stop at home. It is exceedingly difficult, perhaps nearly impossible, to admit an at-home patient to an acute inpatient rehabilitation facility. However, Phil was admitted that day to a rehabilitation unit—this was the benefit of human intervention.

To account for why direct admission to a rehabilitation facility was allowed, one has to understand the patient context. This patient had witnessed the violent death of his son, causing his blood pressure to skyrocket out of control, which led to a major stroke. The patient left the hospital against medical advice because his son's funeral was that day, and the patient refused to miss it.

This example focuses on diverse human-centered AI needs. Performing optimal decision making requires factoring in the entire human context or holistic experience. Knowing when a human should intervene is part of human-centered AI. So how much information is needed and in what format should information sharing occur to help the human end users feel educated on why this decision resulted?

Human intervention looks at the context, including events in the patient's life. Human intervention understands and would negate any AI information recommending support for the predicted level of care being hospital, rehab, and then home. Human thinking allowed the irregular direct admission from home to a rehabilitation facility. Human sociocultural values were given precedence, and this unlikely outcome was allowed to occur, which ended up being the optimal treatment decision for this patient. Human decision making focuses on a careful weighing of all available evidence to come to the best conclusion. Ignoring the way humans make decisions would have resulted in a significantly costlier outcome, both financially and emotionally, for this patient. The patient avoided a repeat emergency department evaluation, an ambulance transfer, a possible repeat inpatient hospital stay, and the emotional toll of repeating a process that was strongly associated with his son's death.

Explainable AI is at play in this scenario because we did not allow AI to be in decision making. It was apparent to the clinicians why AI made its recommendation adhering to clinical guidelines or hospital guidelines, but the doctor could override this decision because of context. Understanding why AI makes its initial recommendation and the supporting evidence helps doctors know when to ignore AI information and when to include it in their decision making.

Humans understanding AI also focuses on the ethical issues related to a lack of knowledge of AI applications. If human end users do not understand at some level how decisions regarding social care or therapy are determined, then how can we ensure that ethical decisions are made, without bias or commercial motivation? (How would someone know their insurer has not created AI systems focused on lowest cost rather than on best care?) In the preceding example, how much information would have to be shared with humans to make the outcome understandable? Given that this information was highly sensitive, what are the ethical responsibilities of sharing this information to enhance end-user understanding?

Human Ethics and AI

AI has been called one of the significant human rights challenges of the 21st century. PricewaterhouseCoopers estimates that AI will deliver approximately $16 trillion to the global economy by 2030 (*https://oreil.ly/KcgZ0*). The Stanford Institute for Human-Centered AI released a report stating that the growing proliferation of AI could lead to societal imbalances. As more organizations utilize AI, individual privacy and data can be considered a commodity, with a power imbalance favoring those organizations with access to AI. The risks of AI without a human-centric approach are high. Ethical questions to consider include:

- How will we create intelligent structures responsibly to avoid higher concentrations of wealth in an elite few, while avoiding poverty and powerlessness for the global majority?
- How will we address the displacement of human jobs taken over by automation?
- Automated jobs economically hit lower socioeconomic classes at a higher percentage. How do we protect this class?
- How do we ensure data privacy?

When building AI models and solutions, stakeholders must recognize that the business goals drive the development and measures for success. We cannot build AI systems that are better than the goals we seek to achieve. We must understand that ethical issues can arise anywhere in the life cycle of AI solution development, from project inception to deployment. This understanding requires that we address several questions:

- If we automate a task, what are the impacts on stakeholders?
- Is this the right problem for AI?
- If the model or AI solution becomes public, does it undermine or build trust in AI?
- Are we deploying the model responsibly?
- Are we avoiding unfair treatment?
- Are we improving the welfare of people by helping them avoid disease, injury, or harm? That is, are we improving their physical/economic/psychological welfare?
- What is the patient benefit?
- Do we use AI in a manner that enables people to make their own decisions? That is, do we respect the autonomy of people such that we don't manipulate them into taking a particular action?

Recognizing that we don't have AI general intelligence today forces us to understand that AI systems will likely inherit biases from data. Users of AI systems must understand both the goals and the limitations of such systems to use them properly. For clinicians, patients, and consumers to trust an AI healthcare solution, they will want to know:

- Is it easy to understand?
- Is it fair?
- Is it accountable?
- Is it transparent?
- Did anyone tamper with it?

Human-Centric Approach

We are seeing a significant trend in which a majority of the workforce is composed of people of color.[8] Most cities in the US will no longer have a racial majority by 2030, according to US Census Bureau projections. This demographic shift makes the lack of diversity in AI systems more obvious. There is a lack of racial and gender diversity in the creation of intelligent systems. Though this bias may be unintentional, there is

---

8 Elizabeth Gravier, "For the first time in US history, minorities make up the most new hires aged 25 to 54—and women are driving the trend" (*https://oreil.ly/1Qjnk*), CNBC Make It, September 11, 2019.

a lack of diversity among AI engineers, and this heightens the possibility of creating AI models that do not reflect the cultural diversity of the social systems their solutions are meant to address. Another way in which racial bias can be injected into AI is that algorithms are designed on available norms, such as the "normal range" of white blood cell counts mentioned previously, which are based on findings among middle-aged Caucasian males. This results in an inherent bias when the AI system utilizes these norms in its processes.

Several corporations champion the examination of implicit bias training and have numerous diversity initiatives. The Algorithmic Accountability Act, legislation introduced to both houses of Congress in 2019, charges the Federal Trade Commission with the assessment of algorithmic bias and allows the federal agency to issue fines based on company size. Mutale Nkonde, coauthor of the legislation, states that even with the steps made to address diversity, we "have failed to move the needle on creating a tech workforce that looks like its users." Nkonde argues for racial literacy and the concerted effort by industry and tech to create a framework to support diversity in its engineers and products. Although at the time of publication this bill has not been enacted into law, it raises the interesting issue of holding algorithms to different standards than humans, with enforcement presumably through existing practices by the federal government.

Further ethical issues arise when individual autonomy or privacy and AI intersect. Harvard Business School professor Shoshana Zuboff, in her book *The Age of Surveillance Capitalism* (PublicAffairs), describes a new age of capitalism. Capitalism combines many data points, including security surveillance cameras, smart home devices, smartphones, biometric devices, and social media used to obtain data on us as individuals and to make predictions about our lives and how we will behave as consumers. Zuboff writes that this is to "know and shape our behavior at scale."

This form of capitalism would consider personal data as a free raw resource to be translated into behavioral data. The ethical threat is that when our behaviors can be predicted and shaped by a handful of top corporations, we humans will face a sense of hopelessness and no longer be in control of ourselves and our behaviors. Humans risk being manipulated by those who control the data for their own economic advantage. Furthermore, we no longer have privacy. All our personal data is used as a raw material without any individual autonomy in its use or access.

Further ethical considerations focus on power. In 2017 Vladimir Putin said, "Whoever becomes the leader in [the AI sphere] will become the ruler of the world." Elon Musk responded that the AI arms race will be the "most likely cause of WW3." Musk and 4,500 AI and robotics researchers have signed a Fight for the Future open letter in opposition to autonomous weapons that act without human intervention. There has been a proliferation of AI among national militaries, including in China and Russia. The National Security Council on AI was created by Congress in 2018. Ethical issues under consideration include how AI will shape the future of power in our countries. To address some of these issues, a board made up of technology executives and AI ethicists and experts created recommendations for AI ethical principles for the Department of Defense. It behooves organizations creating AI healthcare solutions to understand and maintain awareness of such recommendations. Defense and healthcare share a common goal in human safety.

The complexity of the human context that AI must work with and for is challenging. These ethical considerations and potential fears must be addressed proactively through human-centered AI to ensure limitations and enhancement of collaboration with humans. The result will be the ultimate collaboration between humans and AI rather than an extreme world of domination by a few data hoarders and powerlessness for the rest. Retaining the essential aspects of healthcare work such as empathy and touch is essential to making human-centered AI work.

Making Human-Centered AI Work

There is general agreement that maintaining the human element in the way AI is designed, delivered, used, and improved will make it more successful. We want AI to be understandable by nonexpert users and to be designed with social responsibility in mind. To enable this, a true collaboration between humans and AI must occur.

Research on 1,500 companies found that performance indices were most enhanced when AI and humans worked collaboratively. Humans and AI have a greater and more significant value together than they do separately, and their strengths and capabilities augment performance when combined. The *Harvard Business Review* (HBR) makes this point in describing collaborative intelligence, humans, and AI joining forces.[9] Wei Xu takes this even further, arguing that the first challenge is to move beyond simple interaction to "human-machine integration and human-machine teaming."[10] To overly simplify, the basic concept would be humans and AI working together in a dynamic relationship in which dynamic data inputs result in dynamic goals and ongoing micro-adjustments to the relationship where each player takes priority in their role addressing the function they are most adapted to handle.

An example of how this type of human-centered AI occurs currently is through retinal scanning. AI performs the initial assessment of normal versus abnormal findings. The vast majority of scans will be normal. The remaining 30% or so of abnormal findings are reviewed by a human. In this case, human-centered AI focused on where the limitations to its capabilities occurred, the 30%. This is handed over to AI's

---

9 James Wilson and Paul R. Daugherty, "Collaborative Intelligence: Humans and AI Are Joining Forces" (*https://oreil.ly/f536p*), *Harvard Business Review*, July–August 2018.

10 Wei Xu, "Toward Human-Centered AI: A Perspective from Human-Computer Interaction" (*https://oreil.ly/EA03S*), *ACM Interactions* 26, no. 4 (2019).

human partner, who looks at the abnormal findings in the context of the patient's history and clinical findings to determine whether it's a matter of concern. Out of this emerges a partnership between humans and AI, where AI performs quickly, efficiently, and accurately the task it is assigned, and the human performs their more complex and nuanced evaluation, taking in additional human factors that may impact the patient solution. Clinicians benefit in that they are no longer reviewing all of the scans and can instead focus on the scans that require their human capabilities. One can imagine future models in which AI is used to learn to assess other types of abnormal scans as well, and as its fluency in this area increases, dynamic goals and shifts in the human-AI partnership will occur. As human experience and clinical medicine are dynamic, AI will not replace the human; rather, through this symbiotic relationship, the best outcomes will be achieved.

Call centers or customer service centers in healthcare leverage AI using chatbots or virtual assistants. Some insurance carriers have attempted some chatbot use in the past and failed. When chatbot use replaces human agents, the adoption and acceptance by customers often fails to meet expectations. Designing chatbots to replace humans goes against the principles of human-centered AI, which hold that AI should not replace humans but instead should replace or augment human tasks. Several technological challenges must be overcome for chatbots to mimic human behavior, and we will explore that idea in more detail in Chapter 6. However, newer virtual assistants and chatbots for call centers or customer support have been successful. Still, these often complement or operate as an alternative to call center agents rather than replacing them.

Human-centered AI utilizes AI's strength of pattern recognition to change the way hospitals triage. AI can sift through patient data to assess which patient is most in need of care within the next 90 minutes.[11] This enables clinicians to focus on the care they are providing and less on the logistics of who requires attention next. One can envision an ongoing dynamic relationship between humans and AI in this area. As clinical medicine advances and fewer people require actual hospitalization, a sicker population ends up presenting to emergency departments.

Consequently, a large number of resources are used for triaging patients, and determining who is sick versus who is not that sick gets harder. The current practice focuses on biometric variables to determine who is most unstable and therefore requires more immediate care. As additional data inputs arrive that are interpretable by humans, such as pain intolerance or risk of a dangerous outcome, AI accommodating these signals makes a difference. AI will be able to hone its analysis, and caregivers will be able to focus on the sickest of the sick. In the ideal state, feedback loops exist in which other implicit variables, including sociocultural values impacting outcomes,

---

11 Mara Geller, "Emergency Room Triage with AI" (*https://oreil.ly/Hh28r*), Aidoc, June 16, 2020.

are added to the AI knowledge base. The identification of AI limitations would result in human handoffs as well as human oversight.

Summary

Developing human-centered AI for healthcare requires some basic blocking and tackling:

- When building AI, engineers must embrace best practices honed and developed over decades, such as design thinking and change management.
- Human understanding of AI, i.e., explainable AI, is critical to AI success.
- AI must represent all people; therefore, it must cut across many disciplines and embrace a wide spectrum of genders, races, ethnicities, social economic statuses, and ages.
- AI must do no harm and must be fair, transparent, and ethical.

A further consideration is that human-centered AI, as applied to healthcare, has a different set of duties, goals, and stakeholders as compared with other end users. Stakeholders may include provider systems, clinicians, healthcare administrative services, insurers, federal regulatory agencies, payers, or patients. Each stakeholder will have different goals and endpoints for AI. For example, payers may focus on efficiency in care and controlling costs, whereas provider systems may focus on providing efficient patient care. Addressing complementary and sometimes conflicting goals requires practical explainable AI solutions. AI success requires human collaboration and insights.

AI designed for real human behavior aids in the adoption of AI technologies, and that will allow intelligent systems to reach their full potential. Machine learning and algorithms without social context, knowledge of human behavior, or insight into human beliefs lead to an incomplete solution. Creating AI that understands the human perspective and societal goals, along with cultural norms, will ensure the ultimate system. Human-centered AI is not just a goal but an activity that AI stakeholders (developers, users, and consumers) must all actively engage in.

CHAPTER 3

Monitoring + AI = Rx for Personal Health

This chapter describes how intense personalization and continuous monitoring should and can become a reality for healthcare. With AI we can do more than predict, diagnose, and treat a disease. AI can help with continuous monitoring of a person's health, suggesting adjustments before a patient progresses along the disease continuum from healthy to at-risk to chronically ill (or wherever they might be on the continuum). AI has the potential to help with missed diagnoses and misdiagnoses, challenging current healthcare models. It is not a quick fix. This chapter is not about empty hyperbole or endless platitudes, but it does require imagination and a vision of how healthcare can work.

Let's start with an adapted real-life patient scenario. It was the beginning of summer in 2005, and Bethanie, a 28-year-old schoolteacher, was in the best physical condition of her life. However, when several troubling symptoms started to appear, she realized something was not right. Her symptoms began during a trip to help her friend move to Reno. Because of the dry, hot climate in Nevada, she chalked up her excessive thirst and her need to get up in the middle of the night to urinate—which she had never done before—to the fact that she was drinking more water than usual. During the eight-hour drive back home to Orange County, California, she developed an insatiable thirst and found herself stopping for cold beverages many times along the way.

Once back at home, she started waking up every night needing to use the bathroom, at first only twice a night but soon three times a night. She developed a cotton-like feeling in the back of her throat, yet she continued to imagine that the cause was dehydration from her time in Reno. She felt extraordinarily exhausted and wondered if she might be anemic, since she had less energy each day. Her unquenchable thirst continued.

She called her doctor and described all her symptoms, and blood tests were ordered. The next morning she dragged herself to the lab, and when she found its hours of operation had changed, she sat down on the floor outside the office and fell asleep. Extreme fatigue was another overwhelming problem she was facing.

As the days went on without her symptoms improving, Bethanie found it increasingly difficult to get off the couch. She wanted and needed answers. Walking to the bathroom and back made her feel like she'd run a marathon, and the thought of getting up to call the doctor in hopes the results would finally be in was too much. Later she found out her shortness of breath was hyperventilation. She'd had little to no appetite for weeks and soon found her clothes were so loose they were falling off, caused by a 12-pound decrease in weight.

Bethanie's fatigue continued to worsen, to the point that her mother came over to help her and communicate with her doctors. She and Bethanie were finally told over the phone that Bethanie's lab work showed she had diabetes. Her physician interpreted the abnormal lab values and, given Bethanie's age of 28, made the diagnosis of type 2 diabetes, which proved incorrect. (In reality, Bethanie had type 1 diabetes, requiring a completely different form of medication and treatment.) On that phone call, they said Bethanie should feel better a couple of days after starting a prescription for metformin. But several days went by, and rather than improving, she was getting worse.

Bethanie's symptoms were typical of a classic case of type 1 diabetes: unintended weight loss, no appetite, extreme thirst, frequent urination, fatigue, and weakness. Possibly the doctor saw her high blood sugar reading and considered only two factors, a lack of family history of diabetes and onset at an atypical age, before coming to the wrong conclusion. This misdiagnosis could have proved to be fatal or sent her into a diabetic coma. Unbeknownst to Bethanie and her mom, her body was shutting down while she was on the couch, too weak to get up. She needed a prescription to inject much-needed insulin, not the metformin pill.

After hearing Bethanie's slurred speech and lack of attention over a call from San Francisco, Bethanie's sister Melodie, along with their mom, decided it was time for them to call a nursing hotline. Within a few questions, the person on the hotline said that Bethanie needed to be brought into the emergency room immediately—they would notify the hospital so that it would be able to get Bethanie in right away. Almost immediately, the doctors and nurses seemed to recognize a sweet smell on her breath, indicating her current condition as DKA, diabetic ketoacidosis, which supported the fact that she was a type 1, not type 2, diabetic.

Bethanie spent two days in the intensive care unit, and three more days after that in the hospital, and was told she'd been lucky. Eventually, her blood sugar stabilized, and she began to cope with her new health status as a person with type 1 diabetes. Type 1 diabetes requires immediate and severe lifestyle changes, including a different eating pattern and insulin supplementation, usually through an insulin pump or through several self-given injections throughout the day.

Her appetite returned, and when the orderly delivered her first meal, she had the hunger to eat, which she hadn't felt in weeks. Everything looked delicious at this point, even hospital food. A hospital staff person identified herself as a diabetic educator and confirmed that Bethanie could eat everything on the plate, pointing out each item's category: carbohydrates, vegetables, and even a most delicious-looking brownie were allowed. Bethanie devoured everything, and unfortunately her blood sugar skyrocketed. The diabetic educator who had confirmed Bethanie could eat everything on her plate had provided patently wrong advice.

In 2005, smartphones with internet access and search engines were not ubiquitous. Bethanie and her family did not have the means to validate or double-check information. They received a stack of papers and relied on the expertise of the clinicians.

The next morning, as the staff was changing over, Bethanie overheard a nurse outside her room explaining, "They fed her the wrong food yesterday," yet no one ever communicated this to Bethanie. Within a week, Bethanie had two avoidable and potentially fatal experiences with healthcare. Healthcare should have been better and can be better. AI's use in this situation would have been to evaluate Bethanie's symptoms, signs, and lab values and include type 1 diabetes in the differential along with type 2 diabetes. The data backing AI's suggestion to consider type 1 diabetes could have been the pivotal action that would have led to the physician rethinking the possible diagnosis and not making assumptions. AI use in scanning the immense amount of clinical research literature and database research articles also could have provided an additional diagnosis of latent autoimmune diabetes in adults (LADA, or diabetes 1.5), which presents and behaves almost exactly like type 1 diabetes and is underrecognized and not widely known to all clinicians. Either of these scenarios with AI would have led the clinician to rethink their assumption.

The Rx (or prescription) for personal health occurs when intense personalization happens at the moment of need. Intense personalization is the power of one—dealing with a patient not as a segment but as an individual. Intense personalization is when your provider, your clinician, your pharmacist, and everyone involved in your care at each point of your patient journey know your medical history and your interactions with the healthcare system to the extent needed. Intense personalization, also called extreme personalization or hyperpersonalization, requires integrating AI into workflows, where a patient can be reached with the right message on the right device at the right time.

Medical care for many chronic conditions or disease states such as Bethanie's should not require guesswork. Patients should not be at the mercy of misdiagnoses and medical errors. But medical errors are not rare events. A 2016 John Hopkins study (*https://oreil.ly/l2ZYx*) examining medical death rate data over eight years estimated that there are a quarter million deaths per year due to medical errors. According to a

2019 article by Jacqueline Renfrow on the healthcare news site FierceHealthcare (*https://oreil.ly/XSJ9h*),

> An estimated 40,000 to 80,000 deaths occur each year in U.S. hospitals related to misdiagnosis, and an estimated 12 million Americans suffer a diagnostic error each year in a primary care setting—33% of which result in serious or permanent damage or death.

Let's dig a little deeper into the idea of a prescription for personal health.

Prescription (Rx) for Personal Health

The prescription for personal health is intense personalization. Artificial intelligence and real-time data deliver the relevant signals and notifications to the patient and their primary care physician, enabling better healthcare outcomes. This data is not based just on norms, which in a previous chapter we saw can contain bias. Rather, an individual's personalized data can be assessed by AI to determine what is normal for them personally. From there, the physician and patient can develop a personalized monitoring and care plan that addresses the patient as an individual, optimizing not the health of a population but the health of the individual; case by case, this adds to overall health among the greater population.

Let's look at an intense personalization scenario in which real-time data, analytics, and AI are applied in the care of the patient Bethanie, as illustrated in Figure 3-1.

In this scenario, Bethanie uses an app on her phone that is a digital twin, a virtual representation of her.[1] Since downloading the app, she has granted it permission to receive her clinical data, such as her electronic medical records. The app tracks Bethanie's behavior. Bethanie records her weight daily using a wireless scale, which updates her fitness tracker, which in turn updates her digital twin. The AI in the digital twin knows she has a significant and unexplained weight loss.

Daily, the digital twin app asks Bethanie how she feels, and she responds. This takes about 30 seconds. Bethanie uses the app every day for over a year, and it collects a lot of behavioral and fitness data. It knows she has been exercising daily for a year. It knows that her BMI and weight are ideal for her age and height.

Every day the digital twin does a health check in the form of a Q&A session; if Bethanie doesn't feel right, the series of questions collect data on her symptoms. The AI pays attention to her unquenchable thirst, frequent urination, and fatigue. It knows she is drinking far more water over the last week than in previous weeks. The AI knows she has no familial history of diabetes, and she doesn't fit the typical case for the onset of diabetes.

---

1 While a digital twin app doesn't yet exist in any meaningful way, such an app is possible given today's technology.

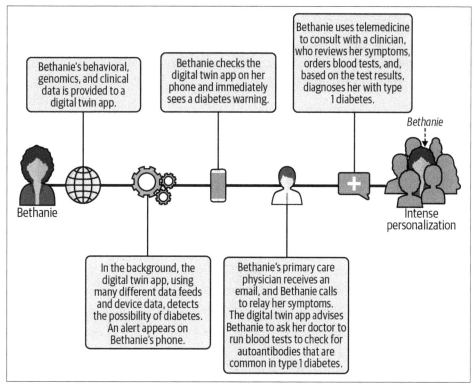

Bethanie's behavioral, genomics, and clinical data is provided to a digital twin app.

Bethanie checks the digital twin app on her phone and immediately sees a diabetes warning.

Bethanie uses telemedicine to consult with a clinician, who reviews her symptoms, orders blood tests, and, based on the test results, diagnoses her with type 1 diabetes.

Bethanie

Bethanie

Intense personalization

In the background, the digital twin app, using many different data feeds and device data, detects the possibility of diabetes. An alert appears on Bethanie's phone.

Bethanie's primary care physician receives an email, and Bethanie calls to relay her symptoms. The digital twin app advises Bethanie to ask her doctor to run blood tests to check for autoantibodies that are common in type 1 diabetes.

Figure 3-1. Intense personalization

In the cloud, multiple deep learning models run disease-state models for hyperthyroidism, anemia, diabetes, and more. The diabetes disease-state prediction model provides a high confidence score but is unable to determine type 1, type 2, or LADA. Bethanie's age and lack of family history are assessed in the model prediction as additional variables, but they are weighted appropriately as to significance and impact on diagnosis based on clinical studies to date.

An alert appears in the app warning Bethanie that she may have a disease: diabetes. It advises her to contact her primary care doctor immediately. At the same time, her doctor's office receives an email alert indicating Bethanie may be having troubling symptoms and signs of diabetes requiring urgent medical evaluation.

Let's assume the primary care physician inaccurately assesses her as a person with type 2 diabetes, as the digital twin doesn't know which type of diabetes she has. Her prescription, metformin, lowers blood glucose through augmentation of the body's own insulin. Bethanie continues to use the digital twin, and she has gotten worse, not better, contrary to what the doctor predicted. Bethanie is weak, but her mom enters data in the app and adds new symptoms, such as Bethanie's slurring and increased fatigue. The digital twin raises the alarm. It instructs Bethanie to have further lab tests, including getting checked for ketones (which would cause the fruity smell of her breath) in her blood and urine. The app also advises that Bethanie should be taken to the ER since her mental status (extreme lethargy) is worsening. The digital twin's alarm, expressed both visually and in words, underlines the need for her to go to the emergency room for care and evaluation.

Other diseases, such as asthma or cardiac disease, could be substituted for diabetes in this scenario. The increased potential for home diagnosis and wearables in the future will accelerate disease detection and management.

Intense personalization in healthcare needs AI, and AI needs lots and lots of data. That data comes from several realms, as depicted in Figure 3-2.

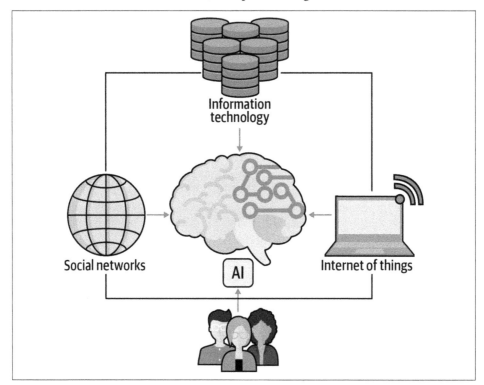

Figure 3-2. Three realms influencing healthcare

Three Realms Influencing Healthcare

Three realms actively create massive amounts of data, what we commonly describe as big data. In the information technology world, EMR systems, claims systems, call centers, and more collect massive amounts of data. The Internet of Things (IoT) continues to explode with wearables and devices at work and at home sending signals, generating health, behavior, and fitness data. Social networks of all kinds, from driving apps to various social platforms, collect data on places visited, social contacts, and more.

Making sense, spotting patterns, and generating insights is what AI does best, and this is what makes intense personalization possible, as exemplified by Bethanie's case study. We live among three realms, each undergoing rapid technological advances in instrumentation, and each becoming increasingly connected. Our physical world comprises intelligent objects, sensors, medical technology devices, smart voice speakers, wearables, and everything belonging to the Internet of Things. People use wearable technology and mobile technologies, instrumenting their movements, behaviors, and actions. This realm of IoT is enabled with apps on mobile devices connecting to the intelligent objects, collecting data, and making sense of it.

The Internet of Things, which includes the subset the Internet of Medical Things (IoMT), comprises billions of connected objects, often purpose-built (connected cars, vending machines, and home appliances, for example) with dedicated functions, and as vast as our imaginations. IoT defines a network of physical objects containing embedded technology to communicate and connect, enabling the exchange of data. IoT devices connect to the internet for data exchange via WiFi, Bluetooth, RFID, and other wireless technologies. Connecting these intelligent objects means we can learn people's behaviors and react with interventional strategies before episodic events.

People are becoming more instrumented as we use laptops, mobile devices, wearables, and IoT in our homes and at work and play. This enables a proactive response when abnormal results from monitored data appear. As of today, reactive treatments are the norm. Clinicians tend to wait for a patient to notify them of worsening symptoms. In personalized AI, sense and respond will become the norm where presymptomatic values or trends in blood sugars occur hours to days before an episodic event. A gradual increase in low blood sugar results in the morning prior to waking, after taking insulin at night, could be an indicator of impending symptomatic and serious hypoglycemia (low blood sugar) occurring while the patient is still sleeping. Simple IoT devices such as connected continuous glucose monitors (CGM) can detect and alert one's physician if such an abnormal trend occurs, and CGMs are routinely used today in diabetic management programs.

Today the instrumentation of people means computers noticing changes in your activity and in your interactions with devices, apps, and other people, which may be early signs of a decline in cognitive abilities. Your voice, collected over decades through the voice speakers in your home or phone recordings made to your health provider, can be used to diagnose depression, Alzheimer's, heart disease, mental disorders, concussions, or even migraines. A digital twin listening to a customer's voice over time allows the detection of Parkinson's disease, depression, schizophrenia, and other disorders.

Products and devices from the medical technology industry are often a vehicle through which patients and consumers interact with healthcare for diagnostics, treatment, and monitoring. These products and devices include pacemakers, pregnancy tests, CT, MRI scanners, and more. New devices are here and more are on the horizon, a network of connected, smart devices and objects that communicate with each other, provide new signals, and automate critical tasks that improve diagnostics and patient care. An entire market has emerged around IoT integration, enabling independently designed applications and data to work together. Healthcare organizations can use or build platforms, defined and explored in Chapter 7, to support an ecosystem of multiple applications, multiple vendors, and multiple devices. The fact that data arrives in different formats doesn't require that we try to boil the ocean creating data standards or data models for interoperability. Of course, it is a huge plus and advantage that standards or models exist. IoT aggregation layers for sensor data aggregation continue to improve, along with existing data aggregation mechanisms.

These new devices create a scenario in which consumers at home gain early insights into potential disease states. No longer are academic institutions and healthcare companies, with their proprietary predictive models, the only means of detecting or predicting disease states. Patients can take greater ownership of their health as they are empowered by data, analytics, and AI to better understand how their condition or disease state is being managed, as well as where they are having problems and where they are having successes. However, this is not a story about an alternative to healthcare by clinicians but instead a story of replacing search engines with questions when an ailment or a condition appears. More importantly, this is about preemptive steps to detect problems before symptoms appear. This represents an augmentation to existing healthcare and to attacking problems before they become fatal or debilitating and expensive. Even more impactful is the ability to attack problems before they come into existence.

Today a typical homeowner has thermometers, bandages, first aid kits, and medicines in their medicine cabinet. In the future, the medicine cabinet in a typical home will be filled with IoT devices focused on disease state detection. For example, electronic noses will drop in price and be used for diagnosis of digestive and respiratory diseases through the breath.[2] Testing saliva at home helps with several disease state detections. IoT home healthcare sensors will drop in price, improve in accuracy, and become part of everyday living. IoT devices such as smart toilets will monitor diseases such as inflammatory bowel disease, prostate cancer, or kidney failure. People who want to keep on top of their health will increasingly adopt these smart IoT devices in their home.

---

2 Carlos Sánchez, J. Pedro Santos, and Jesús Lozano, "Use of Electronic Noses for Diagnosis of Digestive and Respiratory Diseases through the Breath" (*https://oreil.ly/OaEjV*), *Biosensors* 9, no. 1 (2019): 35.

It remains a futurist's role to predict whether an incumbent healthcare company, a start-up, or an internet-born company creates a disruptive healthcare platform, service, or killer app like the digital twin. At its core, healthcare intends to help people live longer and healthier lives. Is one of the killer, successful apps going to be a bracelet that detects cancer, or nanoparticles swimming through your blood to identify disease states? Already we have tests that look for colon cancer DNA in our feces after a bowel movement. Are we that far from taking it a step further? What about smart contact lenses that help people with diabetes monitor their disease states, or something that reverses or slows aging? Maybe a commerce platform combined with personal health data that identifies an individual at risk for a disease, alerts the individual, and schedules a virtual personal assistant before any episodic event occurs? Or how about a platform of apps and services that is contextual yet invisible living in your home, mobile device, or provider clinic? This platform is voice-activated, armed with services, and secure. It provides real-time healthcare by consuming signals from your instrumented body and the spaces you occupy (e.g., home or office) and sensing and responding to promote a healthier lifestyle and detect disease states and episodic conditions before they occur. The platform creates your digital twin, armed with your genetic data, electronic medical record, and data from wearables. It allows you a glimpse into your future health state, 1 year or 50 years from the present day, based on intense personalization. Engineering a platform or services as just described is not science fiction; these killer platforms, services, and apps are within our reach.

Significant advances in computing power, wireless, miniaturization, and the intelligence of ubiquitous, everyday things like watches, sensors, wearables, appliances, and entertainment devices propel technological and cultural revolutions transforming healthcare. These kinds of platforms or services are possible. Who is responsible for monitoring this data, addressing abnormalities with sensor triggers, and incorporating this wealth of data into an individual's healthcare plan (and how to do so) has all yet to be worked out. In the past doctors and other healthcare providers have been held responsible, but with the three realms acting in conjunction, who owns and is responsible for this data is yet unknown and will have to be addressed as this technology is adapted. Yet growth and technological advances continue. At the heart of this technological revolution are the three realms powered by AI and quietly enabling the birth of a new computing paradigm, ambient computing.

Ambient Computing and Healthcare

Many clinicians argue, perhaps correctly, that computers and information technology have not made their work easier (*https://oreil.ly/zcBR8*). In fact, in many instances, computer proliferation and adoption in clinical settings is in the way of doctor-patient relationships. Some argue that it creates the digital patient, as doctors spend more time on screens than with patients. This is why invisible computing, computing that lives in the environment where its presence is hardly detectable, must exist and expand.

The new industrial revolution, the fourth one, represents a fundamental change in the way we work, live, and play. The "Fourth Industrial Revolution" is a phrase often used by economists, policy makers, and technologists to describe innovative technologies in the fields of artificial intelligence, big data, blockchain, wireless, IoT, and more. Underpinning the Fourth Industrial Revolution are distinct computing eras.

Today IoT, big data, miniaturization, blockchain, wearables, social platforms, sensors, AI, and more allow technology to be embedded in people's daily lives. This invisible technology lives in our watches, detecting atrial fibrillation (AFib), a heart rhythm disorder that predisposes to stroke. It resides in cars, sensing impaired driving, or in home sensors that detect movements such as falls or that analyze personal behaviors to determine the best time to send reminders to take medications.

Massive organizational computing and personal computing remain vital for healthcare. Ambient computing, depicted in Figure 3-3, is a game changer and is truly transformational for healthcare. Ambient computing's impact on healthcare creates new models of care delivery and health maintenance. It promises to deliver healthcare to more places, healthcare that is continuous, anticipatory, and intensely personalized. Ambient computing positively impacts the quality of healthcare, creating new, high-quality experiences, and reduces the cost of healthcare while making it more accessible to a broader community.

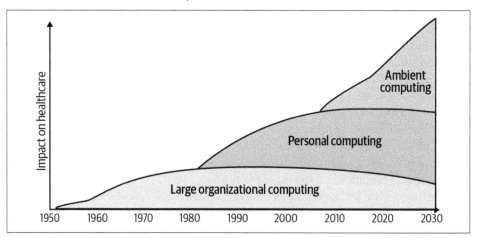

Figure 3-3. Ambient computing

In the future, a personalized healthcare journey, with the home as a scaled platform of care, medication tracking, preventive and behavioral care monitoring, and proactive disease detection, will be ubiquitous and expected by consumers. Creating this journey is achievable through a platform approach with human-centered AI, creating the right experiences at the right time for everyone in the ecosystem—consumers, patients, and clinicians. This comprehensive platform is made possible by pervasive, invisible, contextual computing. The services, APIs, and apps composing the platform make proactive disease management and prevention real while providing a seamless patient healthcare journey.

Such a platform requires lots of data where AI makes sense of the data, separating signal from noise around a potential episodic event or identifying sick patients before they need emergency care. The data fueling this platform originates from the three realms.

Dina Katabi, in a 2018 Ted Talk (*https://oreil.ly/RtC9A*), describes monitoring devices using wireless technology to monitor chronic disease patients in their home. These monitoring devices, intelligent edge computing objects infused with AI, can detect a number of disease states, such as chronic obstructive pulmonary disease, depression, Alzheimer's, or sleep disorders. Sensors or wireless technology detecting movements, such as an elderly person falling, or signals showing a decline of health are solutions we can use today. When implemented, these solutions help patients avoid episodic events causing hospitalization or other bad outcomes. AI and machine learning make these monitoring devices intelligent; patterns and behaviors can be learned, providing a plethora of opportunities to influence behavior, whether it be as simple as encouraging movement or taking medicine at a prescribed time.

Continuous Monitoring Using AI

AI can do more than predict who is at risk for developing a disease. AI can also be used to help determine the best treatment for patients with active disease. For example, start-up companies currently are focusing on the integration of AI into treatment algorithms for patients with chronic kidney disease (CKD). Patients develop CKD due to several different issues. You can get CKD with diabetes or hypertension. You can also develop CKD with problems from an intrinsic disorder of the kidneys.

A patient with CKD will typically, over time, develop worsening of their kidney function. They will need some form of dialysis, such as hemodialysis, a process in which blood is taken out of the patient's body and filtered and then returned to the body (that is, the function of the kidneys is artificially performed outside the body). Hemodialysis is a time-intensive process. A typical schedule for a patient involves them traveling to a dialysis center three times a week and sitting for several hours as their blood is filtered. Conducting hemodialysis over extended periods creates risks associated with the procedure itself. Risks and complications include infection, electrolyte imbalance, and overdialysis (not enough blood volume returned to the patient, with subsequent low blood pressure).

At one time, clinical medicine determined that a kidney transplant was the only option once hemodialysis was no longer possible. However, time and evidence-based medicine have shifted treatment away from hemodialysis to renal transplantation at earlier stages of CKD, before a patient progresses to the point of requiring dialysis. These patients are proven to have better outcomes with early transplant, and an improved quality of life, and overall there is less cost to the healthcare system.

Continuous Monitoring

So how is AI being used here? It's being used to sift through and learn from the incalculable individual patient values/data and patient variables (such as age, relative health, and so forth) to determine who would benefit from early transplants in order to achieve the best outcome. AI can augment the interpretation and actionability of the likely high volume of continuously generated healthcare data. Kidney specialists rely on their intrinsic knowledge of their patient and their own experience to help determine the best time for a kidney transplant operation. Now we have the augmented capabilities of AI assisting providers in making this incredibly critical and lifesaving decision. AI—in tandem with continuous monitoring of variables such as vital sign stability, quality of life, kidney function, medication relied upon to support renal function loss, other medical conditions, and history of previous complications related to kidney function loss—can aid in determining optimal time of transplant. Despite widespread acceptance of the superiority of early renal transplant, however, no guidelines exist for precisely when in the course of CKD progression renal transplant should occur. Preemptive renal transplant too early in the course of renal decline may waste native kidney function and prematurely expose donors and recipients to operative and immunosuppressive risk associated with transplantation. On the other hand, earlier restoration of renal function may slow cardiovascular progression associated with ongoing renal disease and dialysis, with early transplant potentially preventing CKD-associated cardiovascular morbidity and mortality.[3] Evaluating numerous data variables with AI may have a huge impact in determining optimal time for transplant and could be a great tool to facilitate physician care. As illustrated in the preceding example, continuous monitoring augmented by AI is providing new opportunities to help patients live their best and healthiest possible lives. AI and monitoring can also perform real-time monitoring of a person's health, suggesting adjustments in lifestyle before the patient progresses to a disease state.

We think of the health spectrum as starting with wellness or health, and as a person ages, their health progresses through various worsening states if not checked or managed in the interim. Although this construct does not apply to all individuals, it is a

---

3 Morgan E. Grams et al., "Trends in the Timing of Pre-emptive Kidney Transplantation" (*https://oreil.ly/d8hP0*), *Journal of the American Society of Nephrology* 22, no. 9 (2011): 1615–1620.

generally accepted model for describing disease/health progression throughout an individual's life. AI, along with continuous monitoring through IoT, opens up a world of possibility in which we can alter the course of a patient's health by preventing the development or worsening of the disease.

Biometric monitoring is rapidly expanding, and these capabilities, used with AI, challenge current healthcare models in which clinicians respond to the patient at their location in the disease spectrum. This means that if a patient has no significant medical claims, then that patient is assumed to be healthy, with likely no interventions or significant counseling to occur. In a case where there is a known disease—say, diabetes—a clinician will manage per clinical guidelines and patient circumstances to control the patient's diabetes. Monitoring used in conjunction with AI changes this model. No longer are we stuck treating or maintaining a patient where they are in the health spectrum and assuming good health if no significant medical spend or claims occur. Monitoring and AI allow continuous monitoring to prevent disease and make micro-corrections along the health span of a patient to improve their health in never-before-thought-of ways.

Simply put, tracking with AI can help us prevent or slow the development of diabetes in the first place. For the patient with known diabetes, monitoring and AI allows micro-adjustments to treatment based on the continuous feedback loop of monitoring results. Thus, health management has a new tool in its armory for preventing disease and halting disease progression.

Beeps, Chimes, Dings, and Dongs

A well-respected cardiologist and friend of this author (Dr. Siupo Becker) once tried to prove a point in a hospital intensive care unit (ICU). He was trying to demonstrate to management that the nurses were so accustomed to the alarms on the numerous units in the ICU that they no longer responded to the alarms. What alarms? There are ventilators (to help patients continue breathing), intravenous drips, cardiac monitors, blood pressure monitors, drug infusion machines, beds (especially self-turning ones), fall monitors, and more. And with tight staffing, a nurse may be running from one high-needs patient to another. (If you think we're exaggerating about the noise volume, let us share a brief story. While Dr. Becker was training a medical student and preparing to transfer a patient out of the ICU to a step-down unit, the medical student burst into tears. She said all the noise was overwhelming and she couldn't think. It was sensory overload for her. It's good to know your limits. She went on to focus on outpatient wellcare.)

Back to the cardiologist's story: amid all the ICU noise, Dr. Becker's friend decided to enter his patient's room and wiggle all the cardiac monitor cords. Every cardiac alarm triggered. No nurses responded, even after 30 minutes. Good thing there were two doctors in the place. The patient was OK; there was nothing to be concerned about.

It's possible the nurses knew from the readings that this was an artificial abnormality. Regardless, it is the role of the nurse to ensure the monitors are reporting accurately. That is, the nurses are required to check the patient leads (the cords attached to patients from monitors) to ensure all are functioning. One reason the nurses may have become habituated to the alarms going off is "alarm fatigue." One study found that 72–99% of clinical alarms are false. (*https://oreil.ly/2RIgV*) In healthcare, the alerts are signals of interest but in many cases are not deemed urgent or critical enough for intervention.

Alarm fatigue is real. A big concern about AI and IoT devices centers around there being too much data, too many alarms, too much parenting by systems and IT over clinicians' decision making. We can create machine learning models that don't cry wolf, AI that doesn't annoy. We could use AI to let nurses and clinicians know when alarms in the ICU or hospital are of significance and warrant evaluation. Of course this means human-centered design rather than tossing IT solutions over the wall.

Health Continuum

We've briefly touched on the health or disease continuum, but before we combine this with IoT and AI, let us look deeper into what this continuum represents. The health continuum paradigm provides a graphic model of the average person with disease developing and progressing as they age.

At far right in the health continuum shown in Figure 3-4 is a healthy individual; as the person ages, going to the left, they develop a disease and eventually pass away. If there are no interventions, then the model posits that a person progresses in life along this continuum. In actuality, two factors contradict this model. First, there are many congenital issues or other conditions related to birth that would start a person out as a diseased individual. In such a case, we would place that individual at far left in the continuum, at the reduced health or disease stage. Second, not all individuals follow this logical progression in their health. In reality, many people who fall within the excellent health spectrum at the right might "jump" to the poor health or even the disease spectrum without passing through any intervening stages. For example, a teenager may be healthy and very active one day and then within a few days/weeks be diagnosed with type 1 diabetes. Similarly, a very busy and healthy individual may be at optimal health but may immediately "jump" to the far left disease stage after a traumatic injury.

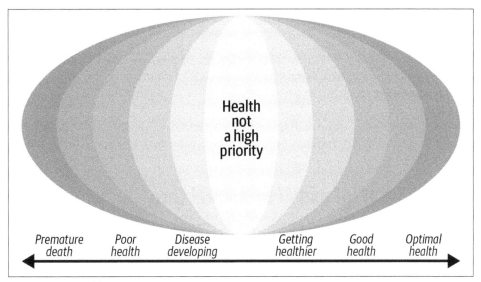

Figure 3-4. Health continuum

What is the benefit of this health continuum, if it cannot be applied to all? It is standard in the healthcare industry to use this model to explain how intervention at the earlier stages of an individual's health journey can either prevent disease or manage it such that the individual stays at the stage they are at longer, without progressing to worsening health. There is a cost-benefit to maintaining the health stage you are at in the continuum and preventing disease progression.

Also, individuals may even improve their stage on the continuum. For example, a type 2 diabetic 50-year-old female with a BMI of 35, hypertension, and high cholesterol may be managed and kept stable in her current stage with the use of medications. This is a typical combination of conditions. If this woman were to exercise, lose weight, adhere to therapies, and improve in these areas, then there is the potential for her type 2 diabetes to be fully controlled through diet, exercise, and weight loss alone. Imagine the improvement to this woman's health and well-being, in addition to the cost savings generated by stopping or decreasing medications. In this case, the health savings would be reflected in a reduced need for physician and specialist visits, and for labs and screenings to monitor her conditions. There would also be reduced cost due to medications being discontinued or reduced in number (diabetic medications are in the top three pharmaceutical spend categories in the US), and the potential cost savings associated with the avoidance of further progression of her clinical disease. It is believed that even with optimal control of multiple conditions over time, progression in the disease spectrum will occur. Improving your health stage in the continuum away from chronic disease means improved health and more significant cost savings. If you then add in the well-being and behavioral health assets gained, you can see the benefits of promoting and understanding the application of AI to the health continuum.

All that said, can alerts from connected devices tied in with AI technology truly change a patient's behavior? A fairly recent clinical literature review (*https://oreil.ly/uHqF3*) compiling results from 51 published studies shows that they can. The review found that reminders and alerts can promote self-accountability in healthcare and increased adherence, with the implication that AI may "reliably assist patients to adhere to their health regimen…, decrease readmission rates, and potentially reduce clinic costs."

Application of IoT and AI to Medical Care

Before the Internet of Things, patients' interactions with doctors were limited to in-person visits, telehealth interactions, portal and email communications, and leaving messages with staff for doctor callbacks. With the advent of IoT-enabled devices, remote monitoring in the healthcare sector is now available. Almost all large health insurance providers have an associated case management arm in which nurse clinicians and physicians are employed to review the care being received by a member (insuree). As technology advances, these case management arms now frequently employ the use of connected devices to help monitor the health of their members with chronic disease. For example, it is routine for case management to have a congestive heart failure (CHF) program, with clinicians following the members' weight and symptoms through notepads and connected scales that feed supplemental information into case management and alert when an abnormality such as increased weight occurs. AI is used to determine when alerts go out and to facilitate the best next action—for example, should the member/patient call their doctor, should a case management clinician call the member, should the member go to the emergency room, and so on. IoT measurement and tracking analyzed by AI provide immediate evaluation of the data, so that over time we can identify healthcare events/diagnose diseases and prevent future events/diseases.

IoT and AI

Another example of an IoT use case is when healthcare payers arrange for connected blood pressure device monitoring for at-risk pregnancies—the premise being that gestational hypertension occurs in approximately 7% of the pregnant population and that 4–20% of these babies end up in the neonatal intensive care unit (NICU). Adding to the healthcare payer incentive to monitor these "at-risk" moms are the increased healthcare costs associated with pregnancy-related complications, including gestational hypertension and its associated conditions, preeclampsia and eclampsia. Anecdotal reports from a team working on managing potential risk in the maternal population at United Healthcare indicate approximately 80–90% compliance with device use and continuation in these connected care monitoring programs. (Study results were not available at the time of the writing of this book.) Maternal blood pressure readings and any abnormalities are communicated to the managing doctors so they can intervene and manage the condition (gestational hypertension), thus preventing complications associated with this disease.[4]

Currently, humans monitor the IoT-generated data in this project. Providers make the actual diagnosis and dictate treatment regimens in this model. In future iterations of this type of IoT monitoring, the IoT data generated by these members would be analyzed by AI. AI could then diagnose and even predict the development of gestational hypertension, preeclampsia, and eclampsia, with AI-guided interventions for timely best-practice treatment or prevention of disease. Further, we could monitor all pregnant females and not just at-risk populations. AI could take that IoT-generated data and learn to identify which factors or trends in data indicate risk of future development of hypertension-related disease and then provide interventions for disease prevention for the entire pregnant female population. Applying traditional clinical rigor would mean including assessments that the benefits to this population in widespread monitoring would outweigh any potential risks, such as false positive findings and unnecessary interventions. But the question and the possibilities are still out there to be defined and resolved.

To truly comprehend the importance of this simple intervention of connected monitoring, one must understand a little more about the maternal health space. Maternal deaths rose by 26.6% in the US between 2000 and 2014. Similarly, hypertensive disorders in pregnancy rose from 529 in 1993 to 912 in 2014.[5] Also, the Healthcare Cost and Utilization Project (HCUP) estimated that the short-term costs associated with managing maternal gestational hypertension/preeclampsia/eclampsia was $6.4 billion in the US in 2012. Neonatal costs related to preterm deliveries as a complication of maternal gestational hypertension are $26.2 billion a year in the US. Although gestational hypertension and its associated conditions are not by themselves the cause of worsening maternal and fetal health and rising healthcare costs, they are significant contributors.

One would think that a mom receiving routine recommended prenatal care would not have issues. However, estimates suggest that up to one-third of women have a missed diagnosis of gestational hypertension. The missed diagnosis is possible. In a pregnant woman's third trimester, during which she is seen weekly by her provider,

---

4 Reports show that the most successful digital strategies are all related to wellness, fitness, or medical reference. Although not focused on maternal fetal health, a report from the UK (*https://oreil.ly/Wahkq*) showed that treatment adherence in chronic obstructive pulmonary disease increased by 94% with the use of connected technology.

5 Centers for Disease Control and Prevention, "Data on Selected Pregnancy Complications in the United States" (*https://oreil.ly/eRtGy*), page last reviewed February 28, 2019.

her blood pressure and other vitals are obtained. Metric collection occurs in a clinic environment. The clinic environment does not mirror a woman's real-life stressors and situations. Blood pressure readings lower with rest, change in position (from standing to sitting and sitting to lying), and decreased stress. Frequently a blood pressure is obtained after the woman has been sitting at rest for 15–20 minutes or longer while waiting to be called back for evaluation. Such circumstances can create falsely low or normal blood pressure readings.

With the advent of IoT, we can now monitor these at-risk patients in real time and in real-life situations to provide timely interventions and treatment. AI would augment this process with continuous analysis and direction to best-practice care or the best next steps in management, thereby preventing maternal/fetal complications and controlling disease and keeping the woman in her managed disease stage versus her progressing to complications requiring high-risk and expensive care, such as Caesarian section, hospitalizations, and so on. Associated with this are the cost savings and health promotion of an infant not requiring preterm delivery and a NICU stay related to gestational hypertension.

From a healthcare standpoint, real-time monitoring and real-time management enabled by IoT and AI keep patients safe and healthy. AI solutions could empower providers to deliver timely and optimal care, increase patient engagement, reduce hospitalizations, reduce the length of hospital stays, and prevent readmissions and emergency department utilization. The simple intervention of connected blood pressure readings with AI analysis and collaboration with providers creates a personalized healthcare solution with tremendous associated cost savings for our healthcare system.

Applying the same approach to many different populations at different times in their lives yields healthier people. For example, fitness bands, blood pressure monitors, heart rate monitors, glucometers, and other devices give patients personalized insights and near real-time management from their providers or clinical support teams. In the case of that middle-aged diabetic female we discussed earlier, we mentioned that she has moved to the healthier end of the healthcare continuum. We can continue to stay engaged and aware of how that patient is doing through her connected devices. If she starts to regain her weight, with data indicating decreased activity and glucometer readings that are routinely increasing, AI leads to the best next actions. Those could possibly include notifying her clinician or her clinical support team through the insurer with a recommendation that they intervene to assess the situation and provide micro-adjustments to her care—thus responding directly to the individual situation in a real-time manner.

Similarly, IoT and AI can be applied to healthy patients to keep them at a healthy stage in the health continuum. Devices may be set to alarm or provide notifications of abnormal results to patients, providers, and clinical support by insurers. In this way, intervention as needed, based on the individual's needs/concerns, can be addressed before a problem worsens. For example, if a healthy patient develops a routine trend toward elevated blood pressure, we can reach out to that patient and determine whether hypertension may be developing. There is the potential to optimize outcomes using AI by amassing data points, assessing best treatment pathways, and monitoring response, all before the actual disease (hypertension) onset.

For the elderly, IoT and AI are being used to help them live healthier lives in an independent setting for longer. By continually tracking their health conditions and safety risks at home, such as falls risk, we can identify any disturbance or change in their health conditions and alert family members, providers, and care management teams. Several pilots have been created that revolve around this type of monitoring combined with AI, and initial results show success in health at home. Taken further, when an abnormality is found or an alarm goes off, a home care clinician is dispatched to the home setting to assess the member and perform adjustments to management. Technology working hand in hand with clinicians provides a form of healthcare not seen in the past.

We've looked at AI and IoT monitoring for improved health from an individual patient, provider, and insurer perspective. Another area in which AI and monitoring are improving health is the autonomous monitoring of patients in hospitals.

Hospital stays are dangerous. A hospital stay carries a 5.5% risk of an adverse drug reaction, an 18% risk of infection, and a 3% risk of developing ulcers. Excluded is the risk of a fall, an injury, or an iatrogenic event (injury or harm that occurs related to hospital/medical care). The longer someone stays in the hospital, the greater their risk of experiencing an adverse event.[6] It is estimated that 1 out of 10 patients experiences an adverse event. On top of this, it's believed that 44% of these events are preventable. 7.4% of these events lead to death.

Companies today use connected monitoring combined with AI.[7] AI predicts and infers behaviors using massive amounts of real-time data to prevent falls/injuries, detect and prevent infections, assess for protocol or process lapses, and so on, with the ultimate goal being increased patient safety and elimination of fatalities associated with hospitalization.

For the individual clinician, for the insurer, for the hospital system, and especially for the individual patient, the evolution of AI combined with connected devices and monitoring has led to a massive paradigm shift in how we envision the future of

---

6 Katharina Hauck and Xueyan Zhao, "How dangerous is a day in hospital? A model of adverse events and length of stay for medical inpatients" (*https://oreil.ly/dQg5R*), *Medical Care* 49, no. 12 (2011): 1068–1075.

7 Cathy Russey, "Google and Care AI Team Up for Autonomous Monitoring of Healthcare Facilities Using AI" (*https://oreil.ly/VOEVB*), Wearable Technologies, November 25, 2019.

healthcare. No longer are we merely doing the best we can, "where the patient is at." We now have the capabilities to move from a reactive healthcare system to a focused, personalized, proactive healthcare model.

Health Determinants and Big Data

Complex relationships exist among several factors influencing or determining health. Medical care, genetics, behavior, socioeconomic circumstances, physical influences, and environment all play significant roles. Learning insights such as the influence of one or more of these health determinants on an individual's health outcomes or which determinants influence each other is complex, requiring more study and research. Figure 3-5 illustrates some of the many health determinants. AI provides the opportunity to make sense of the enormous data saturation coming every day of every year.

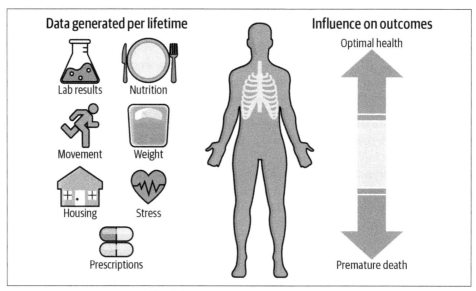

Figure 3-5. Determinants of health

Data collected over time, some quantitative, some qualitative, coming from a myriad of sources in the three realms—that is big data. The opportunity to make people healthier requires making sense of this data tsunami.

A focus purely on medical test results rather than on the many determinants of health limits our ability to reach the optimum health for an individual. Only with AI will we be able to see the patterns and find the causal pathways to understand which determinants influence each other and their effect on health outcomes.

Summary

We are at the tipping point of technology merging with medicine. IoT infused with AI is an early indicator of this merger. IoT and increasingly intelligent devices touching much if not all of humanity makes it possible to extract meaning in context from billions of new data sources, enabling prevention of errors and identification of those heading toward a train wreck of illness. There is hope for identifying the best manner of treating patients, with tools helping providers in their fight to promote the health and well-being of patients. IoT will be more than mobile devices and smartphones and will include simple devices like sensors, air-conditioning systems, generators, and more.

AI embodiments dominate our world, at work, play, and home. Today healthcare providers and patients live in an era in which many predictions of disease states occur before a patient gets sick. The increasing presence of smart things creates vast opportunities in healthcare. Like the Cambrian explosion 500 million years ago, a Cambrian moment of machine intelligence, of AI-fused devices, has arrived, with tremendous, transformational opportunities for healthcare. The world of people is becoming more instrumented. The world of physical objects is getting smarter. The world of systems, processing, and apps is increasingly in the home, enabling more intelligent interactions with appliances, sensors, wearables, and medical devices. Collectively, these three worlds, powered by AI, create a unique opportunity for proactive, noninvasive monitoring for better health. This chapter describes an emerging new computing paradigm and the ensuing opportunities it creates to improve healthcare through real-time tracking, continuous monitoring, and extreme personalization while making healthcare more accessible, efficient, and useful. The new computing paradigm and increasing merger of the world of people, things, and apps enables Rx, a prescription for personal health, helping people live healthier lives.

The internet continues to be a significant general purpose technology (GPT) shaping every industry, made possible by a service, an application, the web, sitting atop this infrastructure, allowing accessibility to a massive amount of information. Services and applications ranging from ride-share applications to digital streaming services, commerce platforms, and social platforms make the internet a force multiplier. Healthcare requires this equivalency, as AI is akin to the internet as a GPT. Amazon, a killer internet app, arrives, showing the power of a digital commerce platform and forever changing the retail industry. Web search engines make it possible to search for text in publicly accessible documents.

The Rx or prescription for personal health requires we think differently about healthcare, and AI affords us this opportunity. AI is not the killer app; it's the GPT, the building block, the engine allowing the creation of healthcare platforms, services, or killer apps. Transforming healthcare occurs with AI services and applications focused on extreme personalization, prediction of disease state onset, mental health, telemedicine, precision medicine, and more. The arrival of AI-embedded killer apps, services, and platforms fundamentally changes how we think about and use healthcare and will be the tipping point for AI.

Our future world will shift from a medicine cabinet of bandages, thermometers, and so on, to IoT medical devices that detect disease states or, used in conjunction with telemedicine, provide clinicians insights as if they were present with the patient. Computing is growing exponentially; let's get medicine and our health on the same trajectory. Our next chapter takes this further by digging into the digitization of healthcare.

CHAPTER 4

Digital Transformation and AI

Healthcare automation plays a key role in healthcare digital transformation by enabling stakeholders to focus on patient care and drive outcomes that make the healthcare system work for everyone. Complex healthcare processes and systems make digital transformation challenging. We define healthcare automation as the use of technology or machines to take on tasks so as to free people to focus on patient care and the health of populations. Digitization is defined as simply converting nondigital data (e.g., faxes or voice) into digital data, which allows opportunities for technology and machines to increase automation. The pandemic shows the value of healthcare automation where resources are limited and AI and other technologies can facilitate improving efficiencies and access to healthcare services. *We define digital healthcare transformation as embracing both healthcare automation and digitization.* It is a broad term that encompasses everything from implementing new technologies in healthcare operations to increasing digitization or new business models. It can also refer to modest activities such as launching a new website or a new mobile app.

Optimizing the impact of technology and improving the entire breadth of organization workflows and processes while improving access to data should be the goal for digital healthcare transformation. Implementing automation-based technology in silos across the organization may be a positive step forward, but reducing redundant applications or eliminating process inefficiencies often produces a far greater impact. Digital healthcare transformation entails increasing self-service technologies for patients, clinicians, and all stakeholders. The implementation of digital tools that make information and data more readily accessible should be a goal. Several studies suggest organizations with successful transformations deploy more technologies than other organizations do.[1] Increasingly, AI as a general purpose technology (GPT) will be a key enabling technology for healthcare digital transformation.

The opportunity presented by artificial intelligence, machine learning, natural language processing, and computer vision to make healthcare better means increasing and improving the automation and digitization of healthcare. AI solutions exist today that help reduce the time physicians spend taking notes, making patient-doctor interactions efficient and helping patients recall the key points of physician-patient interactions. These are examples of giving day-to-day tools a digital upgrade. AI enables clinical documentation that writes itself. Even the processing of patients' voicemail messages for clinicians can be automated, enabling clinicians to take faster action on behalf of their patients.

The large incumbent healthcare companies will lead the way, with a big assist from technology companies. Many technology companies, start-ups, and healthcare companies are in a race to lower the cost of healthcare, improve experiences, provide better diagnostic tools, and reduce friction in the systems. Successful digital healthcare transformation is not all about implementing new technologies or implementing AI. However, digitization and AI are interlocked; the full value of digital healthcare transformation cannot be achieved without unlocking the value of AI.

Agreement on a definition of what digitization is remains as elusive as a definition of artificial intelligence in organizations. However, organizations must have a common definition of both to achieve digital healthcare transformation. In decades past, everyone agreed that moving from analog to binary, from paper to computer readable, or from vinyl records to CDs was digitization. Now we view streaming videos, not CDs, as digital. In the early 1990s, we viewed chess-playing computers as AI, but today we see them as a computational task. Narrow definitions of digital and AI don't serve us anymore. Companies born in the AI era see the internet, mobile, and cloud as table stakes underlying their platforms, systems, and processes. They don't debate what it means to be digital or AI because the two are interlocked and are a natural part of their ethos.

Healthcare digital transformation gets accomplished through the pursuit of two tracks, as illustrated in Figure 4-1. Digital healthcare transformation must better the way clinicians get their work done; this is *people-centric digitization*. Computers must fade into the background, and the applications or systems used by clinicians must become more intelligent and have less friction and easier interfaces; this is *application-centric digitization*.

---

1 See "Unlocking success in digital transformations" (*https://oreil.ly/71oBf*), McKinsey & Company (survey), October 29, 2018.

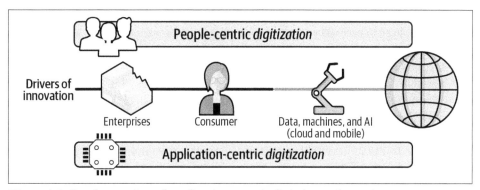

Figure 4-1. People-centric and application-centric digital transformation

People-centric digitization focuses attention on the experiences, workflow, and out-comes of the stakeholders involved in the patient journey. For clinicians and patients, the nirvana state or goal is precision medicine, healthcare tailored to one's specific needs. Enabling doctors to focus on prevention and early diagnosis changes the healthcare outcomes for patients. Patients will be able to get their most basic questions about benefits or insurance coverage answered on a moment's notice. Your medical history being securely stored on your mobile device, your dermatologist connecting with you over video chat to review skin issues, and prescriptions being delivered to your doorstep are examples of people-centric digitization.

Detecting bed moves and falls and alerting caregivers to take immediate action can be achieved through applications or systems that sit silently in the background and detect movements using computer vision and machine learning. This is application-centric digitization.

People-centric digitization recognizes this shift and consumers' expectations for novel, intuitive people-machine interactions. We saw this in banking, where consumers' desire to exchange money with anyone in the world, at any place and at any time, gave rise to mobile digital payment services. Incumbent banks were dragged into mobile banking and mobile payment services because of the needs and demands of their consumers, who started using apps from start-ups providing services previously unavailable from their financial institutions. The same will most likely be the case with healthcare unless an incumbent seizes the opportunity for people- and application-centric digitization.

Digital Transformation of Healthcare

Digital transformation of healthcare is a broad area addressing a wide swath of domains, such as patient care, health and wellness, diagnostics, decision support systems, hospital and provider systems, electronic medical record (EMR) systems, triage, back-office administrative systems, home care, urgent care, emergency rooms, chronic care management, mental health, and more. Digital transformation means using technology to provide real-time, immediate outcomes, whether in approving an insurance claim, approving prescription coverage, or performing a diagnostic. Digital transformation eliminates the need for phone calls by making information readily and instantly accessible, whether you're trying to determine your benefits, get your lab test results, or get approval for a prescription, a test, or surgery. It means substantially reducing misdiagnoses and medical errors thanks to highly interactive decision support systems at play in doctor's offices or hospital settings. Digital transformation means price transparency, so that patients know the cost of a service at the time of inquiry and delivery. The pandemic shows telemedicine becoming a more important experience for patients and clinicians, taking our traditional in-person practice into the digital world. The number of use cases is limitless, but let's explore a few through the lens of three paths.

Three distinct paths (see Figure 4-2) should be pursued by healthcare incumbents and by every organization tasked with making healthcare better, faster, and more accessible and with increasing its efficacy.

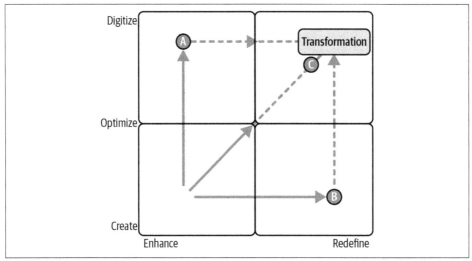

Figure 4-2. Paths to the digital transformation of healthcare

All three paths require employing transitional and game-changing technologies like artificial intelligence. AI enables digital capabilities previously unimagined. For example, we can employ AI to help people adhere to their medications, to use a person's voice as a way to search for healthcare services, to evaluate a patient's specific conditions to determine whether they would be better served by readmission to hospital A versus hospital B, or simply to determine that a patient's best healthcare outcome will be achieved with a specific provider organization. AI allows us to use empirical evidence for where patients will obtain the best outcomes rather than relying on anecdotal comments on social media sites ranking providers. Many of these capabilities cannot be achieved without the application of AI, and this is only a small, partial list.

Organizations that fail to apply the right AI techniques in deep learning, machine learning, computer vision, and natural language processing (to name a few) will not achieve optimal digital healthcare transformation. Often AI alone will not be sufficient. For example, using technologies such as graph databases instead of other database technologies enables organizations to see relationships among data. Seeing the intersection of patients, providers, and clinicians allows organizations to create patient journeys, so that any authorized user can see the steps an individual patient makes as they interact with the healthcare system. Graph and other technologies are discussed in *State of Healthcare Technology* (*https://oreil.ly/LHIFF*) by Kerrie L. Holley et al. (O'Reilly); this ebook provides a summary of healthcare technologies required for optimizing healthcare and accelerating digital healthcare transformation.

Next, we'll discuss the three different paths to the digital transformation of healthcare.

Path A: Creating Digital Operations and Processes

Path A creates and integrates digital operations and processes delivering on the customer value propositions. Customers include the ecosystem in healthcare, including patient consumers, clinicians, hospitals, providers, health services companies, and more. In this path, organizations focus on changing existing processes and their legacy systems supporting those processes to a digital state. Path A concentrates mainly on transitioning from the as-is state to a future state of current operations and processes. That is, you take existing products, systems used for ongoing operations, or legacy systems and focus on how to optimize, increase automation, or apply AI. Undertaking any or all of these three actions improves the path toward increased digitization.

Healthcare digitization is held hostage to several IT applications and systems. For example, electronic medical record (EMR) or electronic health record (EHR) systems provide digitized records of a patient's healthcare encounters. Digitized records of a patient's healthcare encounters were state of the art at one time, but not anymore. Today, time spent on EHR systems reduces the amount of time physicians spend with their patients, negatively affecting patient relationships. Storing data is not a clinical tool; it doesn't provide healthcare. A 2018 Harris Poll conducted on behalf of Stanford Medicine (*https://oreil.ly/iKWfl*) delivered a treasure trove of AI use cases for EHRs: disease diagnosis, disease prevention, and population health management. In this study, 9 out of 10 physicians wanted their EHRs to be intuitive and responsive—a perfect storm for AI adoption.

Currently, physicians type up encounters or enter them into systems on tablets. Providers have to click on different sections of a record to access useful data such as previous medical notes or scanned documents, where a more complete clinical picture of the patient is found. The ICD-10 codes that are used for medical billing are also used in EHRs to identify diagnoses, but a patient's coded diagnosis may not reveal the true issue with the patient. For example, if someone has chosen a code for congestive heart failure (CHF), then the doctor understands that this is a current condition of the patient, but the doctor does not know where the heart is failing, which is usually delineated by the terms *diastolic* or *systolic* CHF. That information also helps to determine the underlying cause of the CHF. These are all-important factors that are not always captured in one code.

A more intuitive and responsive system would simulate what paper charts did in the past. A clear description, often annotated by the physician, would be appended and carried through in the chart or would be immediately accessible for review to give the provider a clearer picture of the patient's medical issue. Once the diagnosis and its implications are clear, then bigger issues such as disease prevention in populations can be addressed. So for diastolic CHF, a physician could look for predisposing sleep apnea or hypertension and address these conditions to prevent CHF from developing. Improving code accuracy has been addressed by ICD-10 but is not enough in itself to fully resolve the issue. Short-term improvements to date include voice as a modality acting as a scribe during patient visits, a highly viable AI engineering effort using deep learning and natural language processing.

In many cases, legacy systems must address poor system availability and stop the mindset that systems that read and write data cannot have the reliability and availability seen in the platforms of the large technology companies, such as Google's search engine, Amazon's commerce site, or Netflix's streaming videos. Historically, incumbent companies spend the lion's share of their budget on customer-visible capabilities, unlike digital-era companies, who make no such choice. Digital-era companies treat performance and availability as first-class constructs, the same as consumer-visible features and functions.

Path B: Building New Capabilities

While Path A focuses on improving existing products, services, systems, and capabilities, Path B is thinking up and deploying new capabilities. For example, clinical coding, as we discussed earlier, takes information about a specific patient case and assigns standard classification codes. Codes for heart disease, diabetes, and other conditions help with medical informatics and research in a variety of applications. Amazon created a new product, AWS Comprehend (*https://oreil.ly/1Vrqp*), to automate this activity using deep learning. This is classic Path B: building a new capability. Arguably, after creating enough new capabilities, Amazon becomes a competitor in healthcare, just as it moved from commerce to technology with the cloud. If an incumbent with a clinical coding product were to decide to improve its product using AI (i.e., deep learning), that would be pursuing Path A—making an existing product better using AI.

This example of clinical coding[2] highlights the variation in what is meant by digital healthcare transformation. Each improvement over time increases the automation of clinical coding and thereby improves digital healthcare transformation. That is, clinical coding can be automated or made digital in a variety of ways, leading to computer-assisted coding systems that increasingly make this an easier task for coders. Some clinical coding systems are superior to/more digital than others because they apply AI in the form of natural language processing. Clinical coding systems that use deep learning NLP are more accurate than those using NLP without deep learning. The application of deep learning NLP to coding systems would help solve the issue raised in the CHF example discussed earlier—hence the interlock of digital healthcare transformation and AI. Perhaps another way to approach this scenario is not to label a solution as digital or more digital but simply to tackle every problem with the intent to maximize the use of AI because both the old and the new reflect automation implementations.

Similar to how we see video streaming and not CDs as the optimal digital experience today, using deep learning NLP for clinical coding rather than just NLP is a more optimal digital healthcare transformation service. The deep learning NLP service over time will get better and faster than an NLP without deep learning implementation. This is what is meant by maximizing AI. In the future, additional AI research may require a different choice beyond deep learning.

Path B builds a new set of capabilities around the desired customer end state and operating model. Path B means thinking about how to use a variety of technologies (e.g., AI, IoT, graph, ambient, augmented reality, and more) to create new products and services. Path B enables enhanced healthcare experiences by defining even better experiences and healthcare outcomes.

Path C: Transforming Business Processes

Path C transforms business processes and often requires taking an enterprise view and eliminating duplicative processing or else imagining a new process. This path is fraught with risk and high rewards. Path C includes moonshot projects, or as Safi Bahcall calls them, loonshots (*https://oreil.ly/iXPhW*)—novel and breakthrough ideas that can cure diseases or transform industries. Real-time healthcare is a moonshot because of the technical, structural, and cultural divisions preventing interoperability

---

2 Thomas H. Davenport and Steven Miller, "The Future of Work Now—Medical Coding with AI" (*https://oreil.ly/ES6Or*), *Forbes*, January 3, 2020.

and data exchange among all stakeholders involved in patient care. Path C may mean acquiring new businesses, i.e., diversification. Path C focuses on the transformation of culture, systems, or business processes.

Paths to the Digital Transformation of Healthcare

Figure 4-2 highlights three pathways to digital healthcare transformation, but these pathways are not a digitization strategy. Organizations should develop and realize a digital healthcare transformation strategy that addresses one or more of the following aspects:

- *Digital healthcare transformation* requires organizations to provide a strategy for achieving their transformation that is focused on problem areas or pain points at which applying AI would make a difference.

- *Cultural transformation* means that organization models and talent must be aligned with the goals for digital healthcare transformation and must focus on data liberation versus silos.

- *Technology adoption* requires decisions on how and when business areas will apply AI and accompanying technologies.

- *Business process transformation* means thinking about what processes need to be reengineered or reimagined.

- *Portfolio diversification* suggests thinking about *digital divestiture,* which may extend digital transformation outside the walls of the organization.

- *Business model innovation* means that the organization must decide if it will change its underlying customer value propositions and/or the business operating model.

There is no single playbook for digital healthcare transformation. David Rogers asserts (*https://oreil.ly/nrZSv*) that digital transformation is about strategic thinking, not a better technology stack. Interestingly, the same can be said for AI—that is, organizations' success with digitization and AI depends on how companies understand, define, and think about it. What works for one organization may not work for another. The next section explores what digital healthcare looks like through examples and use cases.

Digital Healthcare

In general, digital healthcare applies technology, using the data acquired through technology to improve our health and wellness. This technology includes apps, wearable devices, remote or ambient monitoring devices, telemedicine, health-related email, and electronic health records to incorporate a patient's related data into their health management.

The benefits are apparent. For example, if a patient is diagnosed with hypertension, doctors and other caregivers will have real-time or near real-time data on how their blood pressure management is working. This scenario will allow more immediate adjustments or micro-adjustments to the patient's care that would not be possible in our current healthcare model. Typically a patient would start treatment with medication or a lifestyle change and then return to their doctor in several weeks' time to have their blood pressure rechecked. Figure 4-3 illustrates the effect of digitization where digital care is continuous: monitoring the patient's blood pressure, doctor check-in, and suggesting lifestyle changes.

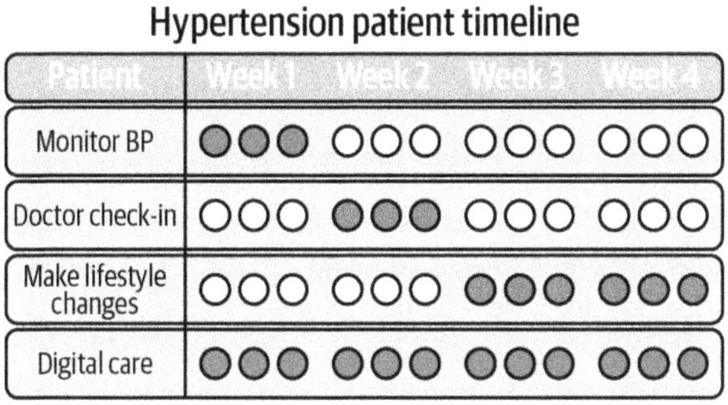

Hypertension patient timeline

Patient	Week 1	Week 2	Week 3	Week 4
Monitor BP	●●●	○○○	○○○	○○○
Doctor check-in	○○○	●●●	○○○	○○○
Make lifestyle changes	○○○	○○○	●●●	●●●
Digital care	●●●	●●●	●●●	●●●

Figure 4-3. Hypertension patient's timeline of care

Micro-adjustments result in improved care for the patient. The doctor will be able to tell if the prescribed treatment worked or if further adjustments are warranted. The less time the patient's blood pressure is out of control, the safer their kidneys and other vital organs are from the damage resulting from uncontrolled hypertension. The doctor has more tools and information to help manage the patient's condition, making the doctor's job more comfortable and efficient.

Digital tools can help pinpoint new issues by identifying medical conditions that would not be apparent otherwise (i.e., would not be captured during a doctor visit). As in the example, digital tools can help monitor the effectiveness of treatment and identify the worsening of chronic conditions. As we discussed in the last chapter, identification of medical issues allows physicians to intervene faster, either treating immediately or preventing the development of medical disease. Better management of disease symptoms occurs, improving patients' quality of life. Patients avoid long-term complications resulting from untreated disease. For hypertension, these complications include kidney and eye injury, as well as increasing the risk for stroke. Avoiding these complications of the disease improves the patient's quality of life and life span. It avoids healthcare costs associated with the development and management of these complications. The sicker a patient is, the higher the healthcare cost, as treating conditions takes more resources.

To take this a step further, let's say that the doctor and patient have the hypertension well managed through medication therapy, and the blood pressure readings are consistently within a healthy range. What else is left to do?

AI Applied to Digital Healthcare

Elevating individual ownership of health through AI helps in the digital monitoring portion of digital healthcare. Digital healthcare can include digital insurance cards, digital check-ins for appointments, digital/virtual visits, and so on. AI adds another dimension to your care. Using the same hypertension example, AI now points out to the patient and their doctor that a weight decrease of 20 pounds could control the patient's blood pressure without medication. In the office, a clinician is usually harried and is potentially running behind schedule, with numerous demands on their time. For example, physicians see patients, supervise other clinicians (such as students and physician assistants), respond to patient emails and phone calls, respond to insurance coverage issues, and address billing complaints, all while covering these same responsibilities for other physicians who are out of the office. Unfortunately, it is easy sometimes for patient care to slip between the cracks. The potential for patient care to improve exists when AI use eliminates or streamlines nonclinical tasks, thus giving doctors more time for direct patient care and reducing their burnout and overload from the stimulus of addressing so many associated patient care items throughout their day. Also, AI could be used to fill the role of safety net for the clinician, to ensure that appropriate and timely care is not accidentally overlooked.

AI can serve many functions in the clinical space. AI augments the physician, reminding them that counseling and perhaps enrollment in a health and well-being program for weight loss might help with nonmedication management of hypertension. Also, AI can be used to provide doctors with reminders about best-practice management for chronic conditions.

In the hypertension example, the patient's blood pressure is well controlled on medication therapy. The patient starts working on healthy weight loss and engaging in regular aerobic exercise. Their connected device provides timely input to their doctor that the regimen is working well, and their blood pressure is now not only controlled but borderline low. AI is used to identify abnormally low blood pressures, taking both the data from the patient's biometric device and input from a tablet that indicates the patient may have been feeling dizzy intermittently. AI analyzes all this information and researches the clinical database and hypertension management guidelines to form a recommendation for intervention by the doctor.

The doctor takes this packaged and easily digestible information to make an immediate decrease in the patient's medication dosage. Over time, with close connected monitoring and AI assistance, the patient is able to stop all medication therapy. The patient's hypertension has resolved as long as the patient continues to adhere to a healthy lifestyle.

As the patient ages, blood vessels become less compliant, genetics starts to catch up with them, and they may require medication therapy again. Over their entire life cycle with this condition, from elevated blood pressure to fully diagnosed hypertension to resolution of hypertension to chronic hypertension, AI and digital connections have been used to provide personalized care with optimal outcomes.

Many of the largest technology companies, aka Big Tech, have invested in the healthcare industry. Whether through acquisitions, startup investments, or their own products, or by democratizing AI or providing cognitive AI and cloud services for the masses, Big Tech will change healthcare. The next section provides a small sampling of the impact on healthcare.

AI, Digitization, and Big Tech

Predictably, technology companies are jumping on the digital healthcare bandwagon —look at Google, for example, with its deployment into the wearables market with Google Wear and its launching of the health platform Fit in 2014. Moreover, Google recognizes the impact of AI on digital healthcare and has created ventures that include the DeepMind unit, such as in AI being used to identify eye disease from imaging scans. Google's parent company, Alphabet, has a health sciences arm named Verily, which is working on such exciting projects as the Aurora study, in which AI is being used to identify physical biomarkers of mental trauma. Verily created a wearable specifically for this study.

While some companies are investing in future AI with digital solutions, Apple has focused on current-day applications. It has been expanding the Apple Watch's healthcare uses with the addition of a falls detection monitor and an ECG monitor. The corporate goal is to create other offerings for providers as well, such as Apple's HealthKit; the Apple Watch would be the relied-upon device to connect patients to their providers for care. Amazon, in partnership with others, has created its own healthcare company, Haven, in an attempt to reimagine the healthcare market and how technology is used.

Big Tech's interest in healthcare is expanding for a variety of reasons. Healthcare has traditionally been recession-proof, with high spend and growing demands on healthcare resources leading to the need for cost-saving strategies and innovative solutions. To date, the market appears to be focused on preventive strategies. For example, knowing the correlation between being overweight and hypertension and identifying an overweight or obese patient before the development of hypertension is a preventive strategy. Other preventive strategies using AI and digital health are being applied to chronic diseases such as diabetes and hypertension. Preventing disease is much less costly than treating illness, and we'll explore that topic further in the next section.

Big technology companies' penetration into healthcare is relatively low compared to the incumbent healthcare companies. Consequently, their expected impact in making healthcare operations or processes more intelligent and measurably moving the needle of digital healthcare transformation is also low unless adoption by healthcare organizations occurs. The increasingly powerful AI and cognitive cloud services provided by many Big Tech companies create enormous upside in making healthcare operations and clinical care processes more intelligent.

Preventive and Chronic Disease Management

The Centers for Disease Control and Prevention (CDC) writes (*https://oreil.ly/9srml*) that 60% of Americans have at least one chronic disease, and these diseases are a leading cause of death and disability as well as of rising healthcare costs. But most chronic diseases could be prevented, says the CDC, if we simply moved around more, ate better, and got regular health checks. We can better accomplish those goals with the help of real-time feedback loops resulting from inputs (e.g., sensors, patches, or wearables) and output signals (e.g., atrial fibrillation, glucose, and others), where intelligent machines understand health signals and provide insights into our intent and behavior. Figure 4-4 illustrates this emerging scenario of turning passive inputs into informed action.

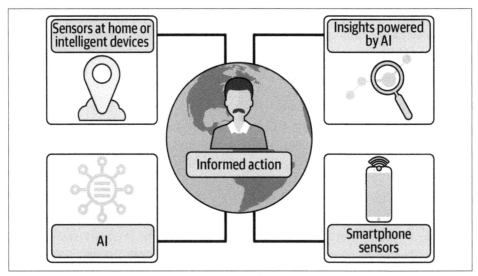

Figure 4-4. Turning passive inputs into informed action

Today, patients and consumers increasingly engage with things that take in more signals and information about their data. For example, a consumer might receive an alert from their Apple Watch of an episode of a heart arrhythmia such as atrial fibrillation and wonder whether it's a false alarm or a real signal. This triggers the consumer to see their doctor and upon confirmation from their clinician, a care pathway for evaluation and management is established. As another example, someone with type 1 diabetes might use patches and wearables to manage their diabetes.

Figure 4-4 illustrates a real-time feedback loop in which AI, using machine learning, turns passive inputs into informed action. Sensors or intelligent objects in the home capture real-time data on falls, rising glucose, ear health, skin health, sleep, and more. Smartphone sensors are on the rise, making continuous monitoring of consumers' health a reality and enabling informed action.[3] Consumers or patients can use targeted alerts to take action before episodic conditions arise. Phones have several sensors allowing capture of data about usage patterns, motion, humidity, temperature, biometrics, and more. Using distributed AI, AI in the phone, the cloud, or edge devices, insights can be provided that will help maintain a consumer's physical and mental health over time.

Wearables, internet-connected medical devices, and mobile devices can help us move more and eat better and can provide signals about our health. This can occur because AI is everywhere and distributed throughout our environments. Sensors in our bodies or our homes and wearables like intelligent watches provide signals. Insights and analytics will be part of a closed feedback loop in which computers will learn from our actions and behaviors and remind us when to exercise, take medicine, see our clinician, or modify a behavior.

All of this represents new data being turned into value. These closed data loops tighten the feedback loop among data, insight, and action. Machines (e.g., sensors, watches, or computers) powered with AI capture data in real time and use AI to process the data at scale. We are maturing from just capturing and storing data to producing insights and recommendations for action.

Wearable devices can track multiple health signals, but the large amount of data and its current incompatibility with most EHRs makes their use unwieldy. Apple's Health Kit is one tool that integrates data from wearables into the EHR.

AI and Prevention

Preventive medicine, lifestyle modification, and AI monitoring solutions abound. They range from stress management solutions to monitoring data associated with our health trackers to detect a potential risk for disease development and offering counseling on management and prevention.

Weight management, stress management, sleep, exercise, and financial support are all the major categories of AI that are in place today. Consumers/patients use this

---

3 See Sumit Majumder and M. Jamal Deen, "Smartphone Sensors for Health Monitoring and Diagnosis" (*https://oreil.ly/3abOD*), *Sensors* 19, no. 9 (2019): 2164.

technology to assess and take ownership of their health. The majority of consumers today are comfortable with and even embrace this technology for wellness.

Not only can hypertension possibly be averted through exercise and maintaining a healthy weight and diet, but a broad range of other conditions can be prevented as well. We can use AI to monitor a patient's sleep—and rather than the patient being required to spend the night attached to monitors at a medical office, at-home sleep studies are now the standard. AI has the capability of identifying abnormal sleep patterns or restless sleep. AI can enhance data gathered from the sleep study and help manage the sleep disorder by using other signals like weight and alcohol intake, which, if the patient is overweight and alcohol intake is elevated, may cause worsening of the sleep disorder and prevent current treatment from being effective. An app takes in manual input on alcohol consumption, and a signal from a connected scale provides information on patient weight. Each of these signals, as reflected in Figure 4-4, is part of a closed feedback loop that provides the patient and their doctor with insight into other factors that may be contributing to the sleep disorder and impacting effective management.

Of course, in this same example, a sleep disorder can also be identified early on, providing the consumer an opportunity to change their lifestyle, modify their diet with weight loss, and have immediate data available to them and their provider on the management of their possible sleep disorder. The Apple Watch ECG app that can identify potential heart rhythm disorders that predispose to stroke is the start of numerous uses of wearables using AI in preventive medicine. This naturally extends to chronic disease management once it develops.

AI and Chronic Disease

Type 2 diabetes and hypertension are two of the most common chronic medical conditions today. The CDC reports that 1 in 9 Americans have type 2 diabetes, and 1 in 3 Americans have hypertension. Each of these conditions is a significant risk factor for heart disease, which remains the leading cause of death in America. 7 out of 10 people having their first heart attack have hypertension, and people with diabetes are twice as likely to have heart disease or a stroke as compared to people without diabetes, and at an earlier age. Sixty percent of patients with hypertension also have diabetes, and the health risk increases exponentially, with the potential for long-term nerve, eye, and kidney damage.

Interestingly, diabetes and hypertension can be "silent" for a prolonged period, until a crisis is reached. People with diabetes may slowly develop increased thirst and urination and not know that this could indicate an underlying disease state. Similarly, hypertension is known as the "silent killer," as patients frequently will present with stroke or other neurological symptoms that are later tied back to undiagnosed and untreated hypertension. Both are managed through a healthy diet and lifestyle and medication therapies.

Patients with diabetes or hypertension self-monitor their blood sugar levels and blood pressure. The data input to healthcare providers and systems through the use of connected devices can be enormous. AI health solutions can track, understand, and report results from this patient-generated healthcare data (PGHD). For example, AI has been developed in which abnormal results are sent to healthcare management systems that can then reach out and provide telephonic counseling to improve disease management.

Alternative interventions through AI include the use of apps and virtual consultants to address abnormal results. One example is teledermatology, an application of telemedicine in which photos of skin conditions are sent remotely to dermatologists for diagnostics. Teledermatology will soon evolve to where a mobile phone can be used to take the pictures. AI embedded in the phone will classify the disease state from images taken over the course of a year. A dermatologist may have told a patient that they would see them again in one year, but the AI on the phone, in examining the photos regularly taken by the patient, sees a suspect mole turning into melanoma.

Besides the use of AI to enhance chronic disease management, AI can also promote and improve self-education for the patient. For example, a patient using a mobile device or laptop can enter a query or question regarding their diabetic diet and what their allowed intake is. Patients can use a voice speaker in their house, an app on their phone, or a virtual assistant with a web application on their computer that uses AI/NLP to provide advice on a diabetic diet. Doctors can access near real-time data and perform micro-adjustments to their patients' care, which will lead to the avoidance of complications of the disease and associated costs.

AI provides benefits to healthcare payers as well. As mentioned earlier in discussing the telephonic case management program, patient members are given customized guidance and counseling. At the same time, clinical decision support is used to guide the patient to the best next step in care action. Should they meet with their provider to discuss starting medication therapy, or should they try shifting to a low-salt diet first? Should they start a weight-loss program? Providers may be contacted for care integration. All of this leads to enhanced disease management and improved quality of life without requiring the patient to self-manage, identify, or necessarily understand the underlying connections that lead to integrated care and improvement in their disease management.

Through these AI modalities come several other benefits: healthcare costs are decreased, and quality of life is increased for patients; there is increased accessibility and application of data to improve disease outcomes, as well as decreased cost from complications associated with the unmanaged or mismanaged disease; permanent end-organ damage is mitigated by improved management; and financial loss from hospital or emergency department visits is avoided because AI allowed intervention and care before a crisis.

Our physical well-being often is easier to detect than our mental health, i.e., our psychological, emotional, and social well-being. We are increasingly able to detect mental illness using artificial intelligence.[4]

AI and Mental Health

The use of AI in disease management and prevention is not limited to diseases like hypertension, or to what are typically bucketed as clinical medical conditions. Mental illness is common in the US, where nearly one in five adults lives with a mental illness —that was 46.6 million people in 2017, per National Institutes of Health (NIH) statistics (*https://oreil.ly/GvsDE*). There are apps that allow AI to check a person's behavioral health by monitoring their smartphone and recording how many social interactions have occurred that day, including social network site visits, texts, and calls, as well as physical activity level and general smartphone use. That data is then analyzed by AI to determine whether depression or other behavioral health disorders are on the increase or are being managed. In this way, AI allows self-assessment and connection to one's provider for near real-time monitoring of one's mental health. Some chatbots provide mental health counseling, and there are apps for cognitive behavioral therapy. The development and use of these tools is essential, as there is a growing gap between the amount of mental healthcare needed and the number of providers who can provide this mental/behavioral healthcare.

Technology usage for mental healthcare is on the rise, and people's comfort level is growing. The meditation app Headspace told CNBC (*https://oreil.ly/Bmo0K*) that, due in large part to COVID-19 and the resulting pandemic in mental and behavioral healthcare, it has seen a greater than 500% increase in inbound interest from companies seeking mental healthcare. AI for mental health makes sense, as more consumers are taking responsibility for their mental healthcare. Again, the COVID-19 pandemic brought digital technology to the forefront, with people in isolation and their states shut down. Estimates show that the mental health burden rose in proportion to the prolongation of isolation associated with social distancing during the pandemic. Because the population was encouraged to stay at home and avoid social contact, digital healthcare grew. COVID-19 may inadvertently drive the increased utilization of digital technologies based on necessity. Time will tell if the trend continues, but we believe the pandemic has changed the healthcare paradigm to digital healthcare made possible with AI.

---

4 "AI in psychiatry: detecting mental illness with artificial intelligence" (*https://oreil.ly/mpEeq*), Health Europa, November 19, 2019.

The coronavirus pandemic shows what is possible with telemedicine. Improvements in the state of "conversational" AI and everything described in Figure 4-4 will make telemedicine soar in efficacy.

AI and Telemedicine

In an ideal digitized healthcare environment, AI takes in all the data from connected devices, and that data is then processed by AI to provide quick and timely interventions in healthcare, all of which is supported by AI analysis of the most up-to-date and relevant treatment options. Connected devices facilitate remote delivery of care, or telemedicine. Telemedicine, as evidenced during the COVID-19 pandemic, has broad reach and has made billions of users aware of a new modality of healthcare. AI has a special and significant role in telemedicine.

The transformation of our healthcare system is already happening. COVID-19 was the impetus behind a rapid and exponential increase in the utilization of telemedicine. AI is being studied and has shown success in decreasing hospital readmissions.[5] In one hospital readmission reduction program, each patient, upon discharge from the hospital, is given a WiFi-enabled device that transmits vital signs and other important patient data (heart rate, blood pressure, temperature, and so on) to their provider for ongoing outpatient management. AI is constantly monitoring this data, and at any sign of abnormality, the patient, their provider, and any other caregiver can be notified to address the finding and hopefully avert a hospital readmission or emergency department visit.

It's all about timely intervention. An example of just such a partnership now in the market is a pilot program between NHS (National Health Systems) hospitals at Dartford and Gravesham and Current Health (formerly snap40) that is aimed at remote monitoring of patient vital signs with AI analysis. The patients in this pilot are fitted with WiFi-enabled armbands and given a chatbot-equipped tablet for medication reminders and remote communication with their providers. The patients receive all their tools prior to discharge from the hospital. In this manner, provider and care teams are able to keep a remote watch on patients, with the ability to perform micro-adjustments to care that keep their patients healthier and out of hospitals.

Telemedicine has now been widely accepted and can provide clinical support to the world of data that AI has opened. This integration provides numerous benefits:

---

5 Wenshuo Liu, "Predicting 30-day hospital readmissions using artificial neural networks with medical code embedding" (*https://oreil.ly/2zpvm*), *PLOS ONE* 15, no. 4 (2020).

- Early diagnosis and timely intervention
- Personalized care
- Remote patient monitoring on a real-time basis

We've discussed early diagnosis and treatment several times throughout the book. Again, early diagnosis allows for interventions either through changes in lifestyle, habits, or diet or via medications prior to complications of disease development and prior to development of long-term damage to the body related to uncontrolled disease. Traditionally, patients would have symptoms and no other associated information leading them to seek care at a doctor's office. With AI, symptoms are paired with personalized patient data generated by the patient's connected devices. Therefore, telemedicine providers have more information at the time of patient evaluation. These teledoctors have the patient to provide a description of their symptoms, data from connected devices (with AI analysis pointing out any abnormal findings), and AI-assisted analysis of clinical treatment guidelines, ensuring the most up-to-date and best care or best treatment or best next evaluation step for each patient based on their own individual data.

Personalized care via AI is possible, as all data generated from connected devices or alternate data input from other devices, such as an iPad with symptom generators and checklists, is derived from an individual patient. Thus doctors can make interventions or treatment decisions based specifically on that patient's data. Information on the impact of each micro-adjustment is immediately available and allows for finer management based on individual patient data. In addition, AI can enhance the treatment algorithms to ensure the best quality of care and the best next step in management for each individual patient. These treatment plans are then monitored through AI to ensure adherence and control of the disease, and if any change occurs, treatments are changed accordingly.

Remote monitoring is a relatively new concept. Traditionally in a hospital, a set of vital signs is obtained on a regularly scheduled basis. If the patient is sick enough, then monitors may be placed such that real-time monitoring occurs, and alarms go off for abnormal readings, leading to clinical evaluation and possible adjustments in treatment. In the outpatient setting, there was no routine monitoring of any vital signs except in rare cases, and this was managed by the patient, who either had further appointments to have monitors placed on them for home evaluation or had to stop in at clinics or other healthcare sites for follow-up readings. AI has transformed the process in the outpatient setting, where devices are now common and use of AI has increased significantly. Today a constant stream of near real-time data is available to both the clinician and the patient. Any abnormalities are analyzed by AI so that early intervention and adjustments can be made. Timely intervention is key, as timeliness prevents long-term complications and allows for fewer intolerable side effects of treatment (since monitoring would identify, say, too low a blood pressure).

Telemedicine is also quickly evolving almost in symbiosis with digital modalities. Telemedicine (or telehealth) has emerged as an essential component of healthcare during the COVID-19 crisis. Although telemedicine administration is now widely accepted, certain related complexities must be managed for its continued success. "Having regulatory experience is imperative, in particular during this time when things are very fast-moving and fast-paced and we're seeing changes in CMS rules and regulations almost biweekly," says Chevon Rariy, director of the Telehealth Program at Cancer Treatment Centers of America.[6] The Centers for Medicare & Medicaid Services (CMS) has instituted new billing and coding recommendations for telemedicine, which allows for the alignment of incentives for the provider and the ongoing growth of telehealth. Telemedicine was once called a "one-and-done" visit. Previously used as an alternative to urgent care medicine, telemedicine is now evolving into a primary care system. Several telemedicine providers are developing or have already deployed primary care provider telemedicine care platforms. Digitization provides support for telemedicine in a patient-provider relationship that is ongoing and not just a one-time visit. Through enabled connections with intelligent devices, AI has the capacity to strengthen this type of meaningful patient-doctor interaction by augmenting the information available to providers and other caregivers so that it extends beyond the telemedicine visit itself.

Specialty telemedicine providers are also emerging. Specifically, diabetes specialists, or endocrinologists, are now being utilized in several different programs to help with ongoing care and the timely micro-adjustment of insulin regimens to provide the best possible care for diabetics. AI again empowers these doctors by notifying them of abnormalities and adherence, as well as supporting doctor treatment/management decisions based on best care practices identified by AI.

Just as digitization has the capacity to enhance telehealth, so too does it have the ability to impact further aspects of the provider-patient relationship, such as medication management. Digitized AI not only can provide meaningful insights on the patient to their doctor but also can be used to understand behavior and drive medication adherence once treatment is prescribed. Instead of issuing blind "take your medication" alerts, AI can be used to find the best time and place to send an alert to take your medication, thus optimizing medication management and adherence.

Medication Management and AI

AI continues to expand its reach and use cases and is taking a leading role in improving medication adherence. Medication adherence is the likelihood that a patient will take the medication prescribed for them as directed, or at all. Why is medication

---

6 "Impact of COVID-19 on Telehealth" (*https://oreil.ly/u3WHe*), *American Health and Drug Benefits* 13, no. 3 (2020): 125–126.

adherence important? Over the past two decades, healthcare costs have been rising exponentially, and prescription medications are a large component of these costs. For example, of the $101 billion spent on diabetes in 2013, half was spent on medications. Meanwhile, studies suggest that one-third to one-half of all patients do not take their medication or do not take it properly, according to a 2017 report by the US Agency for Healthcare Research and Quality (*https://oreil.ly/0OXSI*). This results in nearly 125,000 premature deaths each year and costs the nation about $290 billion in associated hospitalizations and other complications from disease events, per NEHI (Network for Excellence in Health Innovation) and the American College of Preventive Medicine.[7]

The technology response to this problem is digital therapeutics, which encourage patients to take their medications as directed. Studies are using mobile devices and sensors to capture data and provide real-time alerts on medication adherence through browsers, apps, and medical devices. Examples include smart packing and pill dispensers, wearables that provide reminders to take medications and can track medication use, tablet apps providing reminders on refills and taking medications, and even virtual pillboxes with images displaying the size and shape of pills for identification so as to avoid confusion. When connected with sensors and combined with AI, the possibilities for medication and patient management are tremendous.[8]

Medication Adherence

The Medication Event Monitoring System (MEMS) captures when a patient takes their medicine. MEMS uses a bottle cap that fits on standard prescription pill bottles and includes a tiny microprocessor that records the occurrence and time of day when the pill bottle is opened and closed.

A study supported by the NIH (*https://oreil.ly/qWNbD*) used a reinforcement-learning-based medication health program to focus on medication adherence. Patients were randomized using two scenarios:

1. MEMS cap on pill bottle plus text messaging reminding the patient to take the medication and AI management to determine the type and frequency of messaging

2. MEMS cap only, with no AI

---

7 Jennifer Kim et al., "Medication Adherence: The Elephant in the Room" (*https://oreil.ly/a0lEW*), *U.S. Pharmacist*, January 19, 2018.

8 Jae-Yong Chung, "Digital therapeutics and clinical pharmacology" (*https://oreil.ly/6Yt2j*), *Translational and Clinical Pharmacology* 27, no. 1 (2019): 6–11.

The results showed improved medication adherence at three months for both study groups. Of note, medication adherence rose from a baseline of 69–80% to 84–92% with the use of AI.

Management of chronic conditions involves complex behaviors, and patients vary in their medication adherence based on these behaviors. One study of patients who had had a heart attack episode noted that one month after hospital discharge, fewer than 50% of the patients were continuing to take their daily low-dose aspirin as prescribed during the heart attack. Another study showed that of 5,000 hypertensive patients, most patients took their medications only intermittently, and 50% had stopped taking their medications without informing their provider.[9] In the NIH study, there was greater medication adherence when the MEMS cap was accompanied by AI-augmented text reminders. Mobile health services such as text message reminders have been shown to produce up to a twofold increase in medication adherence.

Of note, the NIH study used AI to determine whether patients were nonadherent with medication and to identify what type of messaging and what frequency of texting would spur increased adherence. Within one month, AI had decreased text messages by 46%, due to it learning that more frequent notifications did not lead to increased adherence. AI was also able to tailor notifications to those patients with the greatest need for reminders, and it decreased or stopped notifications to patients who were adherent as indicated by MEMS.

Digital Medication

AI use in medication adherence is not limited to apps, sensors, and wearables facilitating patient and provider/caregiver interactions. It extends into digital *medications*. In 2017 Proteus Digital Health announced that the US Food and Drug Administration (FDA) had approved the world's first digital medication, Abilify MyCite. Abilify MyCite contains a sensor that records that the patient has ingested the pill.

The way this ingestible sensor works is illustrated in Figure 4-5. In this example, a silicon sensor that is the size of a grain of salt is attached to each of the patient's pills. The patient swallows a pill with the sensor, which gets activated by the gastric juices in the patient's stomach.

---

9 Steven Baroletti and Heather Dell'Orfano, "Medication Adherence in Cardiovascular Disease" (*https://oreil.ly/yshJo*), *Circulation* 121 (2010): 1455–1458.

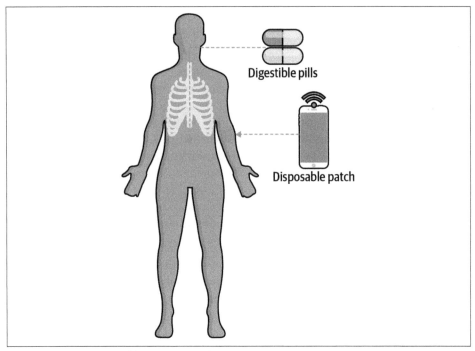

Figure 4-5. How ingestible sensors work

The sensor sends signals identifying the medicine and the date and time that the person took the pill. Like any high-fiber food, the sensor passes through the gastrointestinal tract in several days. Signals are transmitted from the sensor to a disposable adhesive patch on the patient's body. Several metrics are compiled from the sensor and the patient's body, and the analytics and insights are readily available to patients, clinicians, and caregivers.

Abilify MyCite is specific to the medication Abilify, which is used in the treatment of schizophrenia and certain other forms of mental illness. This type of technology is very important, as it is well known that schizophrenics who are not medication compliant have more psychotic episodes and may require more hospitalizations and intensive management, as well as being a potential harm to themselves and others.

The application of AI to digital pills shows even more potential. Not only will medication adherence be tracked, but providers and other caregivers will be able to apply AI to data intakes from wearables and other sensors to provide additional information on whether the medication is working and whether real-time micro-adjustments to treatment regimens must be made. The potential benefits of AI are obvious.

Other ways in which AI is transforming medication management include:

- Improving medication safety (digital data in conjunction with utilization review with AI can detect medication errors)

- Predicting health risks and outcomes (Michigan is working on using patients' medication histories along with EHRs and prescription drug monitoring programs to calculate drug overdose risk and predict the risk of overdosing from a prescribed opioid[10])

- Improving the medication prior authorization process (regardless of improvements, many medications still entail duplicate data entry, delays, and rework after criteria for authorization are not met; AI can be used to extract the relevant data for the prior authorization along with digital information/data that can help augment and streamline the process of authorization by providing and importing the relevant data that may be required for approval of therapy)

Medication management shows what might be developing with digitization. As both AI and IoT advance, the art of what's possible evolves. At the heart of these advancements are the real-time insights into how to possibly change behavior that are gained from previously discarded signals. So many opportunities to digitize are present, and perhaps no bigger opportunity exists than in administrative healthcare tasks.

AI and Digitization Applied to Administrative Tasks

In November 2016 the *Harvard Business Review* published an article by Vegard Kolbjørnsrud, Richard Amico, and Robert J. Thomas entitled "How Artificial Intelligence Will Redefine Management" (*https://oreil.ly/AFaWk*). In the article, the authors explained that AI is expected to automate many of the administrative coordination and control tasks performed by humans and that the transitioning of labor-intensive tasks to AI just makes sense.

In previous sections we've described how administrative tasks continue to comprise a significant proportion of providers' time and prevent clinicians from having the time to spend on face-to-face interactions with patients. AI can simplify humans' lives by efficiently performing administrative tasks and giving providers and other caregivers time to focus on human-based interactions.

Already, AI has made great strides in imaging tasks, such as analyzing X-ray images, detecting cancer, and assisting doctors with clinical decision support and management of patients. Supporting clinicians with some of the "easier" tasks allows time for more human-focused interactions with patients. You often hear patients complain

---

10 Jesse Adam Markos, "Michigan's Enhanced Prescription Monitoring Program and New Analytic Tools for Controlled Substances Help Protect Both Patients and and Providers" (*https://oreil.ly/Ptxtj*), Wachler Associates, n.d.

that their doctor saw them for five minutes and charged them X amount. With AI supporting the doctor, they will have more time to spend with their patients.

Similarly, AI can be a facilitator in population health management, where physicians look for trends in cohorts of patients of similar age and with similar disease conditions, risk factors, and so on. The advent of EHRs has propelled the digitization of healthcare data on broad populations, which AI can then be applied to. AI provides the analysis on those cohorts of patients and parses out the details on which patients need management and/or intervention in care and at what time. Patterns and predictive trends used to rely on data scientists querying healthcare datasets and on clinician review along with clinician experience to determine population health targets. Now AI can either perform this task for us or augment the current process.

Why is this important for doctors? Doctors have long relied on experience and evidence-based medicine guidelines to help facilitate management of large populations. Today AI can augment that management through the above noted analysis. From this broad overview of patient populations, AI algorithms can then analyze millions of data points and comb through the latest published research databases to quickly find relevant patterns and determine next best steps for the doctor and patient. This approach makes a big difference in costs and in patient health. Dr. Robert Pearl, a Stanford University professor, used consensus algorithms, along with oncology data entered in EHRs, and cross-walked them with the hundreds of established treatment regimens to recommend the most appropriate combination of chemotherapy medications for a patient. Furthermore, this same research and use of AI allowed the creation of a predictive model that could identify which cancer patients would end up in the ICU in the near future. AI facilitates doctors in making judgments on management that save in costs and, more importantly, impact people's health and lives.

AI also has the potential to go beyond the human experience through the use of *unsupervised learning*. Unsupervised learning is a subset of machine learning that analyzes data and discovers patterns and anomalies with minimal human involvement. Unsupervised learning has the potential to uncover patterns and trends missed by clinicians based on potential clinician bias.

Last, AI can augment claims and processing as well as prior authorizations (as mentioned previously). All of this results in efficiency and time savings as well as cost savings. AI can empower transactions and data management such that patients should be able to pay for doctor visits in real time, with the claim processed and completed and the needed prior authorizations fulfilled by the time the appointment is over. This all leads to improved quality of life and care for patients and clinicians.

Summary

A lesson of digitization is that organizations cannot apply their old way of thinking to disruptive technologies like artificial intelligence. Digital natives speak the language of digital; they embody the culture of digital in platform, architecture, process, and organization. The mythical digital playbook is just that—mythical.

Digital natives see agility as having a measurable return on investment and high availability of their platforms and products as table stakes. They automate everything. They embrace failure. They constantly evolve their application code. They push new features daily. Experimentation is a way of life. This is the culture of digitization, the ethos of digitization.

Digitization is needed for healthcare, and to have the greatest impact in helping people live healthier lives, digitization must focus on each area shown in Figure 4-6.

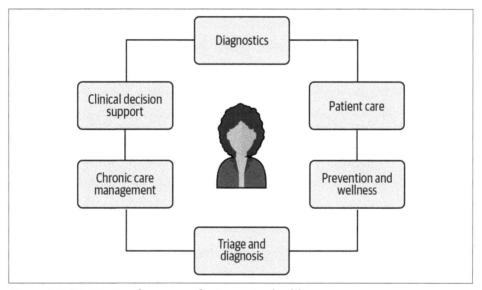

Figure 4-6. Digitization focus areas for improving healthcare

The more digitization can be realized in diagnostics, patient care, prevention and wellness, triage and diagnosis, chronic care management, and clinical decision support, the more we raise the efficiency and effectiveness of clinicians. We make healthcare more ubiquitous and available to wider populations. This is the power of digitization and AI.

In the next chapter we address the use of AI to eliminate or minimize waste, whether that be in terms of clinicians' time or in terms of fraud. So we spend less time on the business of healthcare and more on the back-office and operational aspects of healthcare.

CHAPTER 5

An Uncomfortable Truth

Healthcare waste is frequently defined as healthcare that does not add quality or improve patients' outcomes. The latest data from the Centers for Medicare & Medicaid Services (CMS) indicates that healthcare spend went up by 4.6% in 2019, reaching $3.6 trillion (*https://oreil.ly/pOYOL*). As a share of the nation's gross domestic product (GDP), health spend accounted for nearly 18% of overall spend. The healthcare spend distribution was 33% for hospital care services, 20% for clinician services, and 9% for retail prescription drug costs, with the rest accounted for by several subcategories, including dental care, home healthcare, home medical supplies, and nursing home care.

A 2019 article (*https://oreil.ly/mqF3o*) published in the *Journal of the American Medical Association* (*JAMA*) by William Shrank, Teresa L. Rogstad, and Natasha Parekh estimates that 25% of our healthcare spend results in healthcare waste.[1] That amounts to anywhere from $760 billion to $935 billion in waste. The article breaks down healthcare cost waste into six main areas: failure of care delivery, $102.4 billion to $165.7 billion; failure of care coordination, $27.2 billion to $78.2 billion; overtreatment or low-value care, $75.7 billion to $101.2 billion; pricing failure, $230.7 billion to $240.5 billion; fraud and abuse, $58.5 billion to $83.9 billion; and administrative complexity, $265.6 billion. This amount of waste is high, but it can be addressed by using AI to improve operational efficiency and facilitate clinical care. We won't eliminate 100% of waste, but we can gradually reduce it. We must find better ways to deliver healthcare while improving the quality of care. Achieving this goal will require a change in how everyone in the healthcare ecosystem (i.e., consumers, payers, providers, and governments) thinks about change in healthcare delivery.

---

[1] See also this October 2019 Business Wire article (*https://oreil.ly/eZi5L*) for a summation of the *JAMA* Special Communication.

Healthcare waste takes a heavy toll on providers, consumers, health plans, and clinicians, resulting in higher costs to consumers, and often reduced coverage. A lot of fraud, waste, and abuse, both unintentional and intentional—like a provider charging for services never rendered, billing for brand-name drugs but providing generic prescriptions, physician overbilling, and prescription stockpiling—have legal consequences addressed by various government regulations. AI helps detect patterns surfacing these kinds of waste and fraud, but the capability of AI to reduce waste that affects patient care and clinician efficiency has a greater impact on health.

Everyone expects and wants healthcare when they need it, and there are several regulations that ensure care is provided to someone in need regardless of circumstance. When healthcare is provided but not paid for by the person needing medical help, the cost is absorbed by the healthcare system overall. This is concerning, as the uncomfortable truth is that healthcare costs are rising at an enormous rate, and as those costs rise, access to and use of healthcare will become limited if the healthcare system cannot adjust.

In this chapter, we will cover how AI can reduce astronomical healthcare spend and allow us all to live healthier lives at a lower cost.

Healthcare Waste

We know where waste occurs in our healthcare dollars. We also don't lack an understanding of causes of waste or even solutions for fixing them. However, inertia is often mistaken for gravity—that is, we let the ingrained behaviors of consumers, healthcare services companies, and clinicians convince us that change or transformation is neither viable nor practical.

The previous chapters outline the opportunity for artificial intelligence to improve our knowledge of patients and provide better tools with personalization, while enabling the delivery of more convenient and better care. The desire to achieve these goals makes eliminating waste a priority, because waste makes clinicians less effective and reduces the amount of resources dedicated to making people healthier.

Of course, controlling healthcare costs and waste is not limited to AI interventions and can include getting patients to make better healthcare-purchasing decisions. This is facilitated through transparent tools that let consumers or patients know how much they will be spending on specific procedures, drugs, physician visits, and the like. Private sector (insurer) changes in payment—including value-based payment models, in which physicians and hospital systems are rewarded for better outcomes and controlled costs—can also have a big impact on health spend savings. That said, non-AI-related savings are estimated to be $140 billion over a five-year period, whereas McKinsey has estimated AI-related healthcare spend savings at approximately $270 billion annually (*https://oreil.ly/oXyb3*).

Application of AI to our healthcare spend issue has the potential to yield the greatest benefits and drive the majority of waste control. AI-driven progress does not exist in a vacuum, and disruptors and innovators will learn to integrate several technologies in the era of ambient computing to deliver transformational change.

Healthcare Spend and AI

Overall, greater than 50% of healthcare spend is for clinical care, either in-hospital or outpatient.[2] And a large proportion of identified waste in health spend connects to hospital or outpatient care as well. Twenty-five percent of Americans delay or forgo prescribed or recommended healthcare due to cost concerns,[3] leading to long-term waste as preventive care evaporates for one in four Americans. It is understood that the earlier a person receives medical care (i.e., preventive care) for a condition, the less likely they are to have long-term complications related to their disease. So if someone is diabetic, it makes sense for them to have preventive or screening foot exams and annual eye exams to catch and treat diabetic complications (diabetic nerve-related injury and diabetic eye disease) early, before permanent or more severe complications develop. In this section, we'll review how AI applications in healthcare can reduce healthcare spending by reducing waste.

Using algorithms, heuristics, pattern recognition, deep learning, and cognitive computing that approximates human capabilities, AI can take healthcare to the next level by solving complex problems or analyzing data at scale in a way that humans cannot, which enables AI to support clinicians in predicting diagnoses, facilitating diagnoses, and recommending the best treatment plans.

Clinician efficiency is critical. AI can augment the natural processes that physicians pursue and improve physicians' ability to make decisions, and waste is eliminated as a result. One of the most significant areas of wasteful spending lies in the high variability between physicians and their treatment approach. Not all doctors or providers behave in the same way when confronting the same medical issue. The Dartmouth Institute for Health Policy and Clinical Practice documented significant variation in health spend based on geographic regions and unrelated to health outcomes. The institute's work has led others to conclude that some areas of our country may be more efficient at providing high-quality care at a lower cost. Multiple other studies and analyses were conducted to evaluate additional factors that might impact quality of care, such as provider training, hidden provider bias based on patient socioeconomic standards, and provider gender bias. Their conclusions were clear: different

---

2 Centers for Medicare & Medicaid Services, "National Health Expenditures 2017 Highlights" (*https://oreil.ly/SJ9oW*), released on December 6, 2018.

3 Paige Minemyer, "1 in 4 Americans skip healthcare due to cost concerns" (*https://oreil.ly/CKma8*), Fierce-Healthcare, June 12, 2017.

physicians provide different care, even if all other elements remain the same. AI takes away some of this variability by focusing on evidence-based medicine and application of standards that all providers should follow.

Historically, physicians have relied on their own experience to augment their training when determining the types of testing and treatments to prescribe for patients. AI can bring evidence-based medicine to a new level. In recent times, the inherent variability of this anecdotal type of care has improved with the creation of evidence-based medicine (EBM) guidelines. Generally, EBM guidelines are attached to EHRs and embedded in clinical decision support, a rudimentary form of AI. This must be improved on so that a doctor sees not just recommendations they look up but recommendations that are automatically delivered to them based on the specific patient profile. This would enhance consistency in patient treatment and ensure that the most scientifically proven therapies are chosen. Evidence-based guidelines provide a framework for physicians to follow the clinically proven practices associated with the best outcomes for patients. However, even with evidence-based guidelines in place, extreme variability exists,[4] in part because EBM must be accessed by the clinician rather than it being delivered to them automatically. To boil it down, physicians appear to vary in three main areas: how much the provider knows or understands about the medical issue; how many tests they order; and last, how they deliver that care.[5]

If a physician does not have a good understanding of a condition and the related physical processes, the result will be unnecessary testing and wasted cost. In addition, the treatments provided may be inappropriate, and thus they may be potentially damaging to patients or will be ineffective at best. Let's review a few real-life examples and then see how AI might be applied to these situations.

Dorothy is a 72-year-old whose only health problem is elevated blood pressure, which is controlled with medication therapy. She presents to her doctor with shortness of breath and swelling in her legs. Dorothy had assumed that these developments were a natural part of aging and wasn't too concerned about them until her symptoms worsened in recent months. Her doctor sees Dorothy, and her exam is not abnormal other than her having some swelling in her lower legs. To evaluate further, her doctor orders a chest X-ray, numerous lab tests, lung function tests, and a heart stress test. The total cost, including the physician visit, is several thousand dollars. Her doctor ordered the lab tests because it is unclear if the cause of her symptoms might be kidney failure or lung or cardiac issues. At her follow-up appointment, all the findings

---

4 Gert P. Westert et al., "Medical practice variation: public reporting a first necessary step to spark change" (*https://oreil.ly/cnFvs*), *International Journal for Quality in Health Care* 30, no. 9 (2018): 731–735.

5 Femke Atsma, Glyn Elwyn, and Gert Westert, "Understanding unwarranted variation in clinical practice: a focus on network effects, reflective medicine, and learning health systems" (*https://oreil.ly/YQ7Ep*), *International Journal for Quality in Health Care* 32, no. 4 (2020): 271–274.

are essentially normal. He then orders a scan of her abdomen to evaluate for a mass that might be causing compression of her blood vessels, which could lead to swelling in her legs. Test results reveal no insights. At a loss, he sends her to a heart specialist and a lung specialist.

The heart specialist sees Dorothy and immediately diagnoses (right-side) heart failure. A heart ultrasound confirms the diagnosis. The overall cost of Dorothy's care is over $20,000. If her initial doctor had been able to focus his evaluation, then a referral to the heart specialist with associated testing would have cost around $2,500.

Now let's see how AI could have impacted this scenario. In Dorothy's case, claims data, lost to both the patient's and the doctor's memory, included a sleep study performed several years prior. The study had shown Dorothy to have sleep apnea, a condition in which breathing stops during sleep and which, if left untreated, results in strain to the heart. Dorothy had refused to have treatment as she felt a breathing mask for use with treatment of sleep apnea would be too uncomfortable. Eventually, the untreated sleep apnea caused her heart failure. The application of AI in this situation would have started with raw data input, including all claims data related to Dorothy's medical history. Machine learning algorithms designed to detect multi-disease states would have shown one of her possible diagnoses as heart failure associated with untreated sleep apnea. Imagine the improvement in care and customer experience and the cost saving with AI assisting Dorothy's doctor. AI could have provided recommendations for the best next actions in evaluation and referral to a heart specialist. Quality of care, outcomes, and costs would all have fared significantly better had AI been used.

This scenario illustrates variability in providers leading to increased health spend. If the doctor who initially evaluated Dorothy had considered heart failure as a possible diagnosis, then a heart ultrasound or referral to a cardiologist might have occurred sooner. Avoidance of waste occurs with fewer tests and immediate reference to appropriate subspecialists. This example demonstrates variability in provider knowledge and in quantity of tests ordered. The savings from the use of AI in this one case alone would have been remarkable.

This type of patient example is not uncommon. In the next case, we demonstrate variability in the delivery of care. Linda has kidney disease and requires hemodialysis regularly to control the toxins in her blood. Her doctor has Linda receiving dialysis at a dialysis center that her insurer does not consider in-network. Dialysis quality is controlled by various accreditation processes to ensure that dialysis units meet care standards, so the differences between in-network and out-of-network dialysis units are negligible, other than in the area of cost. Linda's doctor chose the out-of-network dialysis center because it is convenient for the doctor to visit this center if needed. There are several in-network dialysis centers that are just as close and convenient to Linda's home as her current dialysis center. The savings attained by moving to an in-network dialysis center can be as high as $500,000 with no impact on quality of care or outcomes.

As Linda's kidney disease worsens, and dialysis continues, doctors decide on a kidney transplant. Her kidney function is negligible by the time of the operation. Due to ongoing dialysis, she has associated medical conditions that are difficult to manage, resulting in complications with surgery and a lengthy hospital inpatient stay. Eventually, she returns home and is doing well off dialysis. Overall costs for Linda related to out-of-network dialysis, transplant, and complications after surgery are well over $2 million.

In Linda's case, AI could have been used to determine the optimal timing for Linda to possibly receive a transplant even before dialysis was required. AI is the ultimate data aggregator and analyzer. By looking at variables such as Linda's age, overall health status, type and level of existing kidney function, lab results, and urine output and comparing to other patients with similar data patterns, AI can determine the optimal timing for transplant with the best outcomes. By the time Linda received a kidney transplant, she had developed other complications related to her kidney disease and hemodialysis itself. With the application of AI and potential earlier transplants, the cost of Linda's care would have decreased significantly. The potential savings with AI use would have been over $1 million.

We've covered how AI can improve medical costs. What we've also seen from these examples is how AI can aid in the treatment decisions that impact the total cost of healthcare. It should be noted that each time we discuss AI in clinical settings, it merely augments the clinician and does not have agency or operate autonomously. The clinician always makes the final determination on diagnosis and treatment, as AI can go wrong and is solely an aid to clinicians.

Treatment Decisions and AI

As seen in the previous example, AI can drive the best next-step treatment decisions. Similarly, AI can help to drive prognostic evaluations so that patients and providers can make informed decisions on treatment. AI can be used to analyze and assess patient risks and predict the potential likelihood of patient outcomes. As discussed previously, physicians had traditionally based these types of prognoses on their own anecdotal experience and their own clinical literature reviews. Over time, we have been able to perform clinical studies, both looking back in time through collective experience and looking forward and following patients throughout their lifetime, to help make prognoses. We also use standard algorithms that calculate a patient's mortality (risk of death) based on their medical issues and risk factors. AI augments this body of knowledge by being able to take in even more individual factors that can impact prognoses and amassing more significant quantities of data, thereby taking the process to another level.

Why is this important, and how does it help? Because AI can look at so many more factors and amass significantly more influences that may impact a patient's prognosis, even more detail can be brought into the analysis, leading to more accurate predictions on how a patient will do over time. Additionally, AI can also look at the correlation within these different factors, which is something humans may have a hard time processing and identifying. Ultimately, prognosis drives treatment decisions for a patient and their family.

So AI plays a large role in helping us limit waste by providing detailed prognostic information on patients and helping to limit or prevent costs associated with overtreatment. Overtreatment, which is estimated to cost more than $210 billion per year,[6] can be broken down into two main factors: the ongoing expense of providing futile care; and the expense of ongoing care or treatments that do not add value or quality to a patient's life and may even lead to harm. Eliminating overtreatment costs leads to improved patient care at lower costs.

Futile care decisions

The American Council on Science and Health states that 25% of Medicare's annual spend is used by 5% of patients during their last year of life.[7] Medicare patients in their last year of life seem to incur such high costs because in our health system we spend the most money on the sickest patients, and patients who are in their last 12 months of life *are* usually the sickest patients. The problem is that we cannot always tell which patients are in their last 12 months of life. There are three main groups that account for this 25% of Medicare spending: patients diagnosed with cancer who are receiving active treatment; patients who will die in the coming year; and patients who are chronically ill and continue to have high healthcare costs due to progressive disease. The application of AI to this area of prognostication will help to predict the patients with the poorest prognoses and highest expectancy of death within a year. In this manner, there is the potential to offer less expensive but more appropriate care that would enhance the quality of such a patient's life rather than extending treatments and prolonging ongoing pain and suffering that do not add to the patient's outcome.

Futile care, or care without any impact on quality of life or patient outcome, is not limited to the elderly. It also occurs with younger individuals as well. However, as a broad topic, we will limit this discussion to individuals 65 years of age and older. Our general population does not have a realistic understanding of the costs associated with Medicare. It's estimated that the government spends approximately 20% of the

---

6 Heather Lyu et al., "Overtreatment in the United States" (*https://oreil.ly/xgI0P*), *PLOS ONE* 12, no. 9 (2017).

7 Chuck Dinerstein, "The True Cost of End-of-Life Medical Care" (*https://oreil.ly/cjDMa*), American Council on Science and Health, September 28, 2018.

federal budget on Medicare. The public needs to better understand that Medicare is a major factor in healthcare financial waste. We also need a better understanding of the futile care provided to our seniors. A survey undertaken by the Conversation Project (*https://oreil.ly/Sn3yq*) revealed that although 90% of seniors believe they should have end-of-life care discussions with their physicians, fewer than 30% of them have actually done so.

So how prevalent is this futile care? A 2018 *JAMA Health Forum* article estimates that one out of every eight Utah seniors dies in the hospital, and for New York State, the estimated ratio is three times higher.[8] The article's author, Ashish K. Jha, argues for thoughtful care focused on the well-being of terminal patients. It is appropriate for care to be given to those who will likely see a benefit either in quality of life or in quality of outcome. This would be the opposite of wasteful care. AI can facilitate this by helping to predict who will not benefit from care. AI won't make the decision on providing care but will simply provide insights and evidence for caregivers.

Let's review an example. Maurice is an 85-year-old male with metastatic (widely spread) pancreatic cancer. Maurice also has underlying diabetes, heart disease, and high blood pressure and has suffered two strokes, from which he remains wheelchair bound. He has seen his doctor regularly for his chronic conditions but has never had an end-of-life discussion with his doctor. Maurice has not documented his preference to die at home and for no heroic measures to be attempted. Each physician seeing Maurice focuses on their specific portion of his care. His oncologist focuses on the chemotherapy Maurice is receiving and on where it is given. His endocrinologist makes sure Maurice's blood sugars remain stable. His cardiologist focuses on blood pressure control. Maurice's primary care physician makes sure Maurice has all the right subspecialists managing his care. With such fragmented care, there is no one taking overall ownership of Maurice's health and his goals for his own care. Unfortunately, this is not an unusual occurrence.

After one of Maurice's chemotherapy treatments, he develops pneumonia. Maurice lives alone but has family, including a daughter. Maurice is hospitalized and treated for his pneumonia; then, because he is so run down, he is sent to a nursing home to recover. While in the nursing home he spikes a high fever and goes into respiratory failure. Immediately, he is conveyed to the hospital again, where he is intubated and put on a ventilator in the ICU, as he can no longer breathe on his own. Through a cycle of inflammatory reactions due to the underlying pneumonia, Maurice progresses to multi-organ failure. His daughter is called to ask for treatment guidance. Maurice's providers believe he will not recover, but his daughter does not feel comfortable making any decisions regarding the withdrawal of treatment. Although

---

8 Ashish K. Jha, "End-of-Life Care, Not End-of-Life Spending" (*https://oreil.ly/1Tr5i*), *JAMA Health Forum*, July 13, 2018.

counseled by the hospital staff that her father is in dire circumstances, she hesitates and calls in additional family members before a decision is made to withdraw support. Maurice then passes away in the hospital.

Several opportunities for improving the quality of Maurice's life were available here. If any one of his providers had addressed end-of-life care before he was hospitalized, then Maurice would not have been intubated or kept in the ICU for the extended period of time it took for his family to come to a decision. The costs associated with aggressive care of Maurice are not limited to financial waste. Maurice's autonomy and decision-making capabilities were taken away because they were never addressed in the first place. So how could AI have helped in this situation? Given Maurice's underlying widespread pancreatic cancer, AI would have been able to give a reasonable estimate of Maurice's prognosis. This would have prompted his oncologist or his primary care physician to possibly address end-of-life decisions with Maurice, which in turn might have led to reasonable care being provided.

Given Maurice's severe underlying physical limitations after his strokes and his numerous chronic medical conditions, AI would have been able to provide some prognostic information that could have impacted the decision to undergo treatment of his pancreatic cancer in the first place. Although most people would have been able to guess that Maurice's poor baseline status would impact his likelihood to survive cancer and its complications, AI could have provided the hard data needed in the sensitive conversations with family members, where statistics and prognostic information from AI alleviate some of the guilt families feel in making healthcare decisions. If, for example, the family had been told that Maurice was already in poor health, with a less than 30% chance of surviving an additional two years, and that he had less than a 10% chance of surviving treatments for his widespread cancer, then the decision could have been made at that time not to pursue aggressive treatment of the cancer. In this instance, application of AI could have led to decreased personal and monetary waste. Had AI been applied, the focus could have been on optimizing Maurice's quality of life rather than maximizing his quantity of life.

Overtreatment

The second major form of wasteful care is overtreatment in routine healthcare situations. Overtreatment is incredibly common, and the factors that influence this are complex and varied. A few major influences in overtreatment include fear of malpractice lawsuits, patient pressure, expectations in the physician-patient relationship that the physician should "do something," and the inability of providers either to access medical records (patients may come from different systems) or to have adequate background knowledge of a patient's history, leading to repetitive testing and potential overmedication. A survey of more than 2,000 American Medical Association physicians found that 20% of healthcare spend is devoted to "unnecessary treatment" and accounts for $210 billion of the approximately $750 billion spent in healthcare waste.[9]

You may think these numbers are huge and unreasonable, but from the provider perspective, they are typical. Let's evaluate a few scenarios in which overtreatment occurs and the applications of AI in controlling these costs. In the first example we have Susan, an active and otherwise healthy middle-aged female with known migraine headaches. She visits her doctor because her migraines recently seem to have changed in nature, and she occasionally has a tingling sensation or more nausea than previously. Susan looks up her symptoms on the internet and is certain she has either multiple sclerosis or a brain tumor, even though she has no risk factors for either disease. Susan's doctor tells Susan this and tries to reassure her. Susan is adamant and hints that if the provider does not obtain a brain MRI and Susan is later proven correct, she may sue. In this situation, almost any provider will find a way to circumvent any prior authorization requirements from the insurer and order the test.

How could AI have helped in this situation? AI could have given Susan and her doctor the statistical probability of her having any condition other than migraines. The various factors that influence Susan's health could have been assessed, and the best next step in evaluation or treatment could have been guided by AI. This in conjunction with her doctor's reassurance may have allowed Susan to hear and understand that migraine headache symptomatology may change over time as one hits perimenopause. AI analysis may have led to alteration in her migraine management plan as a first step, prior to jumping to a costly MRI. All of this would have led to cost savings and the avoidance of unnecessary treatment/care.

In another example, we have Tim. Tim has moved to a new state for his job, and he is trying to establish care with a new doctor. Tim mentions that he has known high blood pressure and, by the way, has also had a cold for the past two weeks. His new physician has no access to Tim's previous medical records. Tim first asks for a medication refill but does not know the name of the medication. When the clinic contacts his pharmacy, it is closed. Tim believes he might be on Lisinopril. In actuality, Tim's memory is incorrect: he is on Losartan, a different medication that was prescribed for Tim after failing treatment with Lisinopril due to chronic dry cough associated with Lisinopril use. Tim's new doctor prescribes Lisinopril, and the entire process of Tim developing a cough and then changing to Losartan is repeated with Tim's new physician. This was wasteful in terms of time, cost, and quality of life for Tim.

Interoperability of healthcare remains an issue. AI can play a crucial role by offering analytical insights into huge data powerhouses, giving providers more information, including access to critical information, without losing time. One patient may have

---

9 Lyu et al., "Overtreatment" (*https://oreil.ly/Bf3w6*).

hundreds of thousands of healthcare data points, and all this data will have to be collected and then used appropriately through machine learning. This is the role of AI.

Remember that Tim also mentioned having a cold. His doctor tells him that this likely is viral and needs no treatment. Tim states his previous doctor always gave him an antibiotic to cover possible sinusitis and that this has always worked in the past. The overprescription of antibiotics is well known in the United States, and the issue of the growing antibiotic resistance of bacteria and of antibiotic-resistant bacteria outstripping the development of new antibiotics is of increasing concern. Tim's new doctor, knowing that Tim will be filling out an experience survey after their appointment, ends up prescribing an antibiotic to maintain the relationship. Tim develops diarrhea from this antibiotic and is forced to take sick leave from work until his gastrointestinal symptoms resolve. Again, this represents wasteful care. Waste includes the cost of the antibiotic and the time off work. It also represents the potential harm to Tim from this "unnecessary treatment."

So how does AI apply in this situation? Again, AI could have provided the best next step in management by looking at all the variables in Tim's situation and comparing with other amassed data to come to the logical conclusion that no treatment was warranted. If his provider had been able to perform shared decision making, utilizing the findings of the AI analysis to bolster and support his recommendations, a different outcome may have occurred. A discussion between Tim and his new doctor could have led to their mutual agreement that use of an antibiotic was not needed.

Administrative Costs

Beyond patient care, AI has many applications in the healthcare industry that eliminate waste. Administrative healthcare costs are reportedly higher in the US than in almost all other countries. The National Academy of Medicine estimates that the US spends twice as much as necessary on billing and insurance-related costs. In fact, each year healthcare payers and providers spend $496 billion on these costs. Comparisons of administrative healthcare costs in the US to such costs in other countries show the US is an outlier.[10]

You are personally exposed to this waste when you fill out multiple forms prior to receiving care and then fill out more forms to transfer records between medical offices, and then you face multiple bills after your visit. You may wait for weeks or even months before it becomes clear what you owe your provider. You may wait weeks or months to hear whether authorization for a test, medication, or visit to another physician will be covered. And even more time and energy is wasted on following up to

---

10 Emily Gee and Topher Spiro, "Excess Administrative Costs Burden the US Health Care System" (*https://oreil.ly/ujCFB*), Center for American Progress, April 8, 2019.

ensure all appropriate paperwork has been submitted. Providers face administrative waste in charting (documenting in a patient's medical record), medication requests, prior authorization requests, and responding to multiple patient or patient family requests throughout the day—and in covering the same administrative tasks for their partners. Studies reveal that US physicians spend 50% more time on administrative tasks in comparison with Canadian doctors and that the US has 44% more personnel devoted to administrative healthcare tasks.

Administrative waste is so prevalent that clinicians, providers, and consumers see it as business as usual.

Let's consider the following examples:

- Laura suffers from severe diabetes. She has a primary care doctor and an endocrinologist, occasionally seeks treatment at urgent care, and through her insurance has nurse health advocates, all of whom are attempting to manage her care. Multiple health advocates reach out regularly in an effort to help Laura manage her diabetes. Yet none of the advocates coordinate with each other or with Laura's multiple providers. This is waste—a lot of Laura's care, including testing and treatment, is duplicated and uncoordinated.

- Melodie gets blood tests through her insurance carrier's wellness program because doing so benefits her health services account, which she uses for reimbursement of medical expenses not covered by her health plan. Thirty days later, the same blood tests are ordered as part of her annual checkup, and she has a poor experience as a result of getting pricked with a needle more often than desired and because of the duplicated testing.

- Sam, a two-year-old, waits too long in the emergency room, with skin discoloration and high fever exasperating her illness. She has flesh-eating Strep. Because timely treatment is of the essence and the administration of antibiotics and supportive care have been delayed, limbs must needlessly be amputated, and Sam will require expensive medications, custom prosthetics, special garments, and wheelchairs for the rest of her life. This is waste.

We need an agile, adaptive, real-time healthcare system, because healthcare systems today are not efficient and constantly require change to keep updated. These problems are well understood.[11] Healthcare systems that learn in real time and with data and new AI tools will help manage problems better than we can today. Developing and deploying a real-time healthcare system won't be easy; it is not a slam dunk, but

---

11 Institute of Medicine of the National Academies, "Best Care at Lower Cost: The Path to Continuously Learning Health Care in America" (*https://oreil.ly/UsT7i*), September 2012.

it's also not hyperbole to say that it can be done. Let's explore some of the ways this can be accomplished.

Administrative Processes and Waste

Reducing administrative waste in healthcare is all about improving efficiency, and AI can do just that. AI functions include claims processing, revenue cycle management, clinical documentation, assumption of regulatory tasks, and medical record management. Providers report that up to 25% of their time that is taken up by administrative and regulatory tasks could be better spent with patients. A study published by *Annals of Internal Medicine* in 2019 conservatively estimated that $4.6 billion per year is lost due to high physician turnover and lower revenue from reduced clinical hours attributable to physician burnout and time spent on administrative tasks.[12] When AI takes over administrative tasks, efficiencies are created, and the potential burden on physicians may be lessened, alleviating burnout.

Huge strides have already been made in technology utilization in administrative healthcare using robotic process automation (RPA) in combination with AI. Healthcare providers are focusing on cost optimization and using RPA to accomplish it. It is estimated that by 2023, 20% of all patient interactions will involve some form of AI enablement within clinical or nonclinical processes, in contrast to the 4% of patient interactions that involve AI enablement today.[13] The New York-Presbyterian Performing Provider System (NYP PPS) is using RPA and AI on administrative processes in which workflows can be automated and a set of decisions within the process can be improved with the use of machine learning algorithms. NYP PPS has partnered with the RPA vendor WorkFusion (*https://www.workfusion.com*) on these projects. Work-Fusion also has incorporated ML capabilities into its automation platform, which can be utilized to make data-based decisions using supervised learning methods.[14] Although New York-Presbyterian's focus has been on financial processes to date, there are future planned uses in areas such as coding and supply chain management. RPA combined with AI seems to have success in administrative processes due to a number of issues that many provider systems and insurance carriers have, including legacy systems that do not communicate with each other and multiple platforms requiring consolidation.

---

12 Shasha Han et al., "Estimating the Attributable Cost of Physician Burnout in the United States" (*https://oreil.ly/Q676X*), *Annals of Internal Medicine* 170, no. 11 (June 2019): 784–790.

13 N. F. Mendoza, "50% of US Healthcare Providers to Invest in Robotic Process Automation in Next 3 Years" (*https://oreil.ly/BNXNu*), TechRepublic, May 21, 2020.

14 Tom Davenport, "New York-Presbyterian, WorkFusion, and the Intelligent Automation of Health Care Administration" (*https://oreil.ly/tqR6r*), *Forbes*, September 15, 2019.

Increased efficiency, and thus the elimination of waste, is possible through the application of AI to claims and payment administrative tasks. Insurers must verify whether the hundreds of millions and sometimes billions of claims they process are accurate. Reliably identifying, analyzing, and correcting coding issues and incorrect claims saves in cost. Payment of incorrect claims can constitute a significant amount of waste in our system. AI can perform matching of data across different databases to verify this data. This work is otherwise done by utilizing combinations of human and technological support.

A few recent solutions that both alleviate the administrative burden and reduce the waste experienced by providers and patients, as well as streamlining the process and saving waste for insurers, involve medical coverage decisions made in real time while the patient is actually receiving care. AI can be used to help facilitate the different levers that would support immediate medication coverage (for nonformulary or non-first-tier prescriptions) and can also be used in reviewing a patient's medical record to see whether criteria are met in requests for certain tests, studies, or procedures.

What does this look like in practice? As a patient you could get your nonstandard prescription approved during your clinical appointment. Say, for example, that you are on a drug that is not the first choice for treatment of high blood pressure under your pharmacy benefits. AI can scan your individual health record, review past claims for integrated systems, and see whether there are other physical or lab value criteria that would result in coverage of the requested medication. This process normally would have to be done through your doctor reviewing your medical record and available data. The medication could be prescribed and noted as being covered, all during your appointment. AI makes this efficiency of care possible. Some patients wait for days or weeks to find out if medications are covered after their providers have completed the laborious process of requesting authorization. There is risk in the normal process of patients forgoing the prescribed care because they see the process as too onerous and the medication as too difficult to obtain. AI can enhance all such systems to ensure timely delivery of care while also saving on the cost of administrative tasks and enhancing care by supporting adherence to prescription therapies.

Additionally, AI can be used to ease administrative healthcare waste through immediate processing and analysis of prior authorization requests for procedures or tests. Currently, significant cost is associated with the use of human resources in requesting records, reviewing records, channeling authorization requests to appropriate departments, reviewing clinical test or procedure requests, and assessing complicated or unclear cases. Further time and resources are used in the provider office, with office personnel or physicians obtaining the information needed to complete the request. This is not to mention the additional time and resources utilized in communicating to the patient the status of their request and the results of the insurer's review. And then further time and energy are spent in scheduling the requested test or procedure and ensuring the appropriate authorization is associated with the test. The amount of time this process takes can range from days to months. The delay in care could impact the patient's health outcome and shows the huge amount of resources put into what should be simple administrative tasks. AI can address these issues by increasing efficiencies in the system and thereby improving the processes and eliminating waste.

Use of AI Can Ease Doctor Burnout

Doctor burnout is a huge problem in the US and other countries. Approximately one in three doctors experiences burnout at some point in their career, and up to 45% of primary care doctors state that if they could afford to, they would quit their jobs. Added on top of this are 300–400 doctor suicide deaths every year. Although reasons for burnout are as varied and individual as doctors, a large proportion of doctor burnout is due to there being too many bureaucratic/administrative tasks, which increase work hours without enough support. AI is a potential solution. With AI to ease administrative burdens and increase efficiency, as well as remove the responsibility of ensuring that issues such as authorizations are addressed, we could improve the quality of our doctors' lives, giving them back some much-needed time, and generate healthcare savings.

AI can streamline the entire prior authorization process and is in fact being used in some healthcare systems currently. AI enables decision making on test or procedure authorization during a clinical visit. So, just as an example, if a doctor orders an MRI to evaluate a patient's knee instability, the requirements are generated automatically and sent digitally to the doctor for immediate review at the point of care. Also, AI enables the results of the provider's completion of authorization requirements to be rendered at that time, with the patient still in the office. Thus the use of AI removes some human resources from the process, eliminates barriers to care, and avoids delay in the patient's receipt of care. All of this impacts the patient's health and both the patient's and the physician's quality of life, with the added benefit of removing wasteful administrative costs through added efficiency.

As AI improves efficiencies and eliminates administrative processes/tasks, the human resources that were required to perform the intake and processing of information are now less necessary. Is there a risk to job security with AI implementation?

Job Security and AI

In other sections of this book we have touched on how AI could enhance provider functions. This leads to the concern that AI will replace human jobs and experience. We debunked this myth in Chapter 1, and we discussed how the ethics of integration and use of AI are aimed at avoiding the displacement of jobs by automation. However, the concern persists.

In a 2014 report (*https://oreil.ly/ZNsfW*), Deloitte, in collaboration with the Oxford Martin School, estimated that 35% of UK healthcare jobs could be automated out of existence in the next 10 to 20 years. Other studies cite a variety of outside factors limiting the proliferation of technology with displacement of human jobs. These factors include the cost of technology, regulatory and social lack of acceptance, and labor market growth and cost. All told, these factors are expected to restrict actual job loss to around 15%.[15]

To date, there has been no documentation of jobs being eliminated due to AI in healthcare. The healthcare jobs most easily automated include administrative tasks and digital information transfer tasks, among others, but none that are associated with direct patient contact. In general, human resources have been retrained or have developed new skills supporting the AI-augmented processes.

The American Hospital Association's Center for Health Innovation foresees multiple opportunities for new roles and responsibilities for healthcare workers.[16] These include moving on to higher-value functions as workers are freed from routine tasks now automated with AI. Their improved productivity and efficiency allow them to focus on expanded responsibilities. Workers acquire new skills as a result of working with AI.

Clinician Time

Nurses provide more clinician services in hospitals than do doctors. Nurses spend most of their time (38.6%) at the nurses' station, with less than one-third of their time in patients' rooms.[17] In a 2019 survey of nurses and physicians in Iran, the most oft-stated cause of wasted time in hospitals, among 17 possible causes, was paper-based documentation.[18] Stories abound of doctors wasting their time doing paperwork.[19] Natural language processing and deep learning, the basic tools of AI, address many of these challenges. Dictation systems dependent on AI can understand and transcribe healthcare terminology, as compared to pure transcription services, where words are misunderstood because context is not comprehended. Deep learning layered on top

---

15 James Manyika and Kevin Sneader, "AI, automation, and the future of work: Ten things to solve for" (*https://oreil.ly/ziMmI*), McKinsey Global Institute, June 1, 2018.

16 AHA Center for Health Innovation, "AI and the Health Care Workforce" (*https://oreil.ly/17yKZ*), December 2019.

17 Ann Hendrich et al., "A 36-Hospital Time and Motion Study: How Do Medical-Surgical Nurses Spend Their Time?" (*https://oreil.ly/Jcybh*), *Permanente Journal* 12, no. 3 (2008): 25–34.

18 Kamran Bagheri Lankarani, "What do hospital doctors and nurses think wastes their time?" (*https://oreil.ly/sA5QO*), *SAGE Open Medicine* 7 (May 5, 2019).

19 Bruce Y. Lee, "Doctors Wasting Over Two-Thirds of Their Time Doing Paperwork" (*https://oreil.ly/iRaKa*), *Forbes*, September 7, 2016.

of natural language processing takes it to the next level, not only comprehending words and context but also understanding individual physician practices and verbiage; basically, AI learns how the doctor thinks and transcribes their words based on this understanding. To get to this point of interface between physicians and technology requires us to rethink how clinicians' work is done and to reimagine the systems used. Real-time healthcare can eliminate a lot of documentation.

Ambient Clinical Intelligence

AI can be part of the solution, freeing up physicians' time to be spent with patients in clinically meaningful interactions. One elegant potential solution is ambient clinical intelligence (ACI). ACI is touted as a way to reconnect doctors and patients. Instead of a doctor typing on a keyboard or writing in a notebook, microphones, speakers, and biometric monitors would be built into an exam room. A doctor–computer interaction would not be needed, as all data from the interaction would be captured through cloud-based systems. AI is able to discern between individuals in a room and can use speech recognition technology to identify individuals by voice. ACI would integrate conversational AI technologies (applying machine learning, speech synthesis, and natural language processing) in providing diagnostic guidance and clinical intelligence. AI could point out overlooked potential diagnoses based on a patient's history and symptoms, identify potentially dangerous drug interactions while recommending alternative medications, suggest the best next step in evaluations, provide reminders to doctors on diagnostic or treatment guideline recommendations, generate follow-up appointments, and coalesce data/results from interventions and thereby aid the physician in their job. The overall health of patients would also improve, as routine errors that occur during practice could be avoided through the application of AI.

The freeing of physicians from administrative tasks and decreased physician burnout leads to increased clinical time and improvement in overall healthcare, which in turn leads to long-term healthcare savings due to improved health with lower utilization of resources. Microsoft has partnered with Nuance to expedite ACI development and deployment, and Google, Amazon, and Apple are working on similar versions of this technology, which will enhance patient-provider relationships. These are AI solutions being developed. One of the first areas where the application of AI and its obvious efficiencies were realized was in healthcare imaging studies.

AI Use in Diagnostic Imaging and Analysis

AI is especially strong in diagnosing and categorizing images due to its incredible adeptness at pattern recognition. Radiology and pathology are two medical fields in which AI has demonstrated a strong impact and increase in efficiency. Even in these fields, where replacement of physicians by AI is a greater risk, such an outcome is not likely to occur. The use of AI produces a change in how radiologists do their work, but it won't *replace* radiologists.[20]

Radiologists review X-rays, CT scans, MRIs, ultrasounds, positron emission tomography (PET) scans, and any studies that physicians use to visualize the internal workings or systems of the human body indirectly. Pathologists review histology or biopsy slides, which are microscopic studies of tissue with specific patterns that may indicate certain disease or pathology. AI algorithms and pattern recognition can be used to recognize abnormalities that may be missed even by the experienced human eye. There have been numerous studies that show AI is better than some radiologists and pathologists at identifying disease. One would expect AI to have taken over the role of these doctors, and yet it has not.

AI and human intelligence take the same approach to evaluating medical images. The more images one sees, the more one improves in diagnostic capability by learning from mistakes and from accurate diagnoses. However, AI takes it to another level by allowing unlimited data input and a greater level of detail examination, such as pixel density, surpassing the capabilities of the human eye. This takes a field like radiology from an artistic, experience-based science to an objective science.

Radiologists have been a part of the digital world for quite some time. Radiologists frequently work remotely to analyze digital images from anywhere in the world at all times of the day and night. The radiologist's interaction with the doctor ordering the study is now limited compared to the past. In years past physicians would frequently visit the radiology department and review scans with the radiologist. Their interaction would include the ordering doctor providing clinical information to the radiologist, who would further hone their image review and diagnosis possibilities based on that information. AI and the radiologists of today do without this additional support in their study interpretation. An example would be a 35-year-old female on oral birth control who has been increasingly short of breath with elevated heart rate and abnormal oxygen saturations. Based on this information alone and an abnormality found on a lung CT scan, a radiologist would diagnose a possible lung clot, as hormone use is known to increase the risk of blood clotting. If the radiologist had additional clinical information, such as the fact that this same patient has known severe asthma, was exposed to an allergen that caused a sudden change in lung function, and is without any other risk factors for lung clots other than birth control use, an indeterminate finding on the CT scan would then be read as less likely to represent a lung clot.

AI appears to have a step up on radiologists, as even without the additional clinical information that a human would depend on, AI can use its greater data analysis to provide greater description and diagnosis. Pathologists face a similar challenge.

---

20 Thomas H. Davenport and Keith H. Dreyer, "AI Will Change Radiology, but It Won't Replace Radiologists" (*https://oreil.ly/7XXHs*), *Harvard Business Review*, March 27, 2018.

Considering all that, AI would again be expected to replace these physicians, but instead AI is being used to augment their capabilities. AI is providing efficiencies that a human radiologist or pathologist would not be capable of.

The following is one way in which AI is enhancing radiologists' capabilities. As we mentioned, with huge amounts of data interpretation required but with less clinical input from the ordering physicians, radiologists spend more time reviewing images and providing a straight image review with description of abnormalities and no associated interpretation. This has produced a significant gap, as radiologists are truly the specialists in image evaluation and, when provided with full clinical detail, can often provide the most accurate diagnoses. Without radiologists providing clinical interpretation for the ordering doctors, these other doctors (although knowledgeable) will be making their own clinical interpretations without full understanding of the nuance of the imaging detail. AI can help address this gap by providing the radiologist with the basic work of the image analysis and data review. The radiologist or pathologist then has the time required to provide a complete clinical interpretation.

Another way in which AI enhances these fields is by creating more reproducibility, meaning AI provides greater consistency in image review. Humans show great variance in their skills in reviewing images, as their reviews are more subjective than AI-based review. AI edges the field closer to a more objective process, with AI augmenting the physicians. AI can also perform data mining of electronic medical records to provide the radiologists and pathologists with more clinical information that would impact their interpretation of results.

Other areas in which AI adds additional value to the fields of radiology and pathology include identification of negative studies not requiring physician review, comparison of studies to previous scans/tests, aggregation of data from electronic medical records to aid the physician in their interpretation of abnormal results, quality control of studies, and application of decision support to reviews. AI will impact the workforce, yet it cannot replace the physicians, because communication of diagnosis, weighing of patients' values and preferences, clinical judgment, education, policy or regulation application, and interventional procedures are not replicable by AI. AI provides increased efficiency and brings the level of review and recommendations to a higher level. Efficiency removes medical cost waste and frees physicians to be focused on the patients themselves.

In reality, everything revolves around the patient. Better care and enhanced delivery of that care results in better health outcomes. Another avenue for applying AI to patient lives is in the pharmaceutical industry, where new drug therapies are advancing science and saving lives. The downside is delay in drug development or medication approval, as there are many stages in development before new drugs are created or established drugs are repurposed. AI can help address inefficiencies and waste in the pharmaceutical system.

Use of AI in Pharmaceutical Savings

Although not routinely considered a factor in healthcare waste, another large area of healthcare spend is pharmaceuticals. Drug development is a challenge for pharmaceutical companies, as it is estimated to cost $2.6 billion and take more than 10 years to develop and test a single new drug. And the cost of developing a new drug doubles every nine years. Pharmaceutical companies have seen the benefits of integrating AI into their processes to decrease research and development time and to decrease errors, which are both costly and time consuming in the drug development process.

In 2017, many large pharmaceutical companies paired with AI start-ups to work on streamlining their processes. One example of this is AstraZeneca teaming with biopharma company Berg to find biomarkers and develop drugs for neurologic disease. Another example is Genentech (a Roche subsidiary) using GNS Healthcare's AI platform to analyze oncologic medications; this collaboration is working to convert large quantities of cancer patient data into computer models and then use these models to identify new treatment targets for cancer chemotherapies. The overall goal is the application of AI to increase efficiency in current processes, basically by working smarter, not harder, and thereby decreasing time to production of new medications.

Another example of using AI in drug development and creating efficiency in processes, resulting in cost savings, is the work of two Israeli researchers, Shahar Harel and Kira Radinsky, at the Technion–Israel Institute of Technology. The process currently used by pharmaceutical companies is for researchers to first perform preclinical research. That includes looking for specific molecules that may be used in novel treatments based on microorganism and animal research. The molecule search is generated from scientific experience and new hypotheses for treatment based on current therapeutics. Instead of following this current model for drug development, Harel and Radinsky enabled a computer to make smart predictions without human guidance. They fed into their computer system hundreds of thousands of known molecules, along with the chemical composition of all FDA-approved drugs up until 1950. AI then came up with potential molecules based on this massive data input. Amazingly, when Harel and Radinsky instructed the system to suggest 1,000 new drugs based on old drugs, they discovered that 35 of the suggestions were in fact drugs that were approved by the FDA after 1950. This is incredibly promising as a new model for novel drug creation, one that utilizes significantly less time and is able to predict viable medication therapies.

Today most pharmaceutical companies screen large numbers of molecules looking for promising novel drugs. Biomedical researchers then carry out numerous tests to determine if these are viable drugs. This process is incredibly time intensive. AI aids this process by performing the molecular screening, which is labor and resource intensive for humans.

In addition, AI can help with predicting the efficacy and safety of a given molecular form of medication in a biological system. Thus, setbacks in the drug development process due to a novel drug with potential being found to either lack efficacy in an animal system or to cause an untoward side effect in the planned recipient can be predicted and identified ahead of time. AI used in this way creates huge time savings, saves human resources, and gets researchers to a developmental stage in which human input and resources can be more usefully allocated. All of this results in large healthcare cost savings, the timely creation of novel treatments, and improved patient health.

AI can also take existing medications and see where they could potentially be repurposed as alternative therapies for existing diseases or conditions. Fewer than 10% of potential medications actually make it to market. Yet millions of dollars and millions of human resource hours are spent on each of these "failed" therapies. AI can analyze the vast databases of "failed drug therapies" in various stages of development and see if they can be repurposed for use in different disease treatment protocols other than the one they were originally designed for. Often the repurposing is ineffective or is only marginally effective, as in the use of remdesivir in the treatment of COVID-19, but targeted therapeutics often do better.

One of the benefits associated with AI is a lack of bias found in humans. For example, a researcher may have designed a drug for treatment of an autoimmune disease, such as lupus. During the process of drug development, the molecule/drug may have proved unsuccessful for treatment of lupus. The human bias might be that this molecule is used for treatment of autoimmune diseases alone and should be considered only for treating other autoimmune diseases. AI holds no such biases in its analysis and could find uses for this drug as a cancer chemotherapeutic, or even as a treatment for eczema. Such repurposing is common. One example of a repurposed drug is bupropion, which was used solely for treatment of mental health conditions until researchers saw a correlation between patients using bupropion and smoking cessation. Now the drug (under the trade name Zyban) is well recognized as a treatment for tobacco addiction. Bupropion was created in the 1980s, but it was not until the early 2000s that an application was found for its use in helping people to quit smoking.

Instead of waiting years or decades for human researchers to spot correlations between drugs prescribed for their intended uses and desirable if unexpected side effects, AI can perform analyses and find new purposes for existing or failed medications that could benefit patients worldwide, while again producing cost and time savings.

The bioinformatics company Insilico Medicine has used AI to predict where new drugs may prove therapeutic, rather than designing drugs for a therapeutic area. Insilico uses AI to review the large amounts of data from human cells exposed to current drugs and compares the results to nascent or in-development drugs. This process is used to identify applications for these novel drugs other than the uses for which they were originally designed.

It's important to note that the FDA has not yet approved any AI-developed drugs, but the hope is that by finding alternative uses for drugs in the development process or for already existing drugs, an enormous amount of time is saved in turnaround to market. The involved expense is significantly decreased when you can avoid starting from the molecule identification and drug design stage. The time to alternative treatments becoming available for a specific patient condition is also decreased. Efficiency in time, efficiency in process, a decrease in time-intensive human hours of work, and quicker turnaround times for making additional therapies available to patients are some of the benefits of AI in pharma.

Summary

Waste in healthcare is enormous, but AI can be used to redress some of this waste. Efficiency is key. AI can assume the time-intensive tasks that are a necessary component of various aspects of healthcare but that don't require human intuition or critical thinking. AI can augment physician practice and does not pose a risk of replacing those providers. Rather, we should use the capabilities of AI to relieve our providers and our healthcare system so that it can focus on the nontechnological aspects of care. And then we can all live healthier lives at a lower cost.

As we discussed in this chapter, AI can address waste in healthcare through a number of approaches:

- Real-time processing for claims, payments, and benefits processing
- Reimagining the healthcare payment continuum[21] with real-time processing and AI
- Personalization of consumers/patients, resulting in patient empowerment and wellness
- Improving diagnostic accuracy, along with delivering it with speed at scale
- Eliminating redundant administrative processes
- Reducing paper and manual documentation chores
- Modifying patient spending behavior by using AI to reduce doctor shopping and perform effective network steerage to the right provider

Wherever AI is applied, efficiencies are created and medical cost savings are found. The slow adaptation of AI into healthcare is concerning, and AI's use in healthcare is kept somewhat quiet, as the perception of technology in healthcare is that it removes physicians from patients and that care is determined by machines alone. We need to

---

21 "How AI Can Help Reduce $200B in Annual Waste" (*https://oreil.ly/OaV2B*), Optum, n.d.

offer transparency and create a better understanding of how AI is impacting how healthcare is delivered and why the cost savings and reductions in waste are important in achieving the goal of a healthier nation. When we look to the future, we see emerging trends that take the current applications of AI to healthcare to mile-high levels. The future sees AI becoming so inherent to our healthcare systems, providers, payers, and patients that the end result is seamless healthcare.

CHAPTER 6

Emerging Applications in Healthcare Using AI

Since the dawn of man, technology has decreased the work burden on humans while driving efficiencies to free people to pursue other interests. General purpose technologies, which impact economies and societies, continue to make the biggest impact on all industries, including healthcare. Electricity, electronics, mechanization, the automobile, the computer, medicine, the internet, and now AI are examples of general purpose technologies (GPTs), and they were/are all game changers. They are ubiquitous; they are building blocks for continuous innovation; and ultimately their goal is to improve the way people live. AI is a general purpose technology and affords societies the same opportunity to improve healthcare.

One could describe our healthcare system as a sick care system in which care delivery hasn't changed much in recent decades. When someone gets sick or doesn't feel well, they visit their primary care physician, or they make an appointment with a specialist, or they even go diagnosis hunting via internet searches or their favorite health apps. An appointment is made with a clinician, tests are ordered and performed, and treatment follows. This takes time and produces inconsistent results.

Today our healthcare system does not proactively engage people to keep them healthy but instead reacts to episodic events. With the arrival of ambient intelligence, the explosion of smart things, and the underlying use of artificial intelligence, we can change the trajectory of healthcare. We can build more engaging solutions that will help people monitor and engage in their health. Patients are consumers of healthcare, and they can be engaged through devices in their homes, wearables, and social media.

This chapter is about imagining a future in which keeping people healthy is the normal practice. The personalization and connected care discussed in previous chapters become a reality. Patients don't need to be in the same space as their care provider; best practices for care treatments are instantly available to everyone. In this chapter, we introduce the future of healthcare through the lens of potential applications powered by artificial intelligence. The hope is that business executives, clinicians, startups, and others will engage in further AI healthcare development based on the art of the possible—specifically, that they will be energized by ideas and implement those ideas for creating apps, websites, services, or products that will help people live healthier lives.

Improving Human Health

In previous chapters, we've explained how AI-enabled technologies can improve the quality and potentially the quantity of human life. Because this concept is so important, we provide a limited recap here. AI in healthcare can be used to:

- Analyze population health models to identify patients at risk for development of a disease such as diabetes and intervene to prevent development of disease[1]
- Optimize treatment plans and provide best next actions for patients with disease[2]
- Realize personalization, making healthcare and telemedicine more effective
- Augment clinical decision making with AI decision support systems[3]
- Democratize healthcare services by making clinicians' expertise available to previously underserved areas or communities[4]
- Keep people out of the healthcare system through the use of wearables and other digital technologies, with a focus on home testing instead of doctor visits[5]
- Analyze digital images to provide more accurate and efficient identification of diseases such as eye disease or cancer[6]

---

1 Irene Dankwa-Mullan et al., "Transforming Diabetes Care Through Artificial Intelligence: The Future Is Here" (*https://oreil.ly/S8Stf*), *Population Health Management* 22, no. 3 (2019): 229–242.

2 Rajiv Singla et al., "Artificial Intelligence/Machine Learning in Diabetes Care" (*https://oreil.ly/yzrFm*), *Indian Journal of Endocrinology and Metabolism* 23, no. 4 (2019): 495–497.

3 Jessica Kent, "How Machine Learning Is Transforming Clinical Decision Support Tools" (*https://oreil.ly/ryzGN*), HealthITAnalytics, March 26, 2020.

4 Deloitte Life Sciences & Healthcare Group, "Connected health: How digital technology is transforming health and social care" (*https://oreil.ly/IA12J*), Deloitte Centre for Health Solutions, April 30, 2015.

5 Deloitte, "Connected health."

6 Sandeep Ravindran, "How artificial intelligence is helping to prevent blindness" (*https://oreil.ly/bdf62*), *Nature*, April 10, 2019.

- Transform healthcare into real-time healthcare by reducing friction for patients, consumers, providers, insurers, and everyone in the healthcare ecosystem
- Increase efficiency in the development of new pharmaceuticals[7]

Moore's law describes how computer power doubles every 18 months, and we see lots of evidence that AI power will improve at an even greater pace.[8] Doctors, nurses, caregivers, medical schools, healthcare companies, providers, and insurers need to show up and collaborate. *We must think more imaginatively about how we can transform healthcare to improve outcomes.* Fundamentally, the use of AI in healthcare can help us to live healthier and longer lives when built collaboratively and applied judiciously, and with better applications, solutions, and services using artificial intelligence.

Improving Human Lives

Technologies like AI can be tools of opportunity or tools used for abuse. A number of researchers, scientists, and philosophers cover these issues quite well. The clear and evident risk in using AI in clinical settings is in it making a mistake that results in harm to the patient. The widespread adoption of AI risks magnifying errors at a scale not quite previously seen with errors made by one doctor or a single provider. Even just on the administrative side, denying authorization for a life-saving medical procedure or failing to pay a claim could have catastrophic effects for people. It's too early in the life of AI to give it agency or autonomy in healthcare. AI must *serve* humanity, augmenting the work of healthcare workers and helping to improve the healthcare system.

To illustrate how AI in healthcare functions to improve human life, let's make an analogy comparing AI in healthcare to 1920s homemakers—in particular, how home technologies, such as electrical appliances, were expected to improve homemakers' lives.

In the 1920s, household appliances changed women's lives. Women at that time made up the majority of homemakers. Vacuum cleaners and refrigerators were becoming popular, allowing homemakers to do more. Middle-class homemakers who could not afford to hire people to help could buy a variety of appliances to reduce the amount of time they spent doing domestic tasks. It is worth noting that these technological inventions (the electric toaster, the electric iron, and so on) required a GPT—electricity. Two-thirds of American households had electricity by 1924. However, the

---

7 Kathleen Walch, "The Increasing Use of AI in the Pharmaceutical Industry" (*https://oreil.ly/NMPpV*), *Forbes*, December 26, 2020.

8 Cliff Saran, "Stanford University finds that AI is outpacing Moore's Law" (*https://oreil.ly/FacYD*), *Computer Weekly*, December 12, 2009.

introduction of automobiles, a new technology, ended up taking up the time gained from the decrease in housework. It is estimated that the same number of hours spent in the 1920s on housework are now devoted to driving children and others to and from events. The time spent on family tasks is the same; only the technology is different.

Our challenge is to use AI to transform healthcare and improve how healthcare is done. Much as we saw with appliances in the 1920s eliminating some household work and with the internet today, clinicians will increasingly see more of their time freed up by the use of AI, allowing them to spend more time on direct patient healthcare. Of course, if we build AI solutions that force doctors to spend their time figuring out how to work AI islands of systems, we will not see much progress. This is why computing that is invisible or stays in the background, operating with natural user interfaces like voice, must become the norm.

It's noteworthy that electricity was invented in the late 1800s, but it was 50 years, 1925, before it was used in half of all American households. Widespread adoption and application of this GPT happened slowly. In Chapter 1 we defined and described the attributes of a GPT. We expect the GPT of AI to spread much more quickly, as we take proactive actions to make technology infused with AI work for healthcare.

Making Technology Work for Healthcare

So how do we go about actually making technologies work for us in healthcare, and how do we do that with technology that seems to be eating up all of our free time?

The answer is to build the infrastructure and platforms to support the utilization of these technologies to integrate patient data and other health-related systems, with the goal of streamlining patient care, decreasing administrative tasks for clinicians, decreasing human error, decreasing costs, and improving patient outcomes through AI-empowered technologies.

Let's start with an example and then see how applied technologies utilizing AI can change the current landscape of healthcare. This requires ambient computing (discussed in Chapter 3), leading the way to ambient intelligence. The next section defines ambient intelligence and looks at how it manifests through the lens of a patient, a doctor, a hospital system, and a healthcare payer/insurer.

Ambient Intelligence

Ambient intelligence refers to the intelligence revealed in physical spaces that become sensitive and responsive to the presence of people. Ambient intelligence needs smart objects embedded with AI in the physical environment. Ambient intelligence brings together all of the intelligent things to provide intelligent service to patients, consumers, or clinicians acting in these smart environments. Figure 6-1 illustrates a smart environment with ambient intelligence.

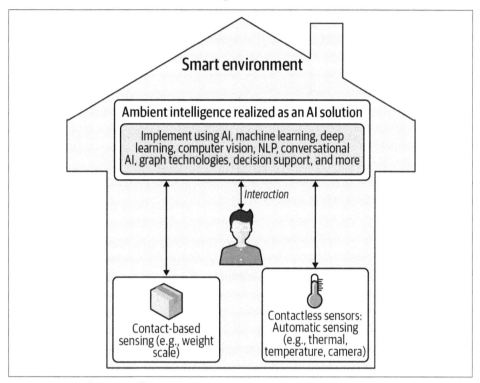

Figure 6-1. Ambient intelligence

Ambient intelligence is made possible by the AI system of intelligence that governs and rules the behaviors in the smart environment. The environment design determines the capabilities that are employed. For example, a smart environment in a home for the aging may have a variety of sensors—cameras, thermal sensors, temperature sensors, and weight scales, for example. The environment senses that the elderly resident has not visited the kitchen in a few days or has fallen and not gotten up. These events are understood by the system of intelligence, and it takes action, calling a caregiver or provider. The elderly resident interacts with the environment through voice or gestures if the environment is designed for that.

This is described as ambient intelligence because it's invisible and seamlessly resides in the environment. The AI system of intelligence integrates the devices, services, people, and technologies, enabling the desired use case such as aging at home. The integration by the AI system of intelligence is often described as a digital mesh. Personalization, learning, anticipation, and probabilistic reasoning all occur with the AI system of intelligence, making the environment intelligent.

Nature magazine describes how this technology could improve our knowledge of the (metaphorically) dark, unobserved areas of healthcare,[9] such as ICUs, where monitoring and improving patients' mobility according to care plans is crucial. Ambient intelligence in hospital rooms or provider offices can augment clinicians in a variety of tasks, including note taking, medical history searches, scheduling, or just answering patients' questions.

Ambient intelligence affords several benefits:

- Seamless and ubiquitous integration of technology with work, life, and play
- Environments that sense and respond based on human presence and behavior
- Homes, care centers, and hospitals that understand human needs
- Everyday objects (e.g., scales, water bottles, toothbrushes, appliances, mirrors) that are smarter and more integrated

Figure 6-2 illustrates a world of ambient intelligence in which AI services live both on the edge and in the cloud. Intelligent objects in homes, care centers, and hospitals operate seamlessly. Instrumented consumers are engaged through the use of apps on their mobile devices and intelligent objects in their homes.

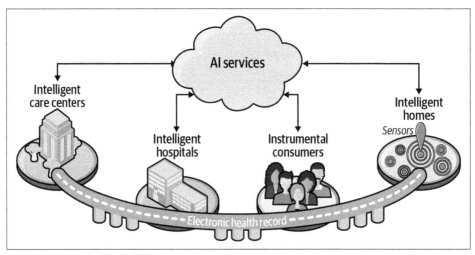

Figure 6-2. Ambient intelligence

---

9 Albert Haque, Arnold Milstein, and Li Fei-Fei, "Illuminating the dark spaces of healthcare with ambient intelligence" (*https://oreil.ly/qKNVl*), *Nature* 585 (2020): 193–202.

Advances in AI and IoT fuel gradual advancement in ambient intelligence. This advancement will come largely from the Big Tech companies and start-ups. The next sections take a look at technology from the perspectives of a patient, a doctor, a hospital, and an insurer.

From a Patient's Perspective

Whether we go to an urgent care center, an emergency department, a hospital, or a clinic office for an appointment or the evaluation of a health issue, we must fill out paperwork. Have you ever wondered where this paperwork goes? Even if we are seeking care within the same health system, if we change where we are seeking care, more paperwork is required.

Lately the situation has improved through the use of tablets to enter this information directly into our records. Yet it does not seem that this information always travels with us. To address some of this administrative burden for clinicians and the wasted time for patients, individual health records (IHRs) have been developed. One large health insurance carrier in the US has created a proprietary IHR system, which its membership utilizes on a routine basis.

A patient's IHR travels with them. It contains all the information, including updated medications and medical and surgical history, that is associated with an individual in their lifetime. AI can first be used here. Before electronic health records (EHRs), there were paper charts housed in massive file storage areas, with old charts being sent to medical information storage facilities, warehouses of individual patient data in paper form. When humans extract data from paper charts, there is room for confusion. Does a pap smear result noted as a histological exam (a test requiring microscopic evaluation) get filed under routine lab results as a scan, or should it be filed under the e-tab of pathology results? When humans perform this task, such a result may not be filed under one or the other tab consistently, making it difficult for doctors to find the latest results. Human entry of data into EHRs has resulted in errors such as echocardiograms (ultrasounds of the heart) being filed under abdominal ultrasounds, which are associated with far different conditions.

AI can solve these problems with intuitive interfaces. AI-enabled technology can automate this process of placing data in appropriate areas through intelligent sorting that would otherwise be time and human resource consuming. AI further enables the electronic record by allowing voice dictation and transcription of notes with the ability to process language. Voice commands, video recording, photos to document stages of disease, or skin findings can also be automatically encoded into the system. There is the further step of ensuring AI is aware of its limitations, and when needed, AI can alert users on tasks that require human assessment or intervention.

So as a patient, we can walk into an office with all our information on file without the need for additional forms, and all our health and medication data is available for our doctor to review in the sections that intuitively make the most sense for the doctor to look at when getting a background view of the patient. Eye scans or facial recognition, along with voice identification software, will identify us as the patient without the need for us to produce a driver's license or otherwise verify our identity. Payment information is in our IHR and directly communicated to the office without our having to fill out forms or produce insurance cards. AI will enable all interactions and documentation of relevant health data during the visit. Ambient computing in the exam room can obtain all vital signs and relevant specific point-in-time patient data as we visit with our doctor. Our doctor and their staff are free to devote time to direct human-to-human interaction, and there is no indication of technology (such as a tablet or other devices) blocking our connection with our doctor. Efficiency through the use of smart devices with AI applications will have then achieved the technology goal of enhancing our lives while saving time for relevant human interaction.

After we complete our visit with our doctor, we normally would head to the checkout area to see whether co-pays are complete and to ensure that any follow-up referrals or tests are ordered and scheduled. In today's system, if a test is ordered, the patient has to wait days or weeks to find out if their insurer has agreed to cover the test. As we've mentioned in previous chapters, technology exists today for immediate completion of prior authorization of both medications and tests/procedures without the need for delay in treatment. At the time of this writing, the same insurer who created its own IHR also has developed the systems to perform these real-time determinations for medication and test authorizations and is rolling these systems out to its network of providers. So we, the patient, would have all of our follow-up tests/procedures, labs, or referrals scheduled and completed prior to leaving the office. Administratively, our co-pay has been automatically deducted from our health savings account (HSA), and our claim for the visit, including physician fees, lab charges, and so on, is complete and paid prior to our leaving the office via charges to the debit or credit card we have on file with our IHR. We do not receive numerous letters at home informing us of charges that we are not able to decipher without the aid of the customer service number on the back of our insurance card.

Customer service representatives (CSRs) go by many names, including *agents* and *advocates*, to cite a couple. Their role is to facilitate any customer/patient complaints, answer questions, and try to redress any human errors that may have occurred during your recent appointment. Consider a scenario in which you need to reach out to customer service: for a recent appointment, you chose an in-network doctor and expect to pay an in-network deductible. However, due to some error, your provider has been marked as out of network. Your bill is incorrect, and you call the CSR. The CSR, if helpful, will place you on hold for 15 to 30 minutes while they call your doctor's office to see what the error is and then fix it in the system, with a new bill being sent to you at your home. AI facilitates all these administrative tasks and prevents such human-related errors. Essentially, the need for CSRs is dramatically reduced, as errors and time-consuming calls will be avoided. Again, technology will have reached its goal of decreasing human work and improving efficiency.

During the primary care doctor office visit, the doctor gives a voice command to schedule an appointment with a specialist. Insurer approval for seeing the specialist occurs immediately, during the visit. The traditional system would have you sign another form, a release of information (ROI), so that your data can be transferred to the specialist's office for review. Clinic office staff would then find your record and download all relevant labs, doctor's notes, and so on, and email the file to your specialist. Again, the opportunity for error here is large, as it is usually medical assistants rather than nurses or doctors who perform this task, and it is harder for them to know what information is relevant. AI uses its intelligence to review your data and pull in all relevant aspects for review by the specialist. With your IHR, you not only have all your records and pertinent information with you, but you also can use your smartphone to relay and confirm that the record has been sent to the specialist. The majority of your time in this future scenario has been spent with people. You sat down and spoke with your doctor while receiving eye contact. You had multiple interactions with technology in addition to interacting with people, but they were so discreet that you barely noticed. You are now all set, with a minimum of delay or hassle, and any barriers to your receiving or pursuing the healthcare you need have been removed with the aid of AI-enabled technologies.

So we've demonstrated how the invisible technology of ambient intelligence reduces friction and improves the patient's experience. Now let's see how it improves the doctor's experience.

From a Doctor's Perspective

It's not possible or practical for any one physician to be an expert, a specialist, in all fields of medicine. The domain is too vast and growing, so medicine is becoming more specialized, with every doctor having a niche area of expertise. There is a shortage of primary care doctors who can guide and quarterback care, something that is often needed along a patient's journey. Although we have covered the disjointed nature, potential waste, and poor quality of care that might result without a quarterback, it's worth looking at this in more detail.

Nowadays we have physicians who are categorized not only by their specialty or area of expertise (such as cardiology for heart specialists) but also by where and when they work. There are *hospitalists* (physicians who practice inpatient medicine only), *nocturnalists* (hospitalists who work only at night), *laborists* (ob-gyn physicians who only deliver babies)...and the list goes on. Because care is now highly fragmented and siloed, the primary care doctor becomes even more important as someone to manage the entire patient care journey. The primary care physician is often akin to a project or program manager when building or engineering something, except in this case it's a patient's care that is being engineered.

To explain this further, if you have diabetes and see a cardiologist, the cardiologist will focus only on your heart problems and will not address your blood sugar issues, expecting that another doctor will manage this condition. However, uncontrolled diabetes is a major risk factor in cardiac conditions, and controlling diabetes can improve your cardiac health. We are entire human beings, not isolated organ systems. Yet in today's systems, the project management role is implied and often not a recognized necessity, though it is a role patients still expect their primary care physician to fulfill. However, physicians are often forced to focus on specific conditions due to time constraints and metrics on their performance, and they may not have the skills to navigate the patient's journey in situations where the patient's care requires multiple physician specialists and/or providers.

How does technology and the need for efficiency play out here? Similar to AI, the primary care doctor is taking in vast amounts of data and processing that information in a short time to come up with complex diagnostic and treatment plans. AI has a role in helping the doctor with this. AI is known for its superiority in analyzing vast databases and taking in information to guide medical management decisions, as well as for having an endless capacity to absorb more data, whereas the human doctor becomes burnt out. Technology comes to the doctor's aid as a facilitator. AI can perform the tasks of assimilating mass quantities of data, reviewing clinical literature and relevant patient information, assessing for medication interactions, and facilitating treatment support, thus diminishing administrative tasks and other work for the physician and increasing the time the doctor can spend with the patient. Just as important, AI can be used to track and retain knowledge of the patient's healthcare journey (their health and healthcare interactions throughout their lifetime).

Once in the patient room, the doctor uses their voice to retrieve pertinent areas of medical history. The doctor is not stuck writing on a tablet or typing into computers in the exam room. All data and work generated between patient and physician are captured through technology. So during a visit with your doctor, your biometrics are obtained through unobtrusive sensors placed throughout the room. Your conversation and the doctor's notes and orders are given verbally to audio sensors that then generate a note documenting your visit and the management plan, which is available to you on your smartphone. Your doctor misses that you are due for a pneumonia vaccination, and your doctor is given a gentle reminder to consider vaccination for you today. Your physician begins to prescribe a new blood pressure pill and is unaware that in specific minority populations it is ineffective and may have severe side effects. AI combs the pharmaceutical literature and identifies this just-released information and relays it to your doctor before you leave the exam room, and your doctor then engages with you to prescribe the appropriate blood pressure medicine.

Instead of your doctor waiting weeks to find out if your new antihypertensive medication is working, connected sensors inform your doctor that your blood pressure is responding well to the medication. AI has reviewed your personal data points and knows what is "normal range for you and per your physician's direction," and it would alert your doctor if significant dips or highs were to occur in your readings, but your activity level and overall energy indicate that you are doing well. Technology has enhanced the doctor's work by making their treatment decision making more informed by your real-life data. Real-time information on interventions is provided to your caregiver, and any micro-adjustments to your care can be performed through technology-enabled communications, with pharmacies receiving direct changes to your medication as needed.

The value of this type of information being relayed to doctors in real time is immeasurable. In close to real time, patients can receive micro-adjustments to care. This prevents big swings in values like blood pressures and blood sugars. In fact, AI-enabled connected devices would mirror what insulin pumps and continuous glucose monitors do for diabetic management. The principles are the same. Inhibiting vast swings in abnormal values of blood pressure or blood sugar will result in less micro-injury, or damage to the human body. It prevents development of symptoms that are associated with large swings in these values and improves the patient's quality of life. By continuously monitoring and managing medical conditions, the doctor has a new tool in their armament for helping patients live healthier and more rewarding lives. Previously hindered by a lack of information, the doctor now has the ability to truly facilitate the type of control that these diseases and patients benefit from.

Because so much is taken care of by AI-enhanced technology, the doctor now has the time to spend assessing the patient and the pertinent data as intuitively grouped by AI, and they have AI to provide reminders and support on best next treatment plans and steps, as AI continuously combs the medical database for the newest and most up-to-date treatment plans and pharmaceuticals.

The doctor's office staff is not burdened by calls to patients, pharmacies, or insurers and is free to facilitate patient care and make sure the patient enjoys their experience within the clinic without hassle. No longer is the patient sitting in the exam room for 20 or 30 minutes waiting for someone to come and explain checkout. The doctor and staff benefit through efficient rooming and movement of patients, which enhances their revenue stream as well. Time is given back to the doctor to do what is most important to them, and that is to develop a relationship with their patient to truly understand their medical and behavioral health needs and to ensure the whole patient/person is addressed in a one-to-one interaction, with nothing acting as a barrier to that interaction.

In previous chapters we have discussed how administrative tasks take up inordinate amounts of time for providers and their staff. With this burden eased by technology and efficient handling of patient needs and wants, the doctor is able to spend time staying up to date on clinical medicine. AI may assist by alerting the doctor to journal articles that anticipate changes in medical care and by providing treatment guideline updates or notifications on drug recalls. This helps ensure that the doctor stays current with ever-changing health systems and clinical updates. Both patient and provider benefit from a better-informed physician. Fewer errors occur with an informed provider and AI assist.

With the ability to micromanage medical conditions, co-managed through AI-enabled tech and physician knowledge, the physician ends up with better quality scores (from patients through online review platforms such as Healthgrades, and from insurers, who use quality scores to determine whom they cover and what type of reimbursement they will provide). Higher quality scores for a provider frequently means higher reimbursement and more patients to care for, thus increasing their revenue.

Last, emerging trends in AI-enabled technology increase the provider's independence, so that they are now free to focus deeply on their patients. Administrative tasks, mindless simple communications, time waiting for a patient to be roomed by medical assistants (which usually takes at least 15 minutes, depending on the practice type), and other distractions and delays are removed. Doctors can run their practices the way they want, with as much AI assistance as they determine is necessary and appropriate. Much is written on physician burnout, but one of the main factors decreasing a physician's quality of life is the feeling that they are an employee bound to a system in which they must churn out patient appointments to gain financial stability.

Just as in the 1920s appliances example, the goal is to decrease the physician's and patient's burden through increased efficiency and enhanced quality of life. Unlike in that example, however, it can be achieved for patients and providers through ever-expanding and developing technologies and their thoughtful application in our everyday lives.

The advantages of ambient intelligence for patients and doctors go beyond the examples provided, as it presents a huge opportunity to improve experiences and care. Of course, this also extends to provider systems, such as hospitals.

From a Hospital System's Perspective

The obvious parallel with AI-enabled technology support of a doctor's administrative tasks exists for hospital systems. Bills and claims, medical coding, patient check-ins, authorization by insurers—all can be streamlined through the use of AI technology.

Differing improvements that impact hospitals are use cases that are currently in development and show promise for expanded use in the future. Beth Israel Deaconess Medical Center (BIDMC) has employed AI to address the issue of delayed hospital discharges.[10] One example of BIDMC's AI initiative involves integrating AI with BIDMC data, whereby the hospital is able to determine the most efficient utilization of its operating rooms. AI is used to perform calculations and make recommendations based on the type of surgery, surgeons' schedules, anesthesiologists' schedules, and patient length of stay in the hospital. This results in increased efficiency in the use of operating rooms, and BIDMC reports that two changes to orthopedic surgeons' schedules led to an "18% reduction in beds needed early in the week."[11] Thus the patient capacity of the hospital is expanded, and patient management and flow through the system is improved.

The cost is astronomical when patients linger in hospital beds due to nonmedical issues, such as an inability to locate the needed durable medical equipment (DME) to help patients once they are back at home, or because of other operational holdups, such as lack of a social worker to identify a nursing home for patient discharge or lack of nursing home availability. This results in a backlog of patients in busy urban populations, where ERs may become further congested with patients awaiting hospital beds—beds that are instead occupied by patients now healthy enough to be transferred out of the acute care hospital to other facilities or homes.

AI tools identify other post–acute care facilities and can analyze the vast databases of available home health agencies, DME providers, patient data, and socioeconomic variables to facilitate timely discharge of patients once they are physically ready. AI can assess and learn from multiple cases over time and recommend the best discharge facility (or home), based on patients' medical and social criteria. This benefits both the patient and the hospital system, as it results in fewer readmissions (being sent back to the hospital because of new issues, or not being prepared to safely discharge home) and decreases costs. Depending on the type of insurance, certain conditions under Medicare are not covered if readmission recurs within a 30-day time period following discharge.

Additionally, AI applied to treatment decisions is already employed in numerous hospital systems[12] and is continually expanding to impact discharge timing in other ways. The health-oriented news website STAT reports (*https://oreil.ly/BJkuF*) that Fairview Health System in Minnesota utilizes an AI discharge tool developed by Qventus that analyzes all variables of an inpatient's stay and can provide facilitated judgments on discharge and timing of evaluations and which evaluation to pursue. The clinicians

---

10 Matt Wood, "Improving Patient Care with Machine Learning at Beth Israel Deaconess Medical Center" (*https://oreil.ly/UMu2t*), *AWS Machine Learning Blog*, March 4, 2019.

11 Beth Israel Deaconess Medical Center, "AI-OK" (*https://oreil.ly/k3LTD*), *Giving Matters*, Summer 2019.

12 Lauren Paige Kennedy, "How Artificial Intelligence Helps in Health Care" (*https://oreil.ly/79Z2g*), WebMD, reviewed by Arefa Cassoobhoy, November 29, 2018; Kumba Sennaar, "How America's Top 5 Hospitals Are Using Machine Learning Today" (*https://oreil.ly/4gBvn*), Emerj, last updated on March 24, 2020.

gather around a hospital dashboard that shows patients with estimated discharge dates and identifies potential barriers to each discharge. For example, a patient slated for discharge on a Friday could instead be discharged on Wednesday or Thursday, if their MRI can be scheduled a day earlier. The outcomes have been astounding (*https://oreil.ly/bu1UX*), with a reported 2x increase in morning discharges from the hospital and an 8–11% reduction in average patient length of stay within the first year.

AI has other current applications in hospitals. AI tools are being used at Oregon Health & Science University (OHSU) to monitor almost all adult hospitalized patients for the development of sepsis (a life-threatening condition that occurs when a patient's immune system responds in an abnormal way to an underlying infection). OHSU uses AI to coordinate care among the main university hospital medical setting and two affiliated community hospitals that make up the OHSU network. By utilizing patient data and hospital census information in partnership with GE Healthcare, the AI system is able to identify potential sepsis in the community hospitals and transfer those members to the university hospital (where more intense care is available). At the same time, less ill patients are transferred to the community hospitals for care, if appropriate. This increases patient safety, as patients will be in the appropriate setting for their level of illness. Since implementation of this AI system, OHSU reports a decline in hospital transfer refusals (which serves as an indicator of more appropriate hospital setting and increased efficiency in the healthcare system).[13]

AI tools benefit hospitals in helping to identify the bacterial cause of certain pneumonias. At BIDMC, researchers studied data from 50,000 intensive care patients admitted from the ER with pneumonia and trained a neural network on the dataset. The AI tool was able to predict the type of bacteria causing the pneumonia.[14]

The benefit of this tool is not obvious, as patients diagnosed with bacterial pneumonia are put on antibiotics regardless. The nuance here is that there is an ever-increasing incidence of antibiotic-resistant bacteria out in the community, and there are few specialized drugs to address these pathogens. When antibiotic resistance is not considered, then the patient gets put on antibiotics that may be of no benefit and could potentially cause harm. Results from traditional laboratory studies, such as sputum (phlegm) samples and sputum cultures, take days or weeks to be returned. AI-enabled technology can predict the type of bacteria so that the best treatment plan is created. This means that patients will heal or respond more quickly, as they are given treatment targeted to their specific bacterial infection. Quicker healing means

---

13 Jennifer Fox and Sam Worley, "A New App Sees Signs of Sepsis Risk in Patients—and Spurs Staff to Action" (*https://oreil.ly/G9zex*), *GE Reports Stories | GE News*, September 26, 2018.

14 "Artificial Intelligence Can Help Predict the Bacteria Responsible for Pneumonia in Emergency Rooms" (*https://oreil.ly/2poZW*), American Society for Microbiology (press release), July 23, 2020.

less time spent in the hospital, and thus quicker turnaround times for beds and more patients running through the system, increasing revenue, and all while providing increased quality of care.

The possibilities for future use of AI tools in hospitals are endless. Oxford University Hospitals is using e-stroke suite technology in collaboration with several surrounding hospital systems. This AI-enabled technology was first deployed in March 2020. The software analyzes brain and surrounding blood vessel images, automatically highlighting the area of probable damage and the associated blocked blood vessel. The rapid analysis of these images with AI assistance helps to determine the type of intervention that should be performed to help the patient achieve the best possible outcome.[15]

In fact, there are numerous physician groups that are calling for the integration of AI into hospital systems. Physician colleagues from several major medical centers published a paper in *BMJ Health & Care Informatics* bemoaning the dearth of AI use in hospitals and calling for appropriate utilization of AI technologies to enhance patient care. As stated in the article, "There is a stark contrast between the lack of concrete penetration of AI in medical practice and the expectations set by the presence of AI in our daily life." The authors call for hospitals to resolve the disorganization within their systems that is holding back the implementation of AI. Their proposed solution is the creation of clinical departments integrating AI into clinical workflows and processes.[16]

Only through true integration and the seamless combining of AI technology with current clinical workflows can AI's utility in healthcare be appreciated and achieved. Increasing efficiency and freedom for hospital systems, providers, and patients will happen through true integration; otherwise we will end up with dysfunctional systems, as in the case of EHRs. EHRs were supposed to improve efficiency and decrease errors while improving quality of care; instead, we had massive amounts of inaccurate data that was entered into nonintuitive and inaccessible portions of patients' echarts. In fairness, EHRs were originally designed as billing tools to help with the codification of clinic visits and their associated charges. The dysfunction arises when we seek to use the same EHRs as clinical databases and to provide insight into a patient's actual medical issues.

Last, let's look at health insurers or payers and how AI could improve the way their work is done.

---

15 Hannah Crouch, "Oxford University Hospitals begins using AI to help stroke recovery" (*https://oreil.ly/ntPQ8*), Digital Health, July 31, 2020.

16 Christopher V. Cosgriff et al., "The clinical artificial intelligence department: a prerequisite for success" (*https://oreil.ly/tacId*), *BMJ Health & Care Informatics* 27, no. 1 (2020).

From an Insurer's Perspective

Health insurance is burdened by many regulatory practices and is subject to state and federal laws and agency regulations. Traditionally, health insurers have been steeped in paperwork. We have discussed in previous chapters how, from a business perspective, AI can be used to streamline operations, decrease administrative burdens, and decrease errors in the multiple transactions that occur with a single consumer/member/patient. A technology like AI can help automate previously labor-intensive processes, leading to lower costs and saved time. Furthermore, AI can be used to understand the consumer better. AI applied to other technologies can be used to predict consumer behavior, predict development of disease, understand consumer preferences, and target offerings with optimized price and product solutions to meet a consumer's particular goals.

AI-empowered technologies can provide the best possible health carrier product tailored to the preferences and possible health risks of the particular consumer. This data was always present but was unharnessed in the past. AI provides the technological answer to making this data usable and accessible for daily application. By tailoring offerings to the individual tastes and health needs of a consumer, insurance coverage becomes more enticing, and its utility has value for the consumer. This may promote increased insurance business, as Gen-Yers and Gen-Zers generally tend to utilize their health benefits less frequently and may not see the intrinsic value in proactive healthcare.

Applied on a larger scale to lines of business such as Medicare or Medicaid, AI has the ability to drill down into data, to region, preferences, socioeconomic status, and other variables that impact healthcare spend. This technology gives insurers the tools to set up different analytic sets and variables so that they can analyze the data in countless ways to provide further insights into markets than ever before possible. The future of AI is to have AI determine which datasets and cuts in the analysis will have the most impact on improving health outcomes. In other words, AI could be used not only to facilitate the analysis itself but also to help determine which subpopulations should receive more focused intensive management. And when people lead healthier lives, the insurers' financial bottom line improves.

The human resources required to achieve what we've just described would be significant. By having AI perform this analysis, there is cost savings and time savings, as AI can efficiently analyze and use its intelligence to determine through learning which models of analysis would generate the best savings opportunities while improving health for customers. Efficiency and time savings could be achieved through AI yet again. This allows the human analysts and scientists to focus on solutions, on troubleshooting, on devising new and creative methods for addressing health that are truly innovative and disruptive to current healthcare and insurer payment and coverage models.

Additionally, AI-enabled technology has application in the emerging technological arena of fraud, waste, and abuse claims. The National Health Care Anti-Fraud Association conservatively estimates over $68 billion is spent on fraudulent claims annually. Others estimate up to $230 billion. Unfortunately, there are doctors out there who are bad actors. Dr. Mark Weinberger was an educated ear, nose, and throat (ENT) doctor who made over $14 million per year in his private practice. His revenue was based on recommending surgeries for hundreds of patients who visited his practice. Later it was learned that the surgeries either were unnecessary (based on a single abnormal sinus CT scan that was used for hundreds of patients to obtain insurance authorization for surgeries) or were never performed.

How could AI-enabled technology help here? AI is commonly used today in fraud, waste, and abuse situations to protect patients and health insurers. Highmark (Blue Cross Blue Shield) used AI strategies to save over $260 million in 2019. The estimated five-year savings for 2015–2019 were approximately $850 million. AI is used by Highmark to analyze changes in provider behavior and billing practices and to help predict anomalies in standard billing practices in a much more efficient manner than traditional tools. Change Healthcare validated Highmark's findings and found that their AI program outperformed the industry standard and saved 10% of medical claims for group customers and nearly 33% more savings than national payers.[17] The advantage of AI is that traditional tools to detect fraud, waste, and abuse are hardcoded and use many algorithms. This makes their use self-limiting, as fraudulent behaviors will change over time based on what is caught by the current health insurer system. The work required to update the rules and algorithms is expensive and human resource intensive. With AI you have a system that learns and can adapt to changing provider behaviors without the same human support.[18]

Similarly, AI can be applied to actuarial and risk models to provide more tailored products that will reduce risk to the insurer and result in increased profits for the insurance company. AI is already used in the car insurance industry to identify "safe drivers" and to provide incentives in pricing with "pay by mile" rates based on the safety of the driver. This same application could be applied to health insurance, and the application of AI to actuarial models is in process, with the predictive modeling capabilities of AI used to determine the pricing of health insurance to a consumer based on their risk. Traditional actuarial models depend on computer models that assume homogeneity in claims data and population analysis. With AI models, individual claims data can be added into the models as well. AI also has the ability to adjust the model based on a change in cost driver, whereas models without AI do

---

17 Jessica Kent, "Artificial Intelligence Saved over $260M in Fraud, Waste in 2019" (*https://oreil.ly/net3K*), HealthITAnalytics, February 4, 2020.

18 "Making the case for using AI for healthcare fraud, waste, and abuse detection" (*https://oreil.ly/DsXJq*), Brighterion, July 7, 2020.

not.[19] Although not active currently, numerous insurers, including Kaiser Perma-nente, are looking toward integration and a more thorough analysis of data through AI to drive down healthcare costs and increase their savings and profits while improving quality health outcomes.

And although the list could go on, we'll wrap up with operational efficiencies of AI. For insurers, reducing their administrative burden through the use of AI virtual assis-tants or other tech to address customer, client, claims, payment, and all other pro-cesses integral to a health insurance system will lead to decreased errors, increased efficiency, more time for insurance workers to perform nonadministrative tasks, the ability to focus on more high-level thinking dependent on human interactions, and the creation of think tanks to address how AI-enabled technology can be applied to improving health outcomes and reducing cost. All of which benefits the insurer and us, allowing us to reach the ultimate goal of using technology to create time for human interaction and advanced thought.

We have examined the use of technology from the perspective of key constituents in the healthcare ecosystem. The next sections review potential new applications, tools, and services afforded to healthcare with applying and adopting AI.

Emerging Applications and Services

Enormous benefits await healthcare companies, hospitals, and clinicians that use AI-infused services, applications, and solutions to help patients with optimal care path-ways, improve clinician's decision making, reduce friction, create improved consumer experiences, and reduce waste. Achieving this future most likely requires collabora-tion among healthcare companies, technology companies, and academia. The path to changing healthcare is a difficult one, requiring investment and imagination, and the headwinds are enormous:

- Old systems and large technical debt decreasing incumbents' agility, increasing their operational costs, and hampering their willingness to change the status quo
- Siloed and redundant applications creating poor experiences for clinicians and consumers
- Providers strapped for cash and unable to afford the required changes to techno-logical infrastructure
- Inability of incumbents to work together to fix systematic problems and reduce friction

---

19 Nicholas Yeo et al., "Literature Review: Artificial Intelligence and Its Use in Actuarial Work" (*https://oreil.ly/wR2Bh*), Society of Actuaries, December 2019.

In spite of these challenges, the opportunity to build intelligent systems that will change the course of healthcare awaits us. AI can power fundamentally new classes of intelligent healthcare systems and predictive applications that providers and patients can use to better diagnose and manage wellness and diseases. AI helps with risk stratification, determining which patients are most at risk of developing a costly disease state or seeing a preexisting healthcare condition worsen. AI can analyze large volumes of data (genomics, behavioral, socioeconomic, clinical, prescription, claims, and more) to learn patterns and predictive models for identifying patients who are more likely to respond to care pathways or treatments. We can change how treatments are selected for patients and move beyond the "one size fits all" guideline into a personalized, intelligent healthcare approach.

The following sections provide brief descriptions of potential applications or products affecting patient, clinician, hospital, or insurer experiences and healthcare outcomes—in fact, many of these concepts will sound familiar to you from our earlier discussions. This is a glimpse of future applications that can reimagine how healthcare is delivered and experienced.

Coordination of Care Platform

Creating a platform that uses AI to do the heavy lifting of patient care activities is an opportunity. This platform can reduce fragmentation of care and medical errors. Care coordination means sharing signals and all healthcare information with healthcare providers. Today, primary care physicians, care centers, hospitals, nurses, and others don't have the time or the ability to effectively coordinate care. Consequently, care is often fragmented and fraught with gaps in patient care. A coordination of care platform can offer integrated care capability, handling the explosive growth in patient data and addressing the negative impacts of silos and the limited sharing of data among providers. This type of platform provides enormous benefits to patients who are dealing with multiple specialists and care providers.

The care platform provides clinical care insights from various sources to transform the workflow and support decision making in the coordination of care. The platform provides new ways to deliver value to patients, new ways for care teams to collaborate, and new ways for the business to operate in what is an increasingly connected ecosystem. Clinical data is captured in real time, point-of-care testing occurs, and a virtual command center provides the capability of seeing the entire care pathway. Real-time scheduling and care team collaboration occurs seamlessly.

The platform for coordination of care has touchpoints via sensors, mobile devices, edge devices, intelligent things, medical devices, and wearables at every point of care (e.g., hospital, home, body, care center) operating seamlessly in concert because of the platform. The platform must provide intake from the various data sources, using AI to facilitate accurate and timely patient monitoring and assessment to augment clinician care. The platform must also provide timely and accurate contextual communication of changes in conditions, symptoms, or patient feedback.

Platforms for clinical care, not point solutions or products, enable organizations to build agile, digital experiences that awe patients and consumers. In Chapter 7 we explore the concept of healthcare platforms. Platforms are the not-so-secret sauce for online digital companies who were born in the computing eras of cloud and the internet. The primary takeaway is to build more platforms with lots of features and capabilities that seamlessly integrate with other platforms not owned or built by your organization. Let's move away from proliferating applications and point solutions and adopt platform thinking.

Disease State Management Platform

Several disease states, such as hypertension, diabetes, behavioral health conditions, and atrial fibrillation, could be better served with a disease state management platform, a platform operated by a virtual care team that collects data from multiple sources and uses predictive models and analytics to assess disease states and the probability of changing state. Figure 6-3 illustrates components of a disease state management platform.

Using sensors and intelligent objects in the home coupled with intelligent wearables, the application continuously collects signals about a patient. AI and machine learning algorithms are used to assess disease states. Patient apps are used to teach wellness and diet changes. This platform is used to manage clinical risk, improve patient care, and prevent episodic events.

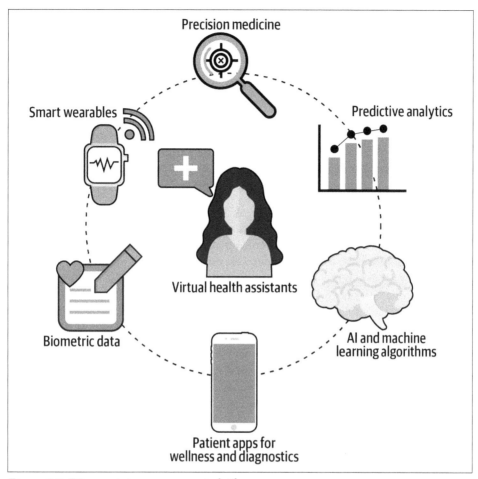

Figure 6-3. Disease state management platform

Human to Machine Experience Services

Conversational AI with cloud and mobile as enablers becomes the basis for many new applications focused on improving patient experiences. Voice-enabled conversations reinvent patients' and consumers' experiences with the healthcare systems. Several new conversational AI applications should emerge to address the following:

- Improving the customer's relationship with their provider and others in the healthcare system
- Providing personalized service

- Directing actionable insights
- Automating activities, such as voice response units

Replacing or augmenting current computer interfaces with natural user interfaces such as voice, gestures, or touch provides significant opportunities to help with aging populations and people with disabilities by simply allowing people to use technology in a way that is comfortable, easy, and fun. Natural user interfaces should make the technology invisible. The opportunity is to create services that can plug into and play with various applications. Such services would be built using deep learning, natural language processing, and automatic speech recognition technology; language model services can be created to change how patients and consumers interact with computers and technology.

One example is the opportunity to minimize or eliminate voice response units with their maze of options that patients or consumers must navigate to review their benefits, make appointments, find a provider, sort out claim denials, and more. Instead of users navigating through a series of prerecorded messages and a menu of options using the phone buttons and voice commands, voice response units can use a conversational AI interface to authenticate users when accessing healthcare services and for subsequent navigation of the various choices or options presented.

The treasure trove of data captured by companies with call centers afford them an enormous opportunity to use language models, automatic speech recognition, natural language processing, and deep learning to create new natural interfaces with people. These services can live and participate in any platform previously discussed, allowing customers and patients to use natural interfaces to engage with technology and computers.

Customer Journey Platform

For the primary care physician, each patient visit usually focuses on the reason the appointment was made. The patient may be undergoing an annual physical exam or may have an injury or illness that needs to be treated. The provider typically sees the patient for that particular reason, charts the visit notes, and then goes on to the next patient. These encounter-based patient records have served their purpose, but new technology is available that offers independent physicians a comprehensive, longitudinal record of the consumer's or patient's health experience.

The clinician should be armed with all the necessary data about the consumer's history and about their most recent experiences with the consumer. The data should be presented in a concise narrative, with facts, insights, and facilitated treatment/diagnostic recommendations that the clinician can digest in five minutes or less so that at the time of the appointment they are ready to focus on the now. A customer journey platform makes this possible. From a consumer or patient viewpoint, accessing the customer journey platform allows them to see every one of their clinical interactions. Imagine being able to see a provider in Chicago, but you live in San Francisco, and when you visit the customer journey platform, you see each interaction. And your primary care physician sees your interactions and pertinent clinical notes. Maybe you had an episodic condition in Chicago, such as kidney stones, and the Chicago physician can also see your clinical interactions through the customer journey platform.

Clinician Decision Support Tools

Clinician decision support tools (e.g., platforms and services) assist doctors, nurses, and clinicians in general with digesting the vast array of digital data, research and otherwise, and helping at the point of care by suggesting treatment pathways for various disease states. Such tools alert clinicians to previously unknown data and insights while detecting potential problems.

Treating patients with the most current medical advice is increasingly difficult to do. Clinicians must grapple with an ever-increasing amount of medical research, best practices, and other relevant data when treating patients. Their ability to keep track and stay current with the latest medical knowledge affects each patient's health, safety, and treatment. Although electronic medical records help manage the rise of information, patient-specific recommendations informed by a clinical decision support system would augment a clinician and improve physician decision making. Patient treatment, care guidelines, testing, and overall patient care could be significantly improved, while reducing errors that impact a patient's health.

Ambient Intelligence Environments

Sensing combined with smart devices and insights creates intelligent environments. Clinical situational awareness increases and becomes a reality with the rise of sensors. A few examples of sensors include:

Galvanic skin response (GSR) sensors
> Detect changes in sweat gland activity, providing insights into the level of emotional arousal in response to one's environment, typically stress. Patients recovering from various surgeries often experience stress or frustration. GSR sensors provide an indication of their stress level and may signal the need to change methods of therapy.

Bioacoustic sensors
> Capture natural acoustic conduction properties in the human body using various sensing technologies. Variations in bone density versus soft tissue and cartilage create distinct signals. This sensor technology enables more novel modalities, allowing hands-free access to patient information.

Digestible sensors
Send data from patients directly to clinicians, helping them to tailor patient care.

Sensor-based wearables
Used to remotely monitor a variety of health conditions, including diabetes, cardiovascular disease, and more.

Ambient intelligence spaces rely on sensors, artificial intelligence, smart devices, IoT, and other technologies to create an immersive, interactive, or automated contextual experience. In healthcare, such a space could be a home or care center in which humans and technology-enabled systems interact in a connected, coordinated manner, with multiple elements coming together to provide a service such as elder care, improve adherence to treatment plans, predict episodic events, and more.

Digital Twin Platform

As discussed in Chapter 3, a digital twin is a virtual replica of a physical thing—in our case, a consumer or patient. What if we had an AI-based platform that could collect, humanize, and analyze the full breadth of a person's health and make it easier to understand and act on it, at a personal level? This is the concept of a digital twin platform. Imagine if each of us had a digital twin that we or our primary care physician could use to model our current health, predict our future health, and pinpoint suggestions for improving our health or preventing future disease states or episodic states. Figure 6-4 illustrates a digital twin platform.

The digital twin should sense and respond and get smarter every day as it consumes more and more signals, using AI to continuously generate insights and predictions. Clinical data, prescription data, electronic health records, genomics data, and behavioral data all provide input and, in many cases, continuous signals. Data from social media sites can securely and with privacy feed the digital twin platform with the permission of consumers and patients. In a research study, Facebook demonstrated a definite link between a person's social media posts and their life events or states, providing a way to understand and predict behavioral states such as depression, risk factors, or future disease states.[20]

---

20 Raina M. Merchant et al., "Evaluating the predictability of medical conditions from social media posts" (*https://oreil.ly/nnbiT*), *PLOS ONE* 14, no. 6 (2019).

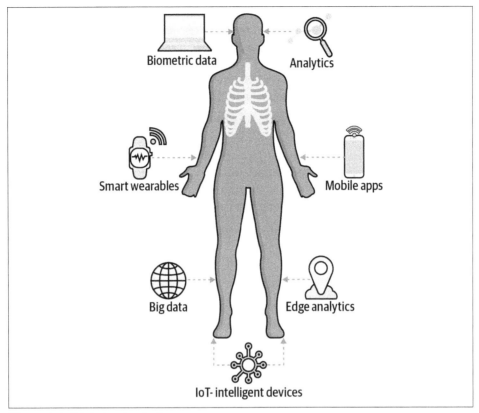

Figure 6-4. Digital twin platform

Clinicians, patients, and consumers can use such a platform armed with a mobile app to engage with their health, be better informed, and be motivated or influenced to live a healthier life. The digital twin can provide a timeline of a patient's health journey. It will help the patient and providers see past, present, and future health using all the data available.

The opportunity of a digital twin platform translates to higher levels of engagement, deeper levels of understanding of patients, and more personalized care plans, coupled with a stronger doctor-patient relationship.

Real-Time Healthcare

In his whitepaper on real-time adjudication for healthcare claims (*https://oreil.ly/ plMMj*), Bill Marvin, CEO and cofounder of InstaMed, a healthcare payment organization, defines real-time claims processing as the ability to adjudicate and respond to a claim in less than 30 seconds. He adds that what makes this real time is that it happens in the presence of the patient or consumer. This is no different than our expectations in banking or retail. Consumers want to be able to check if a knee X-ray is considerably cheaper using an app on their phone, the same way they would compare a price on Amazon with an in-store purchase price. A significant insight from his paper is that real-time adjudication "is a technology feature, not a solution to the existing problem in the industry—a point that has been widely overlooked." Of course, this goes beyond claims processing; it includes price transparency, fraud, and more. It means unscrupulous providers trying to scam the government or insurers for services never provided denied in real time.

Herein lies the opportunity for a new platform or application to reimagine real time in terms of consumer experience, human workflow, decision making processes, integration, and applying technology at the right time. Changing the paradigm, and understanding that the real problem requires a new operating model, is key.

Real-time healthcare, where consumers experience healthcare the same way they experience banking or shopping, is possible.

Internet of Behaviors

The explosion of devices and their increasing interconnection results not only in new data sources but also in new insights about your health and behaviors contributing to health outcomes. The research analysis firm Gartner coined the term *Internet of Behaviors*, or IoB. The IoB focuses on people's actions monitored through wearables, social platforms, locations, and a variety of sensors that may be in their home or on their body. Using AI, data can be synergistically integrated from the multiple data sources to inform healthcare organizations on their engagement with patients. A 61-million-person experiment conducted by Facebook (*https://oreil.ly/49jpo*) suggests real-world behaviors can be influenced by social platforms. In response to the COVID-19 pandemic, we see temperature, location (for contact tracing), and other data being captured and combined to influence behaviors that reduce the spread of the infection.

Of course, ethical debates regarding the implications of applying the IoB must be top of mind. But the opportunity to do good, to create applications that nudge people into healthy behaviors, exists. Richard H. Thaler and Cass R. Sunstein, in their 2009 book *Nudge: Improving Decisions About Health, Wealth, and Happiness* (Penguin), show how we can nudge people in beneficial directions without limiting their freedom of choice. The opportunity exists for healthcare organizations to create solutions that nudge consumers and patients into actions that contribute to healthy lifestyles and outcomes. Thomas Davenport, James Guszcza, and Greg Szwartz wrote an article in the *Harvard Business Review* (*https://oreil.ly/oUrpP*) on using nudges to treat diabetes. The technology, behavioral science, and analytics that make this type of solution viable have arrived.

Summary

The human body is a complex system offering a wealth of data that permeates every aspect of healthcare: ongoing care, urgent care, disease prediction and prevention, patient experience, and wellness. The increasing availability of large swaths of data drives enormous opportunities for creating healthcare platforms described in this chapter.

Today's COVID-19 pandemic shows the power of telemedicine and virtual care. Just as we witnessed a shift in banking from almost exclusively an in-person experience to mobile, online, and physical electronic banking outlets, a similar shift is underway for patient and consumer experiences with healthcare systems. Getting to this end state requires platform thinking, intelligent devices, tools, and services using AI. Several new platforms should emerge.

In the next chapter, we will discuss AI at scale. Every organization's journey to AI adoption will be different, and therefore the journey to AI at scale will also be different. The discussion of AI at scale reviews the role of the Big Tech companies, the new era of computing, and the role of platforms. We will describe the table stakes necessary to be AI-First, as well as the basic elements of platforms necessary to get to AI at scale.

CHAPTER 7

AI at Scale for Healthcare Organizations

Healthcare has an internal compass aligning its goals that is called the *quadruple aim*. The quadruple aim comprises improving the health of populations, improving the healthcare experience, reducing per capita costs of healthcare, and improving the work-life balance of healthcare professionals. The quadruple aim remains elusive. Even with the many successes of AI in healthcare, AI has not yet scaled in a way that materially impacts the quadruple aim. The success of algorithms in real-world clinical settings continues to be modest. Machine learning models are likely to do worse in the real world than in research settings. Yet the excitement of AI's potential remains. There are no silver bullets that deliver on the promises of the quadruple aim. Our discussion in this chapter of AI at scale for healthcare organizations focuses on what business and technology stakeholders can do in partnership to both mainstream AI in their organizations and scale AI to achieve a material impact on the quadruple aim.

Achieving AI at Scale

AI promises to be one of the most impactful technologies of the decade and for years to come, as it improves by leaps and bounds each year. For example, in 2012, machines became as good as or better than humans in several object recognition tasks. This spawned research and efforts to see whether machines could outperform clinicians. Several documented cases show deep neural networks achieving a diagnostic performance on par with clinicians, such as board-certified dermatologists in detecting skin cancer. Certain interventions based on prediction of disease or disease progression remain a challenge within ICUs, but deep neural networks outperformed human clinical intervention prediction baselines. Tasks that decades ago seemed impossible for AI to take on continue to rise: recognizing speech, facilitating predictions and intervention decisions in readmissions, preauthorization approval of claims, categorizing complex problems like medical diagnoses, predicting disease outcomes and/or making a prognosis. However, far too often, these improvements are in the lab and are not fully realized in the real world of healthcare or clinical settings. Organizations can move projects from the lab into the whole world with a focus on AI at scale.

In just a little over a decade, advances in deep learning and language models accelerated NLP, enabling multiple healthcare use cases such as clinical coding, conversational AI, and virtual assistants, which replaced handwriting or typing with voice notes, voice dictation, and more. Healthcare-specific conversational AI occurring between patient and machine or between clinician and machine is within our line of sight. OpenAI, an AI research company, published a text-generating AI that shows tremendous language processing advancement but was described as too dangerous to share because it might be used to spread fake news, spam, and disinformation. The language models created by OpenAI open up innovation for companies employing natural language understanding and processing. These innovations and others provide examples of the rapid progress and improvement in AI. A renaissance of innovation in NLP usage is occurring. AI at scale is possible, offering an opportunity for AI to impact healthcare.

Achieving AI at scale for organizations requires understanding where AI's adoption makes a material difference to one or more components of the quadruple aim. Often leveraging AI with other technologies (e.g., IoT or graph databases) for delivery in workflows will create a more intelligent system. Addressing the following questions helps with setting direction in AI adoption:

- Does the adoption of AI directly affect one or more components of the quadruple aim? Can we describe how AI makes a material difference in the product's success, business process, workflow, or solution?
- Is there sufficient data and access to data to address the problem?
- Do we have the right resources and talent on both the business and the technical side to tackle the problem?

Developing an AI strategy, whether or not it's part of a larger business strategy, is fundamental to getting AI at scale. It's unlikely any two organizational designs will be the same, as they will be unique to the organization's culture and practices. Without execution, strategy means nothing; it's just a useless set of ideas. Organizations that choose not to develop and actively realize an AI strategy will see the success of AI reduced or minimized, as compared to those organizations that take an active approach in addressing the myriad of factors necessary for AI adoption to materially make a difference in an organization. Figure 7-1 highlights several of the elements in an AI strategy that are essential to maximizing AI's success and impact.

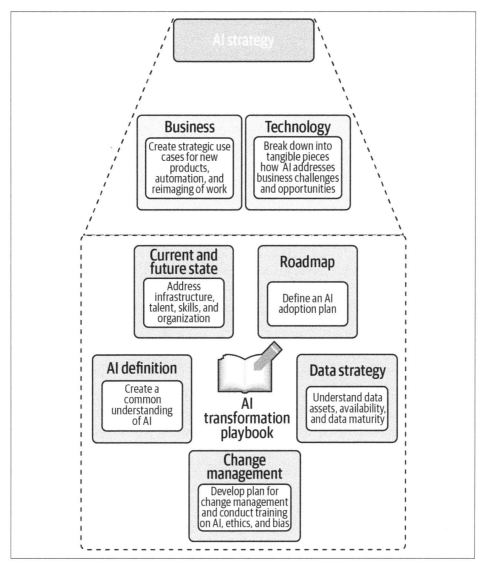

Figure 7-1. Elements of an AI strategy

The absence of an AI strategy is like having a car with no driver, map, or destination; you're just letting the car coast downhill at the mercy of any influential stakeholder's view, definition, and value propositions for AI. An AI strategy's success stems from business and technology teams working together and understanding the challenges while falling in love with the problem rather than the solution. Business stakeholders should compile their wish list, use cases, challenges, or wicked problems in all areas of their business, such as utilization management, network steerage, clinical coding, provider network management, population health management, clinical decision support, remote patient monitoring, or aging at home. Opportunities to reimagine work, automation, or new products will emerge. Each problem will open up the line of sight into various gaps in the system, and in all likelihood AI can be used to address many of them. Technology teams or IT groups should take each use case, challenge, or wicked problem and provide one or more possible solutions to propose to the business stakeholders. Again, loving the problem is more important than loving the solution.

Artificial intelligence is insufficiently precise to identify actionable projects, creating ambiguity in understanding applicable use cases. Hence, attempts to realize the potential of AI may stall. Organizations creating a shared understanding of how AI is defined should develop at least a limited knowledge of AI. Organizations should provide a viewpoint on AI and how it's relevant across the business areas.

Entrepreneur and computer scientist Andrew Ng's innovative work with the Google Brain team and the Baidu AI Group has informed him of what works for large organizations, inspiring him to publish his AI Transformation Playbook (*https://landing.ai/ai-transformation-playbook*). Just like a sports team's playbook that contains the team's strategies and plays, the AI Transformation Playbook provides a blueprint for how healthcare organizations can be more robust in AI, become an AI company, and become, as we call it, an AI-First organization. Although the playbook targets large organizations, all organizations will gain success from adopting all or most aspects of the playbook appropriate for their size.

Achieving AI at scale will require a range of technical work, which will vary based on organizational size. The AI strategy will address current and future states in infrastructure, data strategy and governance, machine learning operations, talent and skill requirements, and organization models, driving a road map for adopting AI.

Figure 7-2, an illustration of the healthcare universe, depicts the various stakeholders involved and addressed by organizations seeking to achieve AI at scale for transforming healthcare.

Each of the stakeholders in the healthcare universe will have different pathways for AI at scale. It will mean something different for each one. For example, providers (provider systems) who are financially constrained may choose to buy AI solutions rather than create bespoke solutions. It's unlikely they will be able to compete for AI talent or build on-premises computing resources. So AI at scale means making good buying choices. Given how old technology is sometimes packaged as new AI technology by healthcare solution providers, it's "buyer beware." Many technology and application providers are taking advantage of the hype around AI by labeling their product capabilities or features as having AI or machine learning capabilities, which is problematic for buyers looking for AI solutions. Such companies market AI as a technology rather than talking about how it promotes business agility and achieves business outcomes, making it difficult for buyers to judge the value of the product's AI features.

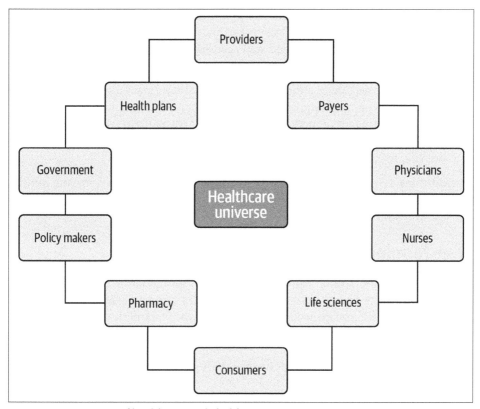

Figure 7-2. Universe of healthcare stakeholders

The evaluation of AI vendor solutions requires AI expertise to understand AI's transitions and determine applicable AI technologies. For example, a clinical coding solution that uses NLP sounds like AI, but it may not be an AI acquisition worth pursuing. That is, if the AI solution uses hardcoded machine learning for NLP instead of the more efficient deep learning algorithm models, it might be a poor purchase choice.

Vendors should be required to provide their definition of artificial intelligence and describe the AI techniques their product uses. They should be able to articulate and demonstrate how their product improves over time or gets smarter over time with data versus rules. Vendors should show how AI is applied to their solution, not just provide a presentation of how their product uses AI. Buyers should look closely at how AI promotes business agility and how data creates a cycle of making the product better as data improves or volume increases.

Describing the machine learning model process for maintaining models helps organizations understand their responsibilities versus those of the vendor. Buyers must recognize their skill requirements to maintain machine learning models and understand their data and compute requirements. Responsibility for maintaining the model may lie with both the vendor and the buyer. Healthcare company buyers must evaluate this during their acquisition stage and staff accordingly.

Buyers need to know that vendors will sprinkle the term *AI* throughout their websites and sales pitches, making it difficult to discern real AI capabilities built from deep learning adoption rather than from traditional machine learning techniques. That is, there is opacity in regard to methods used by vendors when they refer to AI. Analyst firms and others, such as AI subject matter experts within organizations, can help with decision making.

Transforming healthcare won't happen overnight with AI, and significant hurdles exist; however, transformation *is* possible, and the potential value AI brings makes the task worthwhile.

Transforming Healthcare

It has been a few years since venture capitalist and co-founder of Sun Microsystems Vinod Khosla wrote a provocative 100-page paper (*https://oreil.ly/JKSQe*) in which he boldly stated that technology would replace 80% of the work performed by clinicians. In his 2016 paper, Khosla asserted that technology would reinvent healthcare as we know it, and he coined the phrase "Dr. Algorithm." Several critical points articulated in Khosla's paper are reflected in this book and are worth summarizing:

- Opportunities exist for transforming healthcare.
- Technology amplifies clinicians' strengths and increases their competencies.
- A tsunami of healthcare data on populations and individuals makes it possible to improve diagnostics and monitoring of patients.
- Transformation will not be linear but will have different pathways with many course corrections, and we will see both progress and setbacks.

Doctors and others may see these proclamations as implausible. But AI-First healthcare requires us to think differently and to recognize that introducing probabilistic, statistically proven techniques, powered with enormous amounts of data, into clinician practices and healthcare has a huge upside. And we can do even more. We can build intelligent, smart healthcare services and systems using the constellation of AI and other technologies, both software and hardware. Providers (that is, clinicians or hospital provider systems) can be better with the right data-driven and more science-based tools utilizing AI to assist them in the future.

The love affair with machine learning and algorithms is both encouraging and disappointing. Impacting clinical care requires engineering tools, services, and platforms that positively impact patient care—delivering the quadruple aim in healthcare to improve patient healthcare experiences, improve the population's health, improve clinicians' work-life balance, and control costs. Reducing costs is possible with AI tools, services, and platforms. But it's not going to happen if we focus solely on algorithms and try to use AI algorithms to outperform clinicians. When algorithms meet the real world, the test data used to train models, such as detecting cancer in mammograms or identifying cancerous skin lesions, may have high accuracy but low efficacy. That is, algorithms alone won't improve patient care. We need intelligent systems, tools, services, and platforms engineered with a human-centered approach, as described in Chapter 2. Clinicians or technologists need to moderate the love affair with machine learning algorithms while recognizing that building impactful AI tools, services, and platforms demands we do more than apply algorithms.

There are hurdles to achieving AI-First healthcare—bias in models, black-box models, human barriers, resource and cost needs, and resistance to change, to name a few. AI-First means focusing on business outcomes, reimagining the future, keeping humans in the loop, and building intelligent software and things. AI algorithms and models are tools of the trade, not end products.

Achieving AI-First means that healthcare providers and healthcare organizations must define their desired business outcomes, achievable with AI and accompanying technologies like graph, blockchain, genomics, IoT, ambient, and more. Most providers and healthcare entities are a collection of actors, each with their own goals and often performing distinct workflows to accomplish their work on a day-to-day basis. When designing intelligent, smart AI-first systems that will have a clinical impact or address the quadruple aim, understanding existing workflows or business processes is essential. More importantly, we must understand the process, the origins of the process and why it exists, the business outcomes desired, the actor's motivations, and more. Suppose we don't know why operations exist and perform the way they do. In that case, we will likely use AI in highly inefficient ways by engineering outdated workflows, unnecessary workflows, or inefficient processes with AI.

Consequently, a failure to make a meaningful impact with AI feeds the continued dissatisfaction with technology, IT departments, and of course AI. *Failure to understand why clinicians, providers, or healthcare companies do what they do means organizations most likely will miss the opportunity to innovate and make workflow processes intelligent with AI.* Thus, the challenge of delivering clinical impact with AI won't be fulfilled. Reducing healthcare costs will remain a pipe dream.

When thinking about AI-First healthcare, we must understand that users have diverse day jobs, whether that be as a clinician, a call center operator, a business analyst, an executive, an actuary, or something else. And because each user focuses on their own job, they often see problems and the world of healthcare from their perspective alone, almost like Plato's allegory of the cave; human perception cannot derive actual knowledge. Each user tends to view the business, problem, and solution through the lens of their own role, work, workflow, and part of the business process. Often users don't understand technology, what is possible, or the art of what is possible. And it's not atypical that the IT worker tasked with engineering solutions fails to understand what is possible technologically. IT workers may commit malpractice, but no agency or entity governs them or ensures that IT staff (engineers, architects, designers, and so on) provide the best advice or engineer the most optimal solution. Over 30 years ago, Gerald Weinberg wrote, "If builders built buildings the way programmers wrote programs, then the first woodpecker that came along would destroy civilization." The industry has improved remarkably in 30 years, but what has become known as Weinberg's Second Law is unfortunately still true today.

So how do we get better and do AI-First? Ideally, the organization assigns someone, an executive, to own business processes, giving them both the authority and the vision to make each business process work for all constituents in the universe of that business process. A single executive stakeholder should own key business processes in an organization. An executive with business process ownership means they have the authority and oversight to eliminate duplicative business processes and the ability to focus on interconnected systems.

We must also recognize that we have to engineer solutions differently for AI-First. We need to understand that users may not know what's possible technologically, and maybe the IT group doesn't either. Users are too close to the problem to reimagine or visualize their work differently. Recognize that users don't have requirements and that businesses don't have requirements; they have issues and challenges seeking specific business outcomes. Recognizing the real challenges requires us to rethink how we engineer and procure technology.

In his book *Il Principe* (*The Prince*), written in 1513, the philosopher and writer Niccolò Machiavelli states, "It must be remembered that there is nothing more difficult to plan, more doubtful of success, nor more dangerous to manage than a new system. For the initiator has the enmity of all who would profit by the preservation of the old institution and merely lukewarm defenders in those who gain by the new ones." Meeting the critical challenges of delivering healthcare with AI means addressing the human barriers to adoption.

Today providers mostly work around problems with computer solutions. Clinicians use what they know how to do, in part because every time they go to IT with a problem, the answer is always no, or estimates of the effort required to solve the problem are prohibitive in terms of time and cost. As a result, vendors and suppliers often dictate the choice of technologies. Weinberg's Second Law, coined in 1978, told the dark story of IT, which unfortunately still holds true today. Many applications reflect poorly written software, dumb systems, bug-ridden systems, inadequately performing systems, systems that are not user friendly, and, worst of all, systems that don't meet clinicians' needs or help with healthcare. Lest you believe this is solely an IT problem, it is not; often IT builds what the business asks for.

Internet- and cloud-era companies provide a North Star for building software with fantastic customer experience and personalization. Figure 7-3 further describes three concurrent approaches for identifying actionable AI use cases that move organizations closer to AI at scale. Many companies today focus mainly on technology adoption of AI, working on algorithms and models to improve existing products and services. Having a strategic vision for how to reimagine healthcare in the future using AI can be a game changer. Figure 7-3 dives deeper into the three paths.

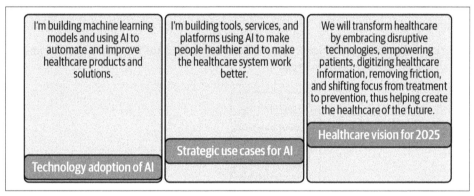

Figure 7-3. Three approaches for AI at scale

Moving forward with any of these three approaches may mean the various actors in the healthcare universe will need to be cajoled, forced, directed, or committed to these guiding principles:

- Embrace and adopt change; break with the past
- Partner rather than duplicate
- Partner rather than build from scratch
- Work with technology companies and/or academia
- Work toward a frictionless, seamless patient journey
- Adopt invisible engines/platforms

Transforming healthcare with AI won't be easy, but the digital natives leave breadcrumbs showing a path forward. Transformation requires organizations to cross a chasm.

The Chasm

In most organizations, a chasm forms with the introduction of a new technology and the excitement of its evangelists. On one side of this chasm are the CIOs, CTOs, and other technologists, who are learning and experimenting with new technologies like AI and seeing their vast potential. On the other side of the chasm are the COOs, lines of business executives, and business stakeholders, who are all less inclined to trust the technical teams or the technology. In these organizations, overpromising and under-delivering is the expectation for their IT departments. Organizations seizing on the opportunities and potential of AI navigate these waters successfully, finding a way to bridge the chasm and advance the business agenda while leveraging new technologies.

Figure 7-4 illustrates the chasm, where teams are successfully crossing the chasm and working together to make progress.

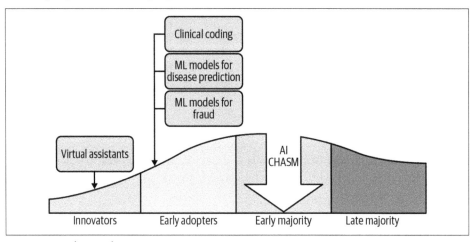

Figure 7-4. The AI chasm

Innovators and early adopters most likely share common organizational characteristics. The organization is not financially constrained and routinely provides the time and budget for exploratory activities. Such organizations have funding directed at research and development. Most likely, the CIO and CTO have an excellent relationship with business stakeholders. This relationship most likely is born out of consistent mutual success delivering value to the business that matters.

With AI, innovators and early adopter teams in the organization avoided the AI chasm. They achieved production, resulting in go-live successes with analytics and data science using machine learning. In production, we see machine learning models for disease prediction helping to manage population health and fraud and abuse detection at scale, such as by finding ghost providers (providers who do not exist but serve as a shell collecting on fraudulent claims) or identifying other abuse and waste within the system.

Members of the early majority who are on the other side of the AI chasm, unable to see value from AI, possess several common characteristics. These characteristics include broken relationships between business and IT, lack of strategic and effective leadership, failure to harness and grow talent, and a focus on operational efficiency at the expense of innovation. A 2012 *Harvard Business Review* article by Maxwell Wessel (*https://oreil.ly/wgYGo*) provides a primer on this topic, arguing that big companies can't innovate because they are designed to be bad at innovation.

Technologists are convinced that AI is make-or-break for the business; they make a strong case for this viewpoint, and the company grudgingly moves forward, with constraints. In this scenario, the organization does not embrace change, although change is essential for innovation. A large chasm is born out of this disconnect between business and IT. The disconnect does not occur because of AI's arrival but rather has taken years or decades to mature. It's often a direct result of a perception that the IT department underdelivers. There exist multiple ways to bridge the chasm, and one of those is invisible engines that are healthcare platforms.

Invisible Engines—Healthcare Platforms

The term *platform* is overloaded and is used to mean different things. There are a lot of platform concepts leading to this vortex of confusion. In the early days of computing, platforms were primarily described in terms of architecture and technology like Microsoft's operating system, Windows, a platform for developers. Today's platforms mainly operate as invisible engines, employed by several internet-era and cloud-era companies.

Underlying many of these companies' products, services, and capabilities is an invisible engine, which we describe as a platform. The engineering activity creating the platform is the invisible engine that finally breaks Weinberg's Second Law. In platform engineering, technical capabilities were once thought of as something the business doesn't care about—nonfunctional requirements, such as keeping an application running 24 hours a day, 7 days a week, or having the ability to drop new code, new features, and new functions into production every hour or to scale the application up and down across the world. All of these attributes are achieved mainly with these invisible engines, which we call platforms.

Platforms come in different types (*https://oreil.ly/bYs7e*), and each type has its own operating mechanics in terms of who owns the user, degree of openness, monetization, and more. Figure 7-5 identifies some platform types.

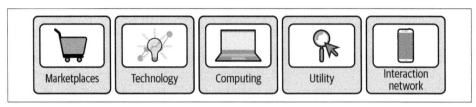

Figure 7-5. Platform types

Technology platforms such as AWS, Azure, and Twilio provide software components, building blocks, or services that can be reused in many different products. The developer of the building blocks owns the user. A healthcare organization owns its product's users, although the product may use one or more of Azure's cognitive/AI cloud services.

An interaction network is a type of platform seen in Facebook, WeChat, LinkedIn, Twitter, and PayPal, among others. This type of platform creates a network of participants (people and businesses) and facilitates digital interaction between them.

Utility platforms such as Google Search, Kayak, and Google Maps attract users by providing a service. The platform owner collects data and often monetizes this data to its advantage. The service provided to the user is usually free, with service fees charged for the use of the platform's analytics.

Computing platforms such as Apple's iOS, Google's Android, and Microsoft Windows connect users of the platform (i.e., the operating system) and third-party developers, typically through an app store.

Marketplace platforms such as eBay, Amazon Marketplace, and Airbnb enable transactions between demand-side and supply-side participants. These platform types support a storefront model in which only the platform owner's products are sold or a marketplace allowing third parties to sell their products using the platform.

Platforms excel at customer engagement, personalization, and operational efficiency, all the qualities we desire in healthcare products and solutions. Platforms are described as invisible engines because the engineering features of these platforms lie beneath the surface.

We make a provocative assertion: *21st-century healthcare companies must adopt platform thinking as a fundamental change, or else society may not see dramatic healthcare improvements.* Platforms allow healthcare constituents to reach a vast number of patients and other consumers, making healthcare better. Platforms enable healthcare services to be accessible via more and different channels, enabling more ubiquitous healthcare.

Platforms must be supported by ecosystems and must leverage application programming interfaces (APIs). APIs are essential tools for healthcare, as they allow one application's capabilities and data to be shared with another. It's how two different programs inside or outside the enterprise communicate. APIs work optimally when infused into a business platform supported by an ecosystem, as illustrated in Figure 7-6.

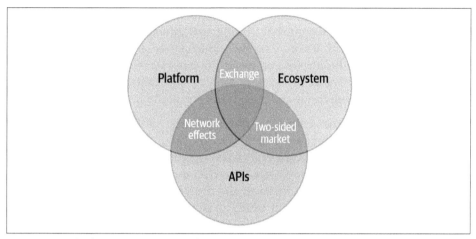

Figure 7-6. Platform, ecosystem, and APIs

The concentric circles of Figure 7-6 are intended to show the symbiotic relationship between a business platform, its ecosystem, and APIs. APIs in this relationship are used for any of the following reasons:

- As digital products to extend the reach of a company's products or services
- As tools for integration
- As vehicles to foster an ecosystem
- As innovation sparks embracing the ideas of third parties
- As onboarding ramps for the business platform, enabling the business platform to extend and expand

The network effect[1] of a business platform enabled and supported by APIs means that third parties (the ecosystem) use the platform in unforeseen ways, creating a symbiotic relationship in which the third parties (healthcare entrepreneurs, developers, start-ups) prosper, the platform adoption expands, and the platform owner grows its impact in healthcare. As the network effects of the platform take hold, the larger the

---

1 In economics and business, a *network effect* is the effect that one user of a good or service has on the value of that product to other people. The Wikipedia entry on "network effect" (*https://oreil.ly/QvVeV*) has more information.

use of the platform, the more valuable the platform is to the various players in healthcare.

Current healthcare application portfolios were designed to address the challenges of the past. Many have become an obstacle to innovation. However, they cannot be replaced wholesale due to costs and risks associated with major change. A healthcare platform is an architectural approach making applications more modular and consumable through different delivery channels, touchpoints, and modalities. Adopting this approach enables healthcare companies to innovate more quickly and adapt applications dynamically; as application features and functions are reassembled, capabilities rise from both inside and outside the organization.

Most healthcare companies embrace a linear business model in which they build things, create the finished product, and then sell the product. The notion of nonlinear business models is key; healthcare organizations in the 21st century must become digital (see Chapter 4), leveraging a network effect through which they can grow the adoption of healthcare products, services, and competencies through third parties. It becomes a symbiotic relationship in which all parties prosper. The healthcare company that created or owns the platform has the most to gain as more and more third parties adopt its healthcare platform. Platforms allow products and services to grow and be extended, with value added by third parties using their time, money, and resources. No single company can build everything on its own.

Companies must decide: will they opt for a product strategy or a platform strategy? Many are defaulting to product strategies disguised as platform plays. But labeling products as a platform doesn't make or create a platform. Platforms provide more value to customers than stand-alone products. Technologies (e.g., the cloud, mobility, analytics, big data, AI, and social platforms) enable the creation of business platforms.

The Road to a Healthcare Platform

Marc Andreessen, entrepreneur and software engineer, defines a platform as a system that can be programmed and customized by outside developers and users, and is adaptable to many needs and niches that the platform's original designers could not have contemplated, much less had time to accommodate. The platform value comes from its features and its ability to connect external data, processes, services, and capabilities. A platform offers a more agile way to connect and share information. Unlike applications or products requiring integrations (often complex custom ones) to combine different data sources, platforms are designed from the start to share information more easily; this attribute truly distinguishes a platform from an application.

Three healthcare platforms reflect this attribute of being designed to share information and embracing APIs and ecosystems. 23andMe is a *pure data healthcare platform* focusing on digesting and performing analytics on vast amounts of data. It offers a direct-to-consumer DNA testing service that also provides several health reports. At one time, it offered its APIs to external developers; that's the beauty of a platform, as organizations can turn it on or off based on their business model. One Drop is a *health engagement platform*. This type of platform often focuses on a specific health condition; for example, One Drop is a diabetes management platform. Health engagement platforms often provide support groups and clinicians access while supporting their users along the entire patient care journey.

One of the most impactful healthcare platforms is Tencent (see Figure 7-7), a *meta healthcare platform* for its comprehensive healthcare landscape coverage.

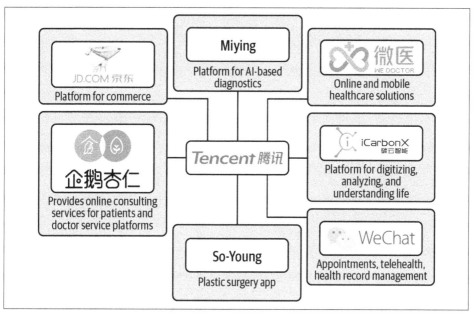

Figure 7-7. Tencent meta healthcare platform

Tencent connects several platforms or mobile apps while providing specific healthcare services in its platform. It brings in different platform types, such as WeChat, an interaction platform for chat, payments, health record management, health-related programs, and other healthcare services. WeDoctor enables online appointment scheduling with providers of all types. iCarbonX, using AI, combines genomics with other health factors to digitize, analyze, and understand life. The Miying platform provides AI-supported diagnostic services. Tencent Trusted Doctors provides online consulting services for patients. Tencent invests in and partners with start-ups to further expand its ambitions as a transformational healthcare platform in China. Tencent launched five years before Facebook and represents one of the earliest digital natives.

Platforms are second nature to digital natives and are key to increasing usability and digitization. Figure 7-8 illustrates the usability of specific healthcare products such as

EHR systems versus that of the platforms provided by digital natives like Google and Amazon.

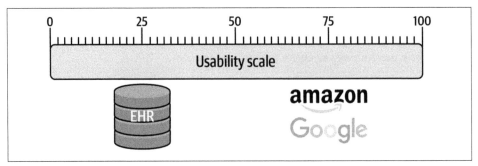

Figure 7-8. Usability scale

If asked whether their EHR system or Google search was more user friendly, most clinicians wouldn't hesitate to say Google. Asked if the consumer experience is better with Amazon or their EHR, clinicians will universally answer Amazon. It is not just EHR products, either—compare vendor products with platforms on any dimension (for example, business agility, time to market, digitization, usability), and the platform wins. Platforms play a crucial role in getting different tools and services to work together (more quickly than custom coding would), promoting composability, the stitching together of features and functions to create new capabilities. Platforms embrace using APIs, delivering outcomes through the assembly and combination of business capabilities.

Both products and platforms comprise a set of software. Platforms promote growth through the expansion of opportunities for connectivity and co-innovation by being programmable. Healthcare organizations' option is to use platforms as centers of innovation, where applications or products can be libraries of business capabilities used to compose many distinct user experiences. Figure 7-9 contrasts an application approach with a platform approach.

Applications or products reflect a closed environment comprising a user interface, application code, and databases. Applications do what their creators intended them to do and nothing more. Enhancing an application often requires waiting in IT development queues, in contrast to a platform, where APIs and SaaS services allow outside partners or developers to inject new features and content into the platform.

Implementing new opportunities and changes is much more comfortable with platforms than with applications or product suites. The addition of new functionality is made more comfortable with a platform avoiding significant rewrites of existing code bases. The pathway to creating a healthcare platform may start with creating a *data fabric*.

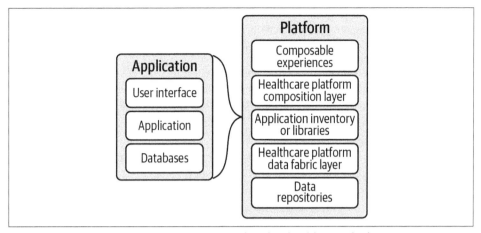

Figure 7-9. Healthcare application contrasted with a healthcare platform

A data fabric comprises an architecture, services, and technologies managing access to many sources of truth—that is, data repositories. Think of a data fabric as a layer connecting multiple data types and sources of data, with APIs for accessing that data. A data fabric provides data ingestion and integration services, supporting real-time, streaming, and batch use cases. It employs graph technology using metadata, creating opportunities for composable services and user experiences. A data fabric allows for dynamic integration and allows a variety of use cases to be woven together, or orchestrated.

Figure 7-10 illustrates that creating a healthcare platform is a journey and must be done incrementally, not with a "big bang" approach. Deciding on the goal and objectives for the platform and the type of platform is paramount—for example, whether to create a data platform like 23andMe, or a mega platform like Tencent, or something in between.

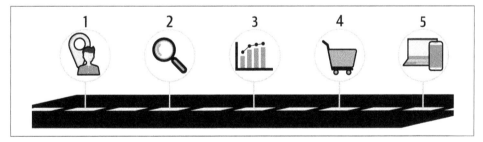

Figure 7-10. Road to healthcare platform

Getting the house in order by ensuring access to data is fundamental to creating a healthcare platform. Organizations must cease copying and moving data around the organization and liberate data so that it can securely and easily be accessed and exchanged when needed, both within and outside the enterprise. This is no easy task, but ensuring that data is accessible through APIs enables flexibility, allowing other parts of the business to compose new capabilities by using the APIs.

Step 1 could simply mean embracing the API economy, as APIs enable healthcare organizations to build products and services faster. Step 2 could be creating a data fabric, so that data is readily accessible throughout the organization, in real time or otherwise, through the use of the APIs. Or it could simply mean making data available to others via APIs in a pure data platform. Liberating data in the organization using APIs as the mechanism for composability is the goal. Step 3 could extend the concept of composability to other capabilities such as access to disease diagnostic models; this step represents the emergence of the composable organization. Step 4 could be creating a marketplace in which both internal and external consumers can compose and create new capabilities using the APIs—that is, digital products. Ultimately, the end point target (Step 5), whether it takes four stages or five to get there, is the creation of the healthcare platform.

Ecosystems

Platforms embrace ecosystems. It's a mistake to see this as new, as previous computing-era companies have embraced ecosystems from their inception. Healthcare organizations know they must create a different experience than in the past with the presence of cloud, mobility, and AI platforms. Facebook opening its platform to developers arguably was pivotal in it overtaking Myspace, as the enhancements from developers, their ecosystem, created added value for Facebook. And there are numerous other examples of the value of ecosystems.

Characteristics that make a healthcare ecosystem vibrant and essential to the expansion and stickiness of a healthcare platform include the following:

- The platform creates or opens capabilities to be accessed by partners, customers, developers, universities, or other constituents.
- The platform makes itself essential and solves a problem for stakeholders in the ecosystem.
- Interfaces are open, standard based, and easy to connect to—that is, they are APIs.
- Innovation and novel use are encouraged, often through "hackathons" or coding festivals.
- Members of the ecosystem are able to add value and capture value through the platform and/or APIs.
- Platform owners are able to capture and monetize value through the platform.

- Platform owners support variety and the ability of the platform to evolve over time.

Application Programming Interfaces (APIs)

Transitional technologies signal the dawn of each new computing era. Early in the computer industry, the transitional technology was mainframe computers and mini-computers; next came personal computers, then the internet, and now mobile devices.

In the past, consumer- or customer-visible features or capabilities took the lion's share of the budget for building solutions. Building for business agility, performance, and availability was second tier, and it was a struggle to get the budget for delivering. But today agility has a measurable line of business and return on investment. In the past, quarterly releases may have been "good enough," but now monthly, weekly, or daily releases are the norm. Rapid response to market changes, customer feedback, and healthcare regulatory environments determines business success or failure. Highly available and agile systems are table stakes.

Digital natives, that is, online companies, were born on the internet and in the cloud. Machine learning and artificial intelligence are their fields of study and the language they speak. APIs and microservices are the constructs for how they build software or deliver machine learning models, and AI First is the way they do business. It's not surprising that many incumbent healthcare companies look to online companies for guidance or with envy, often asking, "Why can't we do that?"

A shift in culture and method of development occurs with digital natives. Online companies build cloud native applications with specific characteristics, where they use small pieces of technology to solve a problem and abandon the third-era computing of middleware platforms. Digital natives replace services often, as business needs change—a throwaway mentality. They embrace failure and experimentation as a way of life. Production is a controlled test environment in which dynamic topologies comprise their applications. At the heart of this is exposing capabilities and their consumption through APIs and understanding when it makes sense to make those APIs digital products.

Summary

It's unlikely that any one company will fix or transform the healthcare system. However, just like in the retail and financial industries, the Big Tech companies and other nontraditional companies will capitalize on the $3 trillion healthcare opportunity to disrupt healthcare. Although we cannot predict the actual disruption, we know it will touch every aspect of the healthcare system in the US.

Digitally enabled patients will be armed with data and empowered to make decisions on their use of healthcare products and services. Providers and clinicians will need to inspire consumers to be custodians in co-managing their health. Figure 7-11 illustrates expectations for the future of healthcare.

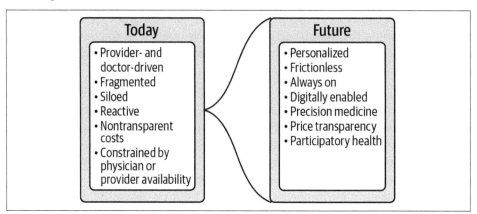

Figure 7-11. Future healthcare experience

The COVID-19 crisis highlights the disparities and challenges in healthcare and the real opportunities for AI to deliver benefits for health systems, healthcare, clinicians, and the public, making existing clinical and administrative processes more effective, efficient, and equitable. At the same time, the COVID-19 crisis reveals significant gaps and deficiencies in healthcare systems, limiting the ability of organizations and nations to manage the pandemic. COVID-19 shows us the power of AI as it has been used to help predict which patients will become ill, select the most effective treatments, and conduct contact tracing (through the use of computer vision and facial recognition technology). Therein lies the opportunity and potential to develop and diffuse AI systems and tools for COVID-19 and beyond.

The potential for artificial intelligence to improve patient care, improve clinicians' productivity, simplify, and make healthcare systems smarter is profound. The increasing volume of data, ranging from clinical data to behavior, genomics, and socioeconomic data, powers AI. The inherent entanglements in the healthcare ecosystem, coupled with the complexity of how diseases interact with individuals, create a perfect storm for applying AI. Adopting AI makes an impact in just about any facet of healthcare, including clinical decision making and healthcare systems redesign. The opportunity to reduce unjustifiable disparities in patient care, avoidable medical errors, inequalities in healthcare access, inefficiencies, and waste expands substantially with AI.

The role AI plays in business and society corresponds to a major shift in the usage of technology, creating a new normal for healthcare. During this new normal, we will see the rapid adoption of AI and business platforms; ecosystems and APIs will be key underpinnings for personalization, automation, digitization, and the widespread adoption of AI. There are no silver bullets; there will be no mythical digital or AI strategy to the rescue.

Companies looking for a silver bullet or a magical agenda, playbook, or strategy for achieving digital transformation or evolution will be disappointed. Companies have diverse paths to increasing digitization. What works for one company may not work for another. We hope we have opened your imagination to the art of what is possible with AI in healthcare.

Some final thoughts include organizations doing any of the following:

- Create an "AI Imagination Center" in which healthcare can be reimagined; create sandboxes to explore and work with technology companies and academia to create something new and better for every constituent in healthcare.

- Define and realize an AI strategy, recognizing that each organization will define AI differently, and that is OK. AI's utility is more important than a definition, and what works for a national or international organization may not work for a local or provincial one. However, having a living AI strategy with goals and measurements can be enormously advantageous. CEOs should have a list of their top three projects employing AI where AI can make a profound difference in healthcare.

- Embrace APIs as digital products. APIs are key to businesses accelerating value, volume, and adoption by enabling healthcare platforms for innovation. APIs ensure a healthcare company's ease in doing business while extending its business capabilities, competencies, products, and services to the widest possible audience. APIs as digital products make adoption of a business's value propositions incredibly simple, while minimizing the incremental effort to pivot and reconfigure new business processes or business models in an ever-changing business landscape.

AI at scale is different depending on budget, size of organizations, resources, and talent. This is why partnering is essential. Last, let's start falling in love with the problems and challenges of healthcare, and then solutions will follow.

Index

A

Abilify MyCite, 115
ACA (Patient Protection and Affordable Care Act), 28
access to healthcare, myths about AI as cure for, 27-29
ACI (ambient clinical intelligence), 137
administrative costs, 32
    administrative processes and waste, 133-135
    AI for eliminating waste, 131-136
    job security and AI, 135
administrative tasks, 117-118
affective computing, 60
AI (generally)
    autonomy, 11
    broad definition of, 4
    emerging applications and services, 162-170
    as general purpose technology, 15-17
    healthcare gaps potentially addressed by, 18
    healthcare myths, 17-33
    healthcare uses for, 146
    human-AI interactions, 11
    improving human lives with, 147
    innovations that become transitions, 11-15
    machine learning and, 1, 4-11
    myths/realities, 1-47
    origins and definition, 2-17
    planning and reasoning, 9
    at scale (see scale, AI at)
AI centaur health, 50-53
AI chasm, 182
AI Stack, 5
AI strategy, developing, 174-176
AI Transformation Playbook, 176
AI Winter, 13
AI-First healthcare, 45-47, 178
alarms, continuous monitoring and, 85
Algorithmic Accountability Act, 68
algorithmic bias, 67-69
algorithms
    limitations of, 42, 178
    machine learning and, 8
    myths about bias, 40
Alphabet, 105
AlphaGo, 9, 13, 50
AlphaGo Master, 13
AlphaZero, 14, 50
Amara, Roy, 18
Amara's Law, 18
Amazon, 105
ambient clinical intelligence (ACI), 137
ambient computing, 81-83
ambient intelligence, 148-151
ambient intelligence environments, 167
Amico, Richard, 117
Andreessen, Marc, 186
anomalies, 41
anthropomorphism, 40
Apple, 105
Apple Watch, 105, 108
application programming interfaces (APIs), 184, 191
application-centric digitization, 96
applications, platforms versus, 188
AstraZeneca, 140
at-risk pregnancies, 88-90
automatic speech recognition (ASR), 58
autonomous AI systems, 11

autonomous weapons, 68
autonomy, human, 60, 68
AWS Comprehend, 100

B

bacterial pneumonia, 158
Bahcall, Safi, 101
Baidu AI Group, 176
Barrett, Majel, 37
Berg, 140
BERT language model, 38
Beth Israel Deaconess Medical Center
     (BIDMC), 3, 156, 158
bias
     and AI's advantage in pharmaceutical
          research, 141
     human sociocultural values and, 58-61
     and lack of diversity in AI systems, 67-69
     myths about AI algorithms, 40
     WBC count statistics, 62
BIDMC (see Beth Israel Deaconess Medical
     Center)
big data
     health determinants and, 92
     as realm influencing healthcare, 78
Big Tech, 105
bioacoustic sensors, 167
black box
     deep learning and, 10
     myth about AI as, 43
black-box AI, explainable AI versus, 44, 55
brain tumors, 23
brain, myths about AI being modeled after, 45
bupropion, 141
burnout, 20, 133, 135

C

CADUCEUS, 3
call centers, 70
cancer
     application of AI to, 22-24
     futile care decisions and, 128
     human-centered AI and, 60
     MD Anderson–Watson AI failure, 61
capitalism, 68
cardiovascular disease, 108, 115
centaur health (see AI centaur health)
Change Healthcare, 161
change management, 56

chatbots, 63, 70
chess, 12, 50
CHF (congestive heart failure), 88
China
     general practitioner/specialist training dis-
          parities, 52
     healthcare access reform, 28
chronic disease management, 106
     AI and, 30, 108-110
     AI and mental health, 110
chronic kidney disease (CKD), 83
claims processing
     processing systems as black box, 44
     real-time, 169
clinical coding, 99-101
clinical decision support tools, 167
clinician time
     AI for eliminating waste, 136-139
     AI use in diagnostic imaging and analysis,
          137-139
     ambient clinical intelligence, 137
computed tomography (CT) scans, 24
computer vision (CV), 9, 40
computing platforms, 184
congestive heart failure (CHF), 88
continuous learning, 6
continuous monitoring
     alarms, 85
     basics, 84
     health continuum and, 86-88
     using AI, 83-88
conversational AI, myths about, 37-38
coordination of care platform, 163
costs, myths about AI decreasing, 29-33
COVID-19 pandemic
     challenges in healthcare highlighted by, 192
     and Internet of Behaviors, 170
     and mental healthcare, 110
     and telemedicine, 111
cross-function validation, 8
CSRs (customer service representatives), 152
CT (computed tomography) scans, 24
cultural diversity, 67-69
cures
     defining, 21
     myths about AI's capabilities, 21-24
customer journey platform, 166
customer service centers, 70
customer service representatives (CSRs), 152

CV (computer vision), 9, 40

D

data fabric, 189
data, ethical stewardship of, 58
decision-making
    clinical decision support tools, 167
    myths about AI as overlord, 38
    treatment decisions and AI, 126-131
Deep Blue, 12, 50
deep learning (DL), 7, 10, 40
deep neural networks, 44
DeepMind, 10, 14, 105
Department of Defense, AI ethical principles
    for, 69
design thinking, 56
diabetes
    medication management, 113
    monitoring and AI, 73-83
    prediction, 62
diabetic retinopathy, 30
diagnoses
    AI performance, 3
    myths about AI's diagnostic abilities, 41-43
diagnostic imaging/analysis, 137-139
dialysis, 125
digestible sensors, 168
digital healthcare, 102-106, 104
digital medication, 115-117
digital mesh, 149
digital transformation of healthcare, 95-119
    AI and digitization applied to administrative
        tasks, 117-118
    AI and mental health, 110
    AI and telemedicine, 111-113
    AI applied to digital healthcare, 104
    AI, digitization, and Big Tech, 105
    defined, 95
    developing strategies for, 102
    digital healthcare, 102-106
    medication management and AI, 113-117
    Path A: building new capabilities, 100
    Path A: creating digital operations and pro-
        cesses, 99
    Path C: transforming business processes,
        101
    paths to, 97-102
    preventive/chronic disease management,
        106

digital twin platform, 75, 168-169
disease state management platform, 164
diversity in AI systems, 67-69
DL (see deep learning)
doctor burnout
    AI for easing, 135
doctors
    myths about AI replacing, 25-27
    technology from perspective of, 153-156
drug creation (see pharmaceuticals)

E

e-stroke suite technology, 159
EBM (evidence-based medicine), 124
ecosystems, 21, 190
electronic health records (EHRs), 99, 107, 159
Elish, Madeleine Clare, 57
emerging applications and services, 162-170
    ambient intelligence environments, 167
    clinical decision support tools, 167
    coordination of care platform, 163
    customer journey platform, 166
    digital twin platform, 168-169
    disease state management platform, 164
    human to machine experience services, 165
    Internet of Behaviors (IoB), 170
    real-time healthcare, 169
ethics
    and framework for human AI, 58
    human-centered AI and, 66-71
    human-centric approach, 67-69
    making human-centered AI work, 69
evidence-based medicine (EBM), 124
existential threat, as AI myth, 34-35
expenditures on healthcare, myths about AI as
    cure for, 27-29
expert systems, 3
explainable AI, 64-66
    black-box AI versus, 44, 55
    framework for human AI, 57
explicit knowledge, 60

F

Facebook, 170, 190
facial recognition software, 41
failures, AI-associated, 61
Fairview Health System, 157
Federal Trade Commission, 68
Ferrucci, David, 40

fetal morbidity/mortality, 20
Fit (health platform), 105
Fourth Industrial Revolution, 82
fraud, 161
full artificial intelligence, 34
fundus photography, 30
futile care decisions, 127-129

G

galvanic skin response (GSR) sensors, 167
gaming, 49, 51
GE Healthcare, 158
Genentech, 140
general practitioners (GPs), 52
general purpose technology (GPT), 15-17
genomics, 23
gestational hypertension, 88-90
GNS Healthcare, 140
Go, 9
Google
    AlphaGo, 9
    BERT language model, 38
    digital healthcare tools, 105
    Majel voice technology, 37
Google Brain, 176
Google Wear, 105
GPs (general practitioners), 52
GPT (general purpose technology), 15-17
GSR (galvanic skin response) sensors, 167

H

Harel, Shahar, 140
Hassabis test, 34
Hassabis, Demis, 34
Haven, 105
Hawking, Stephen, 34
health continuum, continuous monitoring and, 86-88
health determinants, big data and, 92
health engagement platform, 187
health insurance, 28, 160-162
healthcare access, myths about AI as cure for, 27-29
healthcare automation, defined, 95
healthcare costs, myths about AI decreasing, 29-33
healthcare organizations, AI at scale for (see scale, AI at)

"healthcare problem," myths about AI as cure for, 27-29
healthcare spend, 123-126
healthcare waste, 121-143
    administrative costs, 131-136
    basics, 122
    clinician time, 136-139
    healthcare spend and AI, 123-126
    treatment decisions and AI, 126-131
    use of AI in pharmaceutical savings, 140-142
HealthKit, 105, 107
heart disease, 108, 115
hemodialysis, 125
Highmark, 161
HIV (human immunodeficiency virus), 21
hospital readmission risks, 32, 157
hospital stays, risks associated with, 91
hospital systems, technology from perspective of, 156-159
hospitalization costs, 32
human ethics, 66-71
human immunodeficiency virus (HIV), 21
human to machine experience services, 165
human-AI interactions, 11
human-centered AI, 49-71
    AI and human sociocultural values, 58-61
    AI centaur health, 50-53
    AI understanding humans, 61-64
    components of, 54
    defined, 59
    ethical issues, 66-71
    framework for, 55
    humans understanding AI, 64-66
    intersection of AI and humans, 54-66
    origins, 53
hypertensive disorders, 108, 124
    digital tools for managing, 103-105
    gestational hypertension, 88-90
    medication management, 115
    overtreatment and, 130

I

IA (intelligence amplification), 53
IBM Deep Blue computer, 12, 50
IBM Watson computer, 13, 35, 37
IBM Watson for Oncology computer, 61
iCarbonX, 187
implicit bias training, 68

implicit knowledge, 60

individual health records (IHR), 151-153

inefficiency (see healthcare waste)

ingestible sensor (see digital medication)

Insel, Thomas, 45

Insilico Medicine, 141

insurers, technology from perspective of,
    160-162

intelligence amplification (IA), 53

intense personalization
    defined, 75
    as prescription for personal health, 76-83
    three realms influencing healthcare, 78-81

interaction networks, 184

Internet of Behaviors (IoB), 170

Internet of Things (IoT)
    AI and, 88-92
    application of IoT and AI to medical care,
        88-92
    influence on healthcare, 79

J

J. C. R. (Joseph Carl Robnett Licklider), 53

Jennings, Ken, 13, 38

Jeopardy! (TV show), 13, 37

Jha, Ashish K., 128

job security, 135

K

Karpathy, Andrej, 17

Kasparov, Garry, 12, 50

Katabi, Dina, 83

Kelley, John E., III, 37

Khosla, Vinod, 25, 178

kidney disease, 83, 125

Kolbjørnsrud, Vegard, 117

Kozyrkov, Cassie, 40

L

latent autoimmune diabetes in adults (LADA),
    75

Li, Fei-Fei, 53

Licklider, Joseph Carl Robnett (J. C. R.; "Lick"),
    53

lung cancer, 24

M

Machiavelli, Niccolò, 180

machine learning (ML)
    AI and, 4-11
    autonomy, 11
    computer vision, 9
    development requirements, 36
    first program, 12
    limitations of, 178
    myths equating AI with, 35
    natural language processing, 9
    neural networks and, 6-9
    planning and reasoning, 9
    programming by example, 17

Majel (voice technology), 37

malignant melanoma, 23

marketplace platforms, 184

Marvin, Bill, 169

Maslow, Abraham, 36

maternal morbidity/mortality, 20, 88-90

Mayor, Adrienne, 2

McCarthy, John, 2

McCorduck, Pamela, 1

McCulloch, Warren S., 2

McRae, Ian, 32

medical coding, 21

medical imaging, 137-139

medical records, 151-153

Medicare, 127

medication adherence
    digital medication, 115-117
    MEMS and, 114

Medication Event Monitoring System (MEMS),
    114

medication management
    AI and, 113-117
    digital medication, 115-117
    medication adherence, 114

mental health management, 110

meta healthcare platform, 187

Microsoft, 63

migraines, 130

Miying, 187

ML (see machine learning)

model drift, 43

models, algorithms versus, 8

monitoring, 73-94
    ambient computing and healthcare, 81-83
    application of IoT and AI to medical care,
        88-92
    continuous monitoring using AI, 83-88

health determinants and big data, 92
prescription for personal health, 76-83
Monte Carlo simulation, 9
moonshot projects, 101
Moravec's paradox, 16
Musk, Elon, 68
MYCIN, 3
Myspace, 190
myths, AI (generally), 33-39
    AI as existential threat, 34-35
    AI as just machine learning, 35
    AI as overlord, 38
    AI decreasing healthcare costs, 29-33
    AI overpromising and underdelivering, 36
    true conversational AI, 37-38
myths, AI technology, 39-45
    AI as black box, 43
    AI as modeled after the human brain, 45
    AI's ability to see/hear/think, 40
    AI's diagnostic abilities as better than doc-
        tors', 41-43
    algorithmic bias, 40
myths, healthcare
    AI's ability to cure disease, 21-24
    AI's fixing the "healthcare problem", 27-29
    AI's replacing doctors, 25-27

N

narrow AI, 14
National Security Council on AI, 68
natural language processing (NLP)
    acceleration of development, 174
    bias issues, 58
    for clinical coding, 3, 9
    in ICU setting, 5
natural user interfaces, 166
neural networks, 6-9
New York-Presbyterian Performing Provider
    System (NYP PPS), 133
Ng, Andrew, 176
Nkonde, Mutale, 68
NLP (see natural language processing)
nurses, 136

O

One Drop, 187
OpenAI, 38, 174
Oregon Health & Science University (OHSU),
    158

Orion Health, 32
overlord, myths about AI as, 38
overtreatment, 127, 129-131
Oxford University Hospitals, 159

P

paperwork, 151-153
pathognomonic symptoms, 41
pathologists, 138
Patient Protection and Affordable Care Act
    (ACA), 28
patients, technology from perspective of,
    151-153
Pearl, Robert, 118
people-centric digitization, 96
personal health
    ambient computing and healthcare, 81-83
    application of IoT and AI to medical care,
        88-92
    continuous monitoring using AI, 83-88
    health determinants and big data, 92
    intense personalization as prescription for,
        76-83
    monitoring and AI, 73-94
personalization, as prescription for personal
    health, 76-78
pharmaceuticals, 3, 140-142
physician burnout
    administrative tasks and, 133
Pichai, Sundar, 46
Ping An Good Doctor, 52
Pitts, Walter, 2
Planck, Max, 56
planning component of AI, 9
platforms
    for AI at scale, 183-191
    and APIs, 191
    clinical decision support tools, 167
    coordination of care platform, 163
    customer journey platform, 166
    digital twin platform, 168-169
    disease state management platform, 164
    and ecosystems, 190
    steps to implementing, 186-190
Plavix, 22
pneumonia, 158
population health management, 118
preclinical research, 140
Prescott, Tony, 35

preventive disease management, 106
  AI and mental health, 110
  AI and prevention, 107
privacy, 68
procedural programming, 12
programming by example, 17
pure data healthcare platform, 186
Putin, Vladimir, 68

R

racial bias, 67-69
Radinsky, Kira, 140
radiogenomics, 23
radiologists, 26
radiology, 137-139
Rariy, Chevon, 113
readmission risks, 32, 157
real-time healthcare, 169
reasoning element of AI, 10
relation networks, 10
release of information (ROI), 153
reproducibility, in image review, 139
repurposed drugs, 141
retinal scanning, 69
Riedl, Mark O., 53
robotic process automation (RPA), 133
ROI (release of information), 153
Russell, Stuart, 1
Rutter, Brad, 13

S

Samuel, Arthur, 12
scale, AI at, 173-193
  achieving AI at scale, 173-178
  invisible engines: healthcare platforms, 183-191
  transforming health care, 178-183
Sedol, Lee, 51
sensor-based wearables, 168
sensors, 167
Seung, Sebastian, 45
skin cancer detection, 23
sleep monitoring, 108
social platforms/networks
  influence on real-world behaviors, 170
  as realm influencing healthcare, 78
sociocultural values, 58-61
Star Trek, 37
stochastic machine learning algorithms, 44

strong AI, 34
Sunstein, Cass R., 170
superintelligence, 16
supervised learning, 6

T

Tay (Microsoft chatbot), 63
technology (generally)
  ambient intelligence, 148-151
  from a doctor's perspective, 153-156
  from a hospital system's perspective, 156-159
  from an insurer's perspective, 160-162
  making technology work for healthcare, 148-162
  from a patient's perspective, 151-153
technology platforms, 184
teledermatology, 109
telemedicine, 111-113
Tencent, 187
Tencent Trusted Doctors, 187
test data, 8
Thaler, Richard H., 170
thinking machines, 40
Thomas, Robert J., 117
Thompson, Clive, 50
training data, 8
transparency, explainable AI and, 64
treatment decisions
  AI and, 126-131
  futile care decisions, 127-129
  overtreatment, 129-131
triage, 42, 70
Turing test, 34
Turing, Alan, 34
23andMe, 186
type 2 diabetes, 108

U

University of Texas MD Anderson Cancer Center, 61
unsupervised learning, 6, 118
utility platforms, 184

V

values, sociocultural, 58-61
vendor evaluation, 177
Verily, 105

voice-enabled conversations, 165
Voice-First computer, 37

W

waste (see healthcare waste)
Watkins, Elizabeth Anne, 57
Watson computer, 13
Watson for Oncology computer, 61
WBC (white blood cell) count, 62
weak AI, 14
wearables, 105, 168
WeChat, 187
WeDoctor, 187

Weinberg, Gerald, 180
Weinberger, Mark, 161
Weinberg's Second Law, 180, 183
white blood cell (WBC) count, 62
WorkFusion, 133

X

Xu, Wei, 69

Z

Zuboff, Shoshana, 68
Zyban, 141

About the Authors

Kerrie Holley is a former IBM Fellow and joined Optum as their first Technology Fellow, with a focus on advancing healthcare with technology. He holds a number of technology patents and is the author of two previous books.

Dr. Siupo Becker has a clinical background in internal medicine and infectious diseases. She practiced for over 14 years, and is now a senior healthcare executive. Her experience includes providing top Fortune 50 companies with innovative approaches to their healthcare needs. Her skill sets include work in population health management, case management, client retention and growth, and technology solutions and digital health innovation, as well as product development.

Colophon

The animal on the cover of *AI-First Healthcare* is a red-breasted pygmy parrot (*Micropsitta bruijnii*), a member of the smallest genus of parrots. Pygmy parrots are only found on islands near southeast Asia, such as New Guinea, Fiji, and the Maluku Islands. This particular species grows to about 8 centimeters in length and weighs 12–16 grams.

The red-breasted pygmy parrot lives in forest habitat, often tropical or subtropical. While other pygmy parrot species breed near arboreal termite nests, the red-breasted pygmy parrot is unique in that it lives at higher altitudes and builds its nests within tree hollows. The male is more brightly colored than the mostly green female, with a vivid red chest, blue collar, green wings, and orange head and cheeks.

These parrots subsist primarily on lichens, but also eat insects, mosses, and fungi. They spend most of their days foraging through trees by clinging closely to the bark, and have quick, jerky movements similar to nuthatches. Their stiff tail feathers, strong beaks, and oversized feet make them good climbers. The population size is unclear, but red-breasted pygmy parrots have such a limited range that they are likely threatened by deforestation and habitat loss.

Many of the animals on O'Reilly covers are endangered; all of them are important to the world.

The cover illustration is by Karen Montgomery, based on a black and white engraving from Lydekker's *Royal Natural History*. The cover fonts are Gilroy Semibold and Guardian Sans. The text font is Adobe Minion Pro; the heading font is Adobe Myriad Condensed; and the code font is Dalton Maag's Ubuntu Mono.

O'REILLY®

There's much more where this came from.

Experience books, videos, live online training courses, and more from O'Reilly and our 200+ partners—all in one place.

Learn more at oreilly.com/online-learning

Lightning Source UK Ltd.
Milton Keynes UK
UKHW031823200421
382324UK00003B/7